The Spirit of Traditional Chinese Law

The Spirit of the Laws

Alan Watson, General Editor

The *Spirit of the Laws* series illuminates the nature of legal systems throughout the world. Titles in the series are concerned less with the rules of the law and more with the relationships of the laws in each system with religion and moral perspectives; the degree of complexity and abstraction; classifications; attitudes to possible sources of law; authority; and values enshrined in law. Topics covered in the series include Roman law, Chinese law, biblical law, Talmudic law, canon law, common law, Hindu law, customary law, Japanese law, and international law.

THE SPIRIT OF
TRADITIONAL
CHINESE LAW

Geoffrey MacCormack

The University of Georgia Press
Athens & London

©1996 by the University of Georgia Press
Athens, Georgia 30602
All rights reserved
Designed by Walton Harris
Set in 10/14 Trump by Tseng Information Systems, Inc.
Printed and bound by Braun-Brumfield, Inc.

The paper in this book meets the guidelines for permanence
and durability of the Committee on Production Guidelines
for Book Longevity of the Council on Library Resources.

Printed in the United States of America

00 99 98 97 96   C   5 4 3 2 1

Library of Congress Cataloging in Publication Data
MacCormack, Geoffrey.
  The spirit of traditional Chinese law / Geoffrey MacCormack.
    p.   cm. — (The spirit of the laws)
  Includes bibliographical references and index.
  ISBN 0-8203-1722-5 (alk. paper)
    1. Law—China—History.   2. Criminal law—China—History.
I. Title.   II. Series: Spirit of the laws (Athens, Georgia)
KNN122.M33   1996
349.51—dc20
[345.1]   94-39610

British Library Cataloging in Publication Data available

For Catherine and Tom

CONTENTS

CHRONOLOGICAL TABLE
OF CHINESE DYNASTIES

Shang (Yin)	c. 16th–11th century B.C.
Chou	c. 11th century–221 B.C.
Spring and Autumn period	770–475 B.C.
Warring States Period	475–221 B.C.
Ch'in	221–206 B.C.
Han	206 B.C.–A.D. 220
Former (or Western) Han	206 B.C.–A.D. 24
Later (or Eastern) Han	25–220
Three Kingdoms	220–280
Tsin	265–420
Southern and Northern Dynasties	420–589
Sui	581–618
T'ang	618–907
Five Dynasties	907–960
Sung	960–1279
Northern Sung	960–1126
Southern Sung	1127–1279
Yüan (Mongol)	1279–1368
Ming	1368–1644
Ch'ing (Manchu)	1644–1911

PREFACE

In *L'esprit des lois* Montesquieu devotes a surprising amount of space to China, known in eighteenth-century Europe mainly through the reports of missionaries and merchants. The two central points that he makes are that China is a despotism ruled by fear in which the emperor exercises arbitrary power over the life and property of his subjects, and that it is a country governed in every detail by the performance of rites, especially those designed to reinforce the authority of the father or senior. It is in their adherence to the rites that Montesquieu locates the "spirit" of the Chinese people. He writes with some perception: "Respect for fathers was necessarily tied to everything they stood for: [the authority of] the eldest, teachers, magistrates, the emperor. Such respect for the father presupposed a reciprocal love for his children; and therefore the same reciprocity of feeling on the part of the old towards the young, of magistrates towards those under their jurisdiction, of the emperor towards his subjects. Taken together, these [relationships] made up the rites, which constituted the general spirit of the nation."[1]

From Montesquieu's work the reader obtains the impression that the Chinese empire of the eighteenth century knew nothing of law other than the unfettered commands of a despot, but regulated its affairs according to the "rites" that reflected the genuine "spirit" or "genius" of the people. *L'esprit des lois* has probably played a large role in inducing a conviction, common in the West, that traditional China did not have law in any sense resembling that to which Western societies were subject, but rather was governed by a moral consensus given visible expression in the rites (*li*). The view that China did not have law has still not entirely disappeared, even in the writings of well-informed scholars.[2]

In point of fact, as early as the seventh century A.D. China possessed a highly developed and sophisticated system of public law,
both administrative and penal. The penal code itself dealt with much
of what is termed in the West "family law," as well as touching on
aspects of the law of property, contract, and succession. The form of
the penal rules reduces itself to the well-known model constructed
by John Austin, that of "orders backed by threats." The emperor's
subjects are instructed to behave in certain ways; should they fail to
comply, punishments are to be imposed. Such a formulation of the
rules, with its overriding emphasis on punishment, has led to the
view, often expressed by Western scholars, that the traditional law
was concerned only with the enforcement of duties and paid no attention to the rights of individuals.³ While the focus of the Chinese
legislation was undoubtedly on the concept of duty, it seems something of a distortion to deprive it of all reference to right. The very
fact that persons are prohibited from killing or injuring others, or
from damaging or stealing their property, or from refusing to pay their
debts shows that the law is concerned indirectly with the rights of
individuals to security with respect to their persons and property.⁴

We have already noted that Montesquieu located the "spirit" of the
Chinese in their rites rather than in their law. The problem was that
neither Montesquieu nor, it seems, most of the sources that he utilized had a proper understanding either of the role of the emperor
in Chinese society or of the structure of administrative and penal
law by which the empire was governed. The emperor did not have an
unfettered discretion to act as he pleased, but was very considerably
circumscribed by precedent and expected to follow the "right way to
rule" as established by earlier dynasties or his own ancestors.⁵ The
rites and the behavior that they were designed to express were certainly of overwhelming importance in Chinese life at all social levels.
But it is a mistake to think that the law had no role to play. Indeed,
one of its principal functions was to reinforce the rites by attaching
punishments to behavior that contravened those moral prescriptions
deemed most important by Confucian orthodoxy. The "spirit" that
Montesquieu identified in the rites can also be seen in the law. Both
forms of social control cooperated in an attempt to ensure the obser-

vance of conduct held to be morally right and indispensable for the good ordering of society.

To write of the traditional penal law in China in terms of "spirit" is particularly apt because of the strong idealistic character possessed by the law. In effect, it constituted a code of the morally right conduct, which was put forward as a model for all members of society to follow. We may describe the codes as a distillation of Confucian teaching cast into the form of rules equipped with sanctions. Some of these rules, although by no means all, were not regularly enforced by the courts and, indeed, may have been enacted without the expectation that they would have been enforced. In this class of case the idealistic character of the legislation is most strikingly apparent, but we also have to remember that all the rules of the penal code regulating conduct were derived from the fundamental concept of the proper way for each individual to behave. The "way" differed according to one's family and social role as child, parent, husband, wife, official, and so on. But the nature of the behavior deemed appropriate to each role was well defined and, in theory at least, made mandatory through the codes.

It is clear that the rules enshrined in the codes, considered as a whole, constituted an ideal standard of conduct for the elite, the class of scholars, officials, and wealthy merchants. However, the extent to which they were known to, or observed by, the rural masses is uncertain. The central Neo-Confucian values of filial obedience and chastity of women appear to have been widely accepted by all classes, but it is likely that some of the refinements of Confucian behavior, such as the strict observance of the mourning rules, were not regarded as relevant by ordinary peasant households. We have to bear in mind the possibility that not all the law contained in the codes was equally relevant to all sections of society.

The main primary sources utilized for this book are the penal codes of the T'ang, Ming, and Ch'ing dynasties and the decisions of the Ch'ing Board of Punishments from the eighteenth and nineteenth centuries. A variety of nonlegal sources evidencing pre-Confucian, Confucian, and Legalist thinking have also been drawn upon. In view of the fact that knowledge of the traditional Chinese law is still very little diffused in the West, a reasonably full citation of secondary literature in Western languages has been made.

Grateful acknowledgment is made of the help and encouragement afforded by Prof. Alan Watson, Mr. Malcolm Call, Ms. Elaine Durham Otto, Ms. Kim Cretors, Ms. Susan Brook, Ms. Jennifer Rogers, Ms. Kelly Caudle, and the University of Georgia Press's anonymous reader.

The Spirit of Traditional Chinese Law

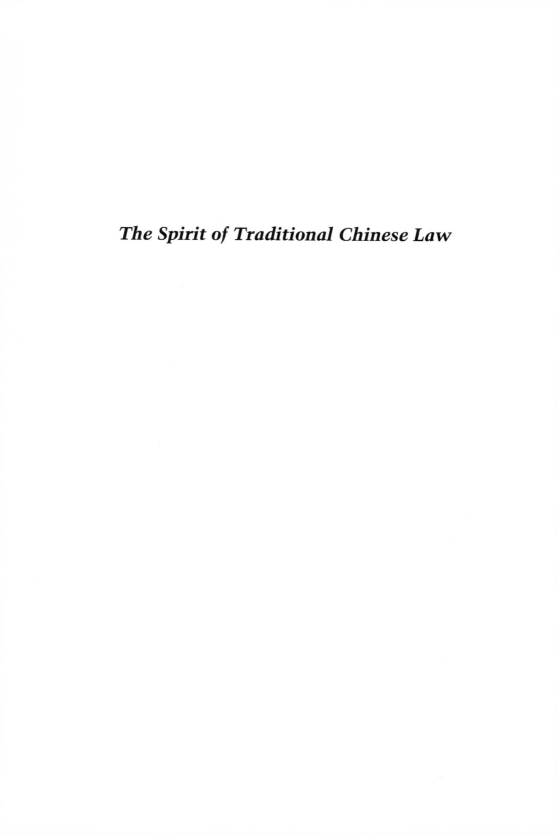

1 Historical Overview of the Traditional Chinese Legal System

The law of imperial China has been described as being Legalist in form and predominantly Confucian in spirit, although marked in some respects by a Legalist spirit.[1] We may ask, what is meant by "spirit" in this context, and to what extent has a combination of the Confucian and Legalist "spirit" inspired the development of the traditional law? Further, is there any other sense in which we may speak of the "spirit of the law"? Does it possess characteristics that cannot necessarily be attributed precisely to a Confucian or a Legalist inspiration? Statements about a Confucian or Legalist spirit at the broadest level refer to the values or techniques, advocated by the Confucian or Legalist schools of thought, that were utilized by the emperor and the government in the drafting of the penal or other legal codes. An investigation into the impact of these values or techniques requires an appreciation of the historical development of the traditional law. In China we are dealing with a well-documented legal tradition from the second century B.C. until the twentieth century A.D., a remarkable feature of which is that a core group of legal provisions survived many centuries of development with little change. The penal code of the last dynasty (Ch'ing) bears a striking resemblance to that of the T'ang, a dynasty founded at the beginning of the seventh century A.D. The values and techniques utilized by the T'ang code had themselves been worked out many centuries earlier.

A combination of Confucian and Legalist perspectives does not necessarily exhaust the whole content of the "spirit of the law." We may still be able to identify certain features of the Chinese law, distinguishing it from Western law, that cannot with certainty be ascribed to specific Confucian or Legalist influence. The remainder of the introduction will chart a brief history of legal development in

China, describe the principal contribution to the law of the Confucian and Legalist schools, and seek to identify certain other characteristics that can be considered under the head of "spirit." These matters will then be explored further in succeeding chapters.

HISTORY OF LEGAL DEVELOPMENT

For our purpose we may distinguish the following stages in the recorded legal history of traditional China: (i) the very beginnings, that is, the laws of the early Chou kings, (ii) the large scale codifications of the law in some Chinese states during the sixth century B.C., (iii) the Legalist-inspired laws of the state and empire of Ch'in, and (iv) the Confucian-inspired laws, beginning with the Han dynasty, fully developed under the T'ang, and continuing throughout the whole imperial period. The early Chou rulers from the beginning of the eleventh century B.C., those venerated as "sage rulers" by the later Confucians, issued or enforced laws that already exemplified certain of the values deemed fundamental in the thought of Confucius and his followers.[2] The earliest document on law and justice in China that is generally regarded as authentic is the *K'ang kao*, a set of instructions issued by King Wu (traditional reign dates: 1122–1116 B.C.) to a younger prince for the government of a fief.[3] Among the worst offenses identified in the *K'ang kao* is the failure to show proper respect to one's father or elder brother.[4] The concept of filial piety occupies a central place in the social and legal system of the state several centuries before its emergence as a main plank of Confucian thinking.

The second stage begins some centuries later. During the sixth century B.C. several of the independent states into which the original Chou kingdom had by this time become fragmented codified their penal laws and inscribed them on bronze cauldrons. Such codifications should probably be seen as part of the process by which rulers attempted to concentrate power in their own hands and to make more effective the central administration of the state. Although nothing precise is known about the content of these codes, it seems that they may have foreshadowed the later overtly Legalist laws of the state of Ch'in by suppressing or reducing the privileges and immunities of the nobles. At any rate, they attracted criticism from orthodox statesmen and thinkers (including, it is said, even Confucius himself), on the grounds that not only was penal law given too conspicuous a role in the government of the people but the distinction between the "noble" and the "base" was eroded.[5]

Of the states competing for hegemony in the period from the sixth to the third century B.C., it was the state of Ch'in that finally obtained supremacy. The Ch'in dynasty was founded in 221 B.C., with the king of Ch'in becoming emperor of the united country. One of the reasons for Ch'in's success was its adoption, on the advice of Lord Shang, of far-reaching penal and administrative codes in the fourth century. The laws imposed severe punishments for failure to comply with the duties imposed by the state and on the whole punished all alike; that is, no section or class of the community was given special privileges or immunities. A similar complex of rules was applied to the government of the short-lived Ch'in empire (221–206 B.C.).[6] During this stage of development the laws of the state and empire of Ch'in were marked by a purely Legalist spirit, hostile to the moral values advocated by the Confucians.

With the fall of the Ch'in and the founding of the Han dynasty, the outlook of the imperial house and the ruling elite began to change. Instead of holding purely to the severely Legalistic perspective of their Ch'in predecessors, the Han emperors and their advisers began to take account of Confucian values and introduce rules designed to implement them. This process continued throughout the Han and later dynasties, culminating in the T'ang. The penal code of the T'ang dynasty is the final product of the "Confucianization of the law," as this process of implementation of Confucian and pre-Confucian values has been described.[7] It constitutes the fourth stage of legal development as identified above.

Confucianism in a somewhat revised form (Neo-Confucianism) continued to be the state orthodoxy under the Sung, Ming, and Ch'ing dynasties. (Even the Mongol Yüan dynasty preserved the essentials of T'ang law.) This not only ensured that the Confucian foundations of the T'ang code were retained but that in some respects they were even strengthened. The result was that the penal codes of all dynasties from the T'ang to the Ch'ing were dominantly Confucian in inspiration.[8] That is, they were designed to give effect to the values of the state orthodoxy, but still retained traces of their Legalist origin.

THE LEGALIST SPIRIT

This is not the place to provide an exhaustive account of the Legalist school or of the views of its principal proponents, Lord Shang and Han Fei Tzu, on the role of law. It is sufficient here to sketch the main propositions that emerge from the writings ascribed to Lord Shang and Han Fei Tzu and consider the extent to which they influenced the legal system of imperial China.[9] First, there is the insistence that the ruler must rely on penal law and the imposition of heavy punishments as the main instrument of his government of the people. A principle frequently invoked is that, were the smallest offense to be met with severe punishment, in the end the people would cease to offend and recourse to punishment itself would become unnecessary. At the same time, the ruler must delegate his authority to responsible and efficient ministers and officials, while retaining in his own hands the "twin handles" of reward and punishment. Conversely, moral considerations should be rigorously excluded in the conduct of government. Lord Shang held that regard for the "six lice" (that is, care for old age, living on others, beauty, love, ambition, and virtuous conduct) or the "ten evils" (that is, rites, music, odes, history, virtue, moral culture, filial piety, brotherly duty, integrity, and sophistry) will guarantee the ruin of the state.[10]

This program was more or less thoroughly implemented by the state and empire of Ch'in, but only in part survived the replacement of the Ch'in by the Han. What survived was recognition of the need for complex penal and administrative codes that enabled the emperor to govern the country through a hierarchy of ministers and officials, all ultimately responsible to him. What did not survive was the rigorous exclusion of moral considerations from the penal code or the requirement that even small offenses should receive heavy punishment. From the time of the Han, rulers used the penal code to achieve what was anathema to the Legalists, in that they allowed factors of benevolence and individual merit or position to influence the incidence of punishment. Further, punishment, although it retained a deterrent function, was carefully proportioned to the gravity of the offense.

A corollary of the Legalist insistence that the ruler, despite the necessity of delegation, retain firm control of the administration, was the need to ensure that his delegates acted only in accordance with the authority conferred on them and that they did not trespass on the prerogatives of the ruler. Hence, the imperial legal systems all retained the original Legalist insistence that the powers of officials appointed to particular posts be defined in detail and that punishments be prescribed for transgressions, whether inadvertent or not. The discretion permitted an official was strictly limited. Until the end of the Ch'ing officials, including those acting as judges, were given very limited discretion in the handling of their duties, and they were made liable to punishment in respect of any decision not in conformity with the rules of the penal or administrative codes.

A hallmark of Legalist thinking was that there should be equality before the law. All, with the exception of the ruler himself, should be subject to the regular punishments if they committed offenses. Lord Shang, when in power in Ch'in, applied this policy even to the heir-apparent, thus ensuring his own downfall when the latter came to the throne.[11] Once the Ch'in empire had ended, the principle of equality before the law disappeared entirely. The codes of subsequent dynasties conferred extensive privileges with respect to the punishment of officials and members of their families and gave special consideration to such factors as age, youth, and infirmity.[12]

On the question of legislative technique, the Legalists stressed that the rules enacted by the ruler for the punishment of offenses should be clear, intelligible to the ordinary people, and properly communicated to them. Only then could order satisfactorily be maintained in the state. These were qualities that all dynasties sought to achieve in their legislation, though proper comprehension of the laws by the officials was perhaps regarded as more important than knowledge by the people. The T'ang code, for example, was a model of precision and clarity that would have been perfectly intelligible to the officials entrusted with its administration. One doubts, however, whether it would have been, except in terms of a certain broad understanding, readily comprehended by the ordinary villagers. While the clarity of drafting and coherence of structure evident in the T'ang code to some extent were inherited also by the later codes, certainly by the latter part of the Ch'ing dynasty problems were caused by the increase in the number of specific situations with which the legislator sought to deal. As the mass of legislation increased, it became doubtful whether even officials could adequately master the complex distinctions it came to contain—a phenomenon well known, of course, in modern Western societies.[13]

The Legalists attached importance to the values of consistency and uniformity in the application of the law. Good order might be maintained in the state only if the people knew that certain conduct would invariably be followed by a certain result. The ruler had to ensure that his officials throughout his realm not only applied the same set of rules but also applied them in the same fashion. Only if this were done would the people have the necessary trust in the ruler and his law. None of the imperial dynasties appears to have deviated from this approach. In the eighteenth and nineteenth centuries the Ch'ing Board of Punishments from time to time expressed sentiments endorsing the values of consistency and certainty in the application of the rules of the penal code.

THE CONFUCIAN SPIRIT

The Confucian school, founded by Confucius himself in the sixth century B.C., in contrast to the more radical Legalists, drew upon and developed traditional attitudes and values, especially as stated by the early Chou rulers or exemplified in their deeds. The three foremost early Confucians—Confucius himself, Mencius, and Hsün Tzu—all emphasized teaching and moral guidance rather than penal law as instruments for the government of the people, though Hsün Tzu was prepared to concede a greater role to law than Confucius or Mencius. Only through teaching could a proper sense of virtuous conduct be inculcated in the people. The Confucian emperors and statesmen of the Han and later dynasties all recognized the practical need for the existence of a wide-ranging penal code. They accepted that teaching and moral guidance alone would not suffice to secure good behavior among the people. Yet penal laws, while necessary, should principally be used to supplement and reinforce the lessons to be obtained from the teachings and guidance furnished by the ruler and his officials. The consequence was that the penal codes became, to an extent rarely found in any other society, vehicles for the enforcement of the moral values held by the ruling elite and, to some extent, by the population at large.

From the founding of the Han in 206 B.C. until the fall of the Ch'ing in 1911, Confucianism for most of the time was the orthodox doctrine of the state; that is, it constituted a set of moral values that the state sought, through both persuasion and coercion, to inculcate in the people. This does not mean that Confucianism enjoyed constant and uniform success or that it underwent no changes. Some emperors were swayed more by Buddhist or Taoist beliefs than Confucian, especially in the centuries between the collapse of the Han and the beginning of the Sung. The Sung dynasty saw a revival of interest in Confucian scholarship and philosophy. From this stemmed a movement known as Neo-Confucianism, which continued to develop during the Ming and Ch'ing dynasties. One consequence of the revived Confucianism was what has been called an increasing "moral puritanism" in official attitudes, which in turn had an effect on the content of the penal law.[14] Nevertheless, the values to which Confucianism subscribed did not change in their essence. It is this fact which, more than any other, accounts for the astonishing similarity between the penal laws of all the dynasties from the T'ang to the Ch'ing.

Confucianism stamped itself upon the law in a number of significant ways. Of these the most important was the legal bolstering of the human relationships held to be necessary for the well-being of society. Early Confucianism had already stressed the bond between ruler and minister or subject, as well as that between father and son, husband and wife, and elder and younger brother. By the time of Neo-Confucianism, the first three of these had become crystallized in the concept of the "Three Bonds," a pivot in the moral and political thought of all classes.[15] The relationship between ruler and subject will receive attention in any legal system. No sovereign will tolerate acts of rebellion and the like. Hence, there is nothing specifically unique in the mere fact that the penal codes deal with offenses against the emperor and the state, though the way in which they determined punishments for those offenses presents some unique features. What may be considered unique is the complex of penal rules designed to regulate in detail the relationship between husband and wife, that between parents and children, and that between senior and junior relatives. These rules were designed to protect the institution of the family, understood as comprising not only the living members but also the deceased ancestors. The rules on adoption, for example, were designed to ensure the "purity" of the family line, so that the sacrificial offerings to the descendants would be acceptable to the ancestors.[16]

Whereas the codes pay considerable attention to the obligations entailed by family relationships, their treatment of property and commerce is sparse. We might be tempted to conclude generally that, Confucianism itself being indifferent to these matters, the legislators likewise tended on the whole to ignore them. Such a conclusion would probably be too simplistic. Certain of the rules on property found in the codes, such as those on inheritance and the powers of the family head with respect to property, almost certainly owe their inclusion to the Confucian concern with the maintenance of proper relationships within the family. Others, such as those on the use of land or the regulation of debt and transactions in the market, look at first sight as though they reflect the concern of the legislator for the maintenance of good order within the society rather than any specifically Confucian goal. In fact these rules, as well as some that appear to be purely administrative, such as those on the regulation of state granaries and storehouses, may owe their origin not simply to a concern for good order but to the particularly Confucian concept of "nourishing the people" (yang min).

Early Confucians, including Mencius, had already stressed the duty of the ruler to see that the people did not starve.[17] An obvious aspect of this duty was the need to ensure that the people had a proper share of the country's resources, sufficient to keep then adequately fed, housed, and employed. No doubt prudential as well as benevolent considerations entered into the calculations of the legislators. A contented populace was less likely to cause trouble to the ruler than one starving and burdened with debt. Nevertheless, one cannot discount the influence on the ruler of his image in Confucian orthodoxy as the fount of benevolence and humanity.[18]

"Benevolence" and "humanity" are the expressions most commonly used to render into English the Chinese term *jen*. The virtue of *jen*, particularly prized by the Neo-Confucians, had a considerable influence on the code. It can be said to underlie the important set of rules that conferred privileges on the old, the young, and the mentally or physically handicapped. Persons falling within these categories were in many cases granted either complete immunity from, or a reduction in, the standard punishment for the offense that they had committed. The legal commentaries explain these rules in terms of respect for the aged and pity for the young or infirm, but the governing concept is that of *jen*, which dictates humane treatment for the subjects of the emperor. Other rules that provide for mitigation in punishment are occasionally identified in the commentaries as examples in the highest degree of *jen*. The impression conveyed by such language is that not only the rules expressly so qualified but the penal code as a whole are products of the ruler's humanity and benevolence, constantly manifested in his concern for the people's welfare.[19]

Another important Confucian virtue is that of self-cultivation, by which individuals were encouraged to reflect on their conduct, discuss with their relatives those matters in which they had gone astray, and form the resolution to repent and reform. The value of repentance itself is given effect in the codes through the rules on confession. Where a person had committed an offense, had afterwards genuinely repented, and of his own accord had informed the authorities before its commission had publicly come to light, he was, under certain conditions, to be exempt from punishment or at least be permitted a considerable reduction. Family relationships were again taken into account, in particular the obligation of close relatives to care for and help each other. Not only were persons allowed to conceal offenses committed by their close relatives—with certain obvious exceptions such as rebellion and the like—but they were also allowed to confess on behalf of the erring relative. Confession by a person on behalf of a relative within the prescribed category was deemed to be confession by the offender himself, and it attracted the appropriate immunity or reduction in punishment. Even an accusation directed against a relative of an offense that the latter had actually committed was construed as a case in which the offending relative had himself confessed, so entailing for him any appropriate cancellation or reduction of punishment.[20]

Implicit in the Confucian conception of the family as well as in that of the relationship between ruler and subject is the notion of hierarchy. Members of the family stood toward each other in relationships under which one could always be classified as the senior and the other the junior. A son was junior with respect to his father or mother or other relative of his parents' generation, a younger brother was junior with respect to his elder brother, and a wife was junior with respect to her husband. Certain obligations were inherent in these hierarchical structures. The superior (senior) owed kindness, affection, and protection to the inferior (junior), whereas the inferior owed gratitude, submission, and respect to the superior. It was the latter aspect of the relationship that received the greater prominence in the codes, marked, on the one hand, by the fact that offenses committed by juniors against seniors were always treated more seriously than offenses committed by seniors against juniors and, on the other hand, by the fact that the duty of respect was given a very wide legal definition. This was evident particularly in the relationship between child and parent or paternal grandchild and grandparent. In these contexts, an infinite variety of acts could be classed as "disrespectful" and so entail punishment by the state of the offending child/grandchild, sometimes, but not always, at the instance of the parent/grandparent. In the Ming and Ch'ing dynasties, the concept of "filial piety" and the duty of obedience that it entailed were taken to extreme lengths, a reflection of the strict moral stance adopted by Neo-Confucianism. Another example is supplied by the Ming and Ch'ing emphasis on the chastity of women.

A final general observation is in point. Confucian rulers and officials had always expressed a preference for education rather than law as the means by which the people should be guided. A constant refrain in official declarations on the law is that punishments should supplement, reinforce, or clarify teaching. This preference may be at least in part responsible for the distrust of lawyers and legal specialists that characterized the traditional Chinese legal order. Those in charge of the administration of justice, from the district magistrate upwards, with the exception of a few high officials staffing the central judicial agencies, were not specialists in law. They were general administrators who had received their education primarily in the Confucian classics. Although they were expected to be familiar with the provisions of the penal code, and indeed were subject to punishment should an examination reveal their ignorance, their knowledge might be no more than superficial and certainly not adequate to deal with all the legislative subtleties and intricacies.[21] As a result, in Ming and Ch'ing times, magistrates and prefects tended to rely on the services of private persons who had made a special study of the law, employed on their personal staff and paid from their own resources. These "legal secretaries," as they were termed, often wrote the draft of the judgments in legal cases that their employer was required to submit for scrutiny to higher authority.

Equally, the development of a legal profession whose services might be available to members of the public was actively discouraged by the state. Private legal specialists, other than those employed by the state or its officials, were regarded as a dangerous source of trouble, liable to be involved in the fomenting of litigation and the bringing of false accusations. The Ch'ing code established severe punishments for persons described as "litigation tricksters" or "pettifoggers" (sung kun) who were found to have made a practice of promoting litigation before the local magistrate.[22]

ATTRIBUTES OF SPIRIT NOT NECESSARILY LEGALIST OR CONFUCIAN

Not all the characteristics of the penal codes can be readily classified as Legalist or Confucian. Admittedly, there is a certain danger in the kind of classification attempted here, in that there may be a legitimate doubt as to whether a particular feature should properly be regarded as Confucian/Legalist or not. Hence it has seemed better to treat independently certain attributes of the codes, on the grounds that they do not betray obvious signs of an origin in specifically Confucian or Legalist thought. These attributes in turn may be divided into two groups: those that seem peculiarly distinctive of the traditional Chinese law in the sense that they differentiate it from Western systems, and those that mark the handling of issues central to any developed legal system. In the first group we include the attributes of conservatism, symbolism, and the value attached to human life. In the second group, we include the technical construction of the codes, the rationality of the legal process, and the purposes of punishment.

Distinctive (Non-Western) Attributes

Features of the codes that make a striking impression on the Western student are the related phenomena of their unique conservatism and the fact that a number of rules seem to have been included irrespective of the difficulties of enforcement or, indeed, even with no expectation that they will be enforced.[23] The conservative nature of the codes has already been touched on in the context of Confucian moral orthodoxy. One reason for the preservation of the same rules, despite great social and political change over many centuries, is undoubtedly that they are grounded in the basic Confucian morality, which did not significantly change. Yet there also seem to be aspects of conservatism that cannot be treated as specifically Confucian in themselves. The respect for the past and the decisions of the ancestors, deeply ingrained in traditional thought, in itself entailed a reluctance to change. There was the inherent respect not only for the institutions established by the founding emperor of the dynasty but also for the achievements in government of previous dynasties, particularly those of the T'ang dynasty. The T'ang penal code was still esteemed as a model by legal scholars at the end of the Ch'ing dynasty.[24] This evaluation was based not just on respect for a great dynasty but also on the intrinsic excellence of the T'ang code itself.

The "symbolic" aspect of the codes is related to the "conservative" in that a number of the rules inherited by the penal codes of successive dynasties have a "symbolic" rather than a "practical" function. By this we mean that their presence in the codes is not to be explained by the fact that they are intended to be enforced, but rather by the fact that they express a certain message. The content of the message may vary and, indeed, cannot always be identified with certainty. Two examples may illustrate the point. Certain parts of the family legislation in all the codes were probably never enforceable throughout the empire as a whole, and they may never have been promulgated with the intention of enforcement. These are the rules specifying the circumstances under which a divorce is permissible or a marriage is to be dissolved, prohibiting the marriage of persons with the same surname, and regulating the class of persons who might be adopted as sons. The prime object of such rules was to affirm in the most solemn way the fundamental family values. Again, it is doubtful whether the rules requiring the standardization of weights and measures could ever have been seriously intended to be enforced. Yet from early times it was regarded as one of the regular duties of the ruler to secure such uniformity. Hence the codes had to contain rules that evidenced the concern of the ruler for the fulfillment of his obligations.

A distinctive feature of the penal codes is the value attached to human life, albeit in a somewhat paradoxical fashion. First, the general presumption of the law is that a person responsible for the loss of another man's life must in turn forfeit his own by way of compensation. Although this principle might be displaced by considerations of status, as where a senior had killed a junior, by and large the law attached great importance to it. Even a person who accidentally killed another was, at least in the later law, formally sentenced to death, although in most cases it was possible to redeem the sentence by payment of money to the family of the deceased.

Regard was had not only for the life of the victim, but also for that of the person deemed responsible for the death. Where the law required the imposition of a sentence of death, whether in cases of homicide or not, the greatest care was taken to ensure in any particular case that the sentence had properly been imposed. For example, under the Ch'ing all capital cases were reviewed in detail by the Board of Punishments, and all death sentences required explicit imperial confirmation. Emperors in all dynasties frequently commented that a life once taken could not be restored.

The paradox lies in the fact that, although the codes required the imposition of a sentence of death, in many cases procedural devices were employed to secure the commutation of the sentence into life exile or less. Broadly speaking in cases of homicide where extenuating circumstances were present, that is, in particular where there had been no actual intention to kill, a review body would recommend to the emperor that the death sentence proposed by the courts and initially confirmed by imperial edict should not be implemented.

The respect paid by the codes to the value of human life can, at least to some extent, be seen as another example of symbolic expression. It was important that the code should formally provide that persons who had killed another should in turn forfeit their lives. Yet such rules were not always intended to be literally enforced. Where grounds for mitigation were present, devices were found to transmute the nominal capital into a noncapital sentence. Implicit in this approach is the law's regard for human life in its broadest context, a regard that ensured appropriate modification of the strict principle requiring forfeiture of the killer's life.

Essential Issues

One issue that faces any developed legal system predicated on a code is the organization of the code and the interrelationship between the rules of which it is composed. The latter question raises the problem of legal shorthand. What devices are to be used to facilitate cross-references between rules? As early as the T'ang dynasty the penal code showed considerable sophistication both in its basic structure and in its cross-referencing. Indeed, the organization of the T'ang code, as its substance, provided the model for all the later codes. It was divided into two main sections, one containing general principles, the other, the specific offenses. The former comprised the general rules governing the application of the punishments, such as those defining the various privileges or defining certain common terms. The latter, arranged roughly according to subject matter, described each offense and the standard punishment to be imposed. This basic framework already discloses a high level of abstraction.

The description of the specific offenses yields an unusual combination of the general and the specific. Since the object of the legislators was to leave as little discretion as possible to the law-enforcing agencies, it was necessary that each offense be described in detail, so that the court could immediately match the facts with the offense and ascertain the correct punishment. At the same time, a full description in each case of all the ramifications of the offense with all its particular circumstances would have entailed not only enormous length but much repetition and duplication. To avoid this, the legislators practiced a technique that we have termed "economy of means." A relatively small number of rules were used in various combinations to permit the calculation of the appropriate punishment for a very large number of situations. The ability to achieve this result was facilitated by the development of a sophisticated "legal shorthand." A series of key terms, each of which entailed a reference to, and invocation of, a particular group of rules, was frequently employed in the description of an offense or the stipulation of its punishment.

At all stages of its development the law appears to have been characterized by a spirit of rationality and fairness. This is evident particularly in the conduct of the legal process. The earliest source (the *K'ang kao*) shows that an individual's guilt was to be determined by the application of the law to the facts as ascertained through a scrupulous examination of the evidence. Methods of proof were rational, based on the investigation of the circumstances of the case by the officiating magistrate and the interrogation of the parties and the witnesses. At no time, even in cases involving allegations of sorcery or witchcraft, was there resort to ordeals or oracles. Decisions of the Board of Punishments reported from the eighteenth and nineteenth centuries are models of legal reasoning. The greatest care was taken to see both that the full facts had been brought to light and that the correct rules of law had been applied.

The one obvious exception to the general rationality and fairness of the legal process is the use of torture. Nevertheless, the law, at least in theory, strictly regulated the degree to which torture (normally beatings) might be employed in the interrogation of suspects or witnesses. The penal codes established the limits within, and the methods by, which torture was to be employed, and prescribed punishments for officials guilty of misuse. During the Ch'ing, in homicide cases in which it suspected that the lies and deceit of the parties or witnesses had prevented disclosure of the full truth, the Board of Punishments was prepared to instruct the provincial authorities to use severe methods (torture) to elicit the truth. In practice, especially in politically sensitive trials, excessive and illegal employment of torture did occur.

As a final issue we have the conception of punishment. The object of a penal code is to secure the compliance by the people of certain standards of conduct through the threat of punishment should the required standards not be met. Such a statement does not, however, tell us anything of the ulterior purpose of punishment that the legislator had in mind. Was it purely to deter persons from acting in the prohibited way? Was it to inflict pain in the conviction that the offender had deserved to suffer (retribution)? Or was the infliction of punishment intended to have a curative effect and bring about the repentance and reform of the erring individual? The Legalists had been interested only in the deterrent, whereas the Confucianists not only had stressed in addition its reformative possibilities, but had also used language hinting at the desirability of retribution.

Although the penal codes do not articulate a theory of punishment, one can draw certain inferences from the conditions under which punishment is imposed. The feature that immediately strikes the eye is the care with which each offense is given a punishment graduated to the seriousness with which the act in question is regarded. Seriousness is evaluated by reference not just to the intrinsic nature of the deed but also to the social or family standing of the perpetrator.

The necessity of finding exactly the right punishment for the offense emerges even more clearly from decisions of the Board of Punishments in Ch'ing times. These consistently emphasize the point that the facts and the punishment must match if an equitable result is to be achieved. All this suggests that the legislators were strongly influenced by a notion that may be understood as "retribution" in a broad sense. More exactly, we should distinguish between "retribution" in a strict sense, which pays attention to the moral wickedness displayed by the offender, and "requital," which pays attention to the degree of harm done by the act. Punishment is graduated according to the degree of moral wickedness and the extent of the harm.

The reformative or deterrent possibilities of punishment were also exploited. Prevalent throughout the imperial period was the notion that punishment itself might be used to induce shame and repentance. A corollary was that, where an offender could be shown to have repented prior to discovery of the offense, the law recognized that in principle there was no longer a need to punish. Punishment was also conceived as a deterrent. Resort to punishment to secure proper conduct on the part of the emperor's subjects was deemed necessary, where teaching and moral guidance had failed to produce the desired effect.[25]

2 Varieties of Law

Traditional Chinese law as such is too broad a concept for unitary treatment. It has to be broken into a number of categories, each of which possesses its own distinguishing features. In the first place, we have to distinguish between the official and the unofficial law. The "official" law is that which emanates from the emperor in whose person was concentrated all legislative, executive, and judicial power. Traditional China did not know the Western concept of "separation of powers." Whereas the emperor delegated many of his administrative and judicial powers to his officials (while retaining ultimate control), he reserved for himself the legislative function. Naturally, he took advice from his ministers as to the topics for which legislation was required, but it was his authority that conferred on the rules so established the force of law. Official law may itself be divided into two main components: penal law and administrative law.[1] The former prescribed punishments for the behavior made mandatory by the state, and the latter defined the duties of the officials and the way in which they were to be performed. By contrast, "unofficial" law was the customary law of the people, rules that developed in localities or among associations of merchants and traders for the handling of matters of common concern. Neither of the standard words for law (*fa* or *lü*) was ever applied to rules of this kind.

Of these varieties only penal law is relatively well known in the West or has received any systematic treatment by Western scholars. A number of reasons can be adduced for this preference. There is first the matter of accessibility, both as to sources and comprehension. It has been relatively easy to gain a thorough knowledge of the penal codes or at least of their central provisions, because they are relatively manageable in size and possess a definite structure and internal coherence. Less well known have been the reports of judicial decisions found in the great Ch'ing collections.[2] Nevertheless, they also are increasingly studied both by lawyers and historians.[3] By contrast, collections of materials on administrative law not only are of formidable bulk but appear to be of impenetrable complexity. Further, the concept and the role of penal law have been more readily comprehensible in the West than the intricate ramifications of administrative law. Penal law displays a logic that is paralleled in the West, that of prescribing conduct through the stipulation of sanctions for deviant behavior. Although one can easily grasp the notion of a set of rules prescribing the duties of officials or the functions of administrative agencies, the sheer complexity of the Chinese administrative system has made it exceptionally difficult for Western students to acquire a general familiarity with the legal principles that govern it.[4]

Second, there has been the question of basic human interest. Penal law is generally perceived as having a much greater bearing on the human condition, and therefore as possessing a greater intrinsic interest, than administrative law. In the case of traditional China, the penal law has provided one of the richest sources for an understanding of the fundamental morality of the people or at least that of the governing elite. At the same time the reports of decisions of the Board of Punishments in criminal cases have proved to be of great interest to historians seeking details of the lives of ordinary people.[5] The first to translate the Ch'ing penal code into a Western language, G. L. Staunton, made reference to this point in 1812. In his preface to *Ta Tsing Leu Lee; being the Fundamental Laws and a Selection from the Supplementary Statutes of the Penal Code of China* (p. xxv), he quoted from Montesquieu the famous passage on the need for the laws of each nation to match the way of life of the people of the country, to echo their morality and their customs.

The study of unofficial law has also had limited appeal in the West. This may be due in part to the fact that the data are contained in such a variety of source materials, most extremely difficult to access, that the very existence of customary rules, lying altogether outside the realm of the statutory law, either remained a matter of assumption or was only occasionally glimpsed in written accounts of disputes or litigation. After the fall of the Ch'ing, a major project was started to compile collections of the customary rules governing property and commercial transactions in the various provinces of China. The results of this project were published and even translated into a Western language.[6] However, very little study of it appears to have been made. Unofficial law still seems to Western scholars a peripheral matter of small interest in comparison with the official, especially penal law.

This book will be confined largely to the penal law. But something will be said here briefly of the other varieties. The point to be borne in mind is that much more study in the West is needed before either administrative law or unofficial law in traditional China can be properly appreciated.

ADMINISTRATIVE LAW

Administrative law was well developed in China very early.[7] This can be seen in the surviving fragments of the Ch'in rules.[8] It was the Ch'in state and empire that laid the administrative basis built on and refined by succeeding dynasties. The central problem faced by the ruler of an empire so large and diverse as China was the maintenance of effective control throughout its various provinces and districts with the help of merely a handful of skilled literate personnel. The fact that the great dynasties, except in times of major political unrest and rebellious activity, succeeded in this task is due to a combination of three factors. First, there was a clear principle that the function of the officials despatched from the center for the administration of the provinces should be strictly limited. They were to be responsible for the collection of taxes, the organization of public works, and the maintenance of order through the control of serious crime.[9] Other matters were largely to be left to the regulation of the family, clan, village, or guild.[10]

Second, there was put in place an effective means of communication between the central administration and the officials in charge of the provinces, prefectures, and districts. A fast and efficient government courier service transmitted documents. From the lower end of the chain of command flowed a stream of reports and requests for authorization, from the higher end, orders, authorizations, and requests for information. Detailed rules defined the situations in which documents should be issued, specified their form, and prescribed the times within which they must be transmitted. We may cite here in particular the complex system for the submission of memorials to the emperor, their handling within the offices of the central government, and the production of an imperial edict in response.[11]

Third, there was the perfection of a system of delegation and accountability. At the most general level, the emperor delegated his executive and judicial, though not his legislative, functions to his officials. They exercised their powers in his name and were accountable to him. At the more specific level, further delegation occurred within the hierarchy of officials. The magistrate in charge of a district was responsible to the prefect in charge of the prefecture to which the district belonged, and the prefect in turn was responsible to the governor of the province containing the prefecture. Each administrative level was required to supervise and review the proceedings of that subordinate to it in the hierarchy, and the working of the whole system was regularly scrutinized by censors or specially commissioned imperial investigators. Accountability was strict in the sense that commission of an error entailed liability and punishment, even though no intent or corruption was present. Furthermore, not only the official who made the mistake but all others in the administrative unit or even in subordinate or superior units who had associated themselves with the mistaken decision were made individually liable. By and large, despite the endemic problems of corruption and incompetence, the system in times of tranquillity and peace worked well. Its pivot, expressed in Legalist terms, was the retention by the emperor in his own hands of the "twin handles of reward and punishment."[12]

What was the position of the emperor in the administrative structure? In theory he was supreme and hence above the law. He could make the law, override existing laws, and upset administrative decisions taken in his name. Yet, although autocratic, the emperors on the whole observed the law.[13] The very existence of the complex bureaucratic machinery constituted a check on the arbitrary exercise of autocratic power. Over the centuries certain hallowed ways for dealing with difficult questions arose. The issue was submitted by memorial to the emperor. He referred the memorial to the appropriate agency of the central government with a request for its advice. The matter would be considered by the appropriate body with reference to the way in which such questions had been handled in the past or in terms of the existing laws and regulations. Where a new piece of legislation was being considered, care would be taken to assess its relationship to the existing law and to ensure that no change was introduced that upset the principles for the proper distribution of punishment. The emperor normally accepted such advice. In other words, he was guided in his actions primarily by reference to what was already accepted as good law. It is true that on occasion he might modify a capital sentence referred to him by the central judicial agencies for his approval, but he always did so with reference to the facts of the particular case and explained in his edict the reasons for the change he had made.[14] Sometimes, indeed, he would even accept a remonstrance by his officials that the change was not proper and accept that he had to act in conformity with the existing law.[15]

The emperors themselves, despite the occasional abuse of power, did not regard themselves as being in a position to act according to their own desires. They were conscious that they had been entrusted with the Mandate of Heaven and that they were therefore bound to respect the laws of heaven and the enactments of their ancestors. Effectively this meant that they could not tamper with the essential framework of the laws that had been inherited from the past, were known to comply with the dictates of heaven, and had been repeatedly confirmed by their imperial forebears. The K'ang-hsi Ch'ing emperor in his valedictory edict issued to the people after his death declared: "The rulers of the past all took reverence for Heaven's laws and reverence for their ancestors as the fundamental way in ruling the country. To be sincere in reverence for Heaven and ancestors entails the following: Be kind to men from afar and keep the able ones near, nourish the people, . . . protect the state before danger comes and govern well before there is any disturbance, be always diligent and always careful."[16]

UNOFFICIAL LAW

Under this umbrella is grouped much of what in the West is termed private or civil law.[17] In particular, it comprises the rules governing the use of property, whether according to private agreement or local usage, and the management and devolution of property within the family. To a limited extent matters of contract and property were regulated by the penal code,[18] but on the whole they were left to private negotiation and the custom of localities. Several reasons can be adduced for the government's "hands off" attitude.

First, there was the conviction that the primary objectives of the penal law should be the maintenance of good order and the reinforcement of basic moral teaching. The latter objective was the more important since observance of the basic moral requirements was believed in itself to entail the stability and prosperity of the realm. There was a moral imperative resting on the ruler to act for the welfare of the people, to "nourish the people," as was stated in the K'ang-hsi edict just quoted. From this perspective may be explained the inclusion in the penal codes of the rules on debt and usury, dealings with land, the borrowing and pledging of property, and the sale of goods in the markets.[19] Regulations on these matters were conducive to the well-being of the people in that, if followed, they would minimize the chance of friction and dispute. Such topics were regarded as of sufficient importance to be cast into the form of behavior prohibited under threat of punishment.

The state also had a strong practical reason for limiting the subject matter to be enforced under the penal code. The persons on whom the main responsibility for the application of the law rested were the district magistrates. They already had large areas of territory and large numbers of people to administer. As a matter of practicality it was impossible to require them to deal with a potentially unlimited range of disputes arising from property and commercial transactions or dislocated family relationships. The government's concern for efficient administration had two consequences. On the one hand, only a strictly limited number of "civil" matters were included in the penal code, thus theoretically necessitating action by the magistrates should the formal rules be breached. On the other hand, magistrates were discouraged by the government not only from intervening when breaches of the penal code in civil matters occurred, but even from acting as arbiters in any kind of civil dispute. (We may also recall the point that a number of the provisions inserted in the code were never seriously meant to be enforced.)

The government was in something of a quandary with respect to its policy in civil matters. It recognized that it had an obligation to prevent the people from resorting to indiscriminate violence. Consequently, it was aware of the danger should no official means for the settlement of disputes be provided. The preamble to the article on intimidation in both the Ming and Ch'ing codes stated that "all persons who have quarrels and disputes ought to forbear from seeking redress otherwise than by complaining to the proper officer of government and submitting the justice of their cause to his decision."[20] How was the government to achieve this objective without overburdening its regular officers? From time to time certain special expedients were adopted with a view to providing mechanisms within the local community for the settlement of disputes arising from contract, property, or family relationships. One of the most far-reaching of these was that established by the founding emperor of the Ming dynasty. He appointed a number of respected elders in each village and conferred on them not just the authority to deal with civil disputes but also quite an extensive criminal jurisdiction.[21] In fact, this attempt ended in failure. Throughout the Ming and Ch'ing dynasties the government tried various experiments to make wealthy and influential people in the villages responsible for preventing and settling disputes.[22] None of these proved to have long-lasting success.

Despite official discouragement, people did constantly bring their disputes before the local magistrate in default of any other effective agency that might resolve them. The more conscientious and able magistrates, while doing everything possible to discourage the people from engaging in ruinous litigation, were prepared to act as arbiters or mediators in the disputes submitted to them.[23] They either referred them back to the village for local mediation or suggested a compromise solution. Magistrates were not interested in developing a system of legal rules that might be applied to a range of disputes. In this they contrast sharply with the Roman jurists of the first to third centuries A.D. who developed a highly refined system of civil law. The Chinese magistrate, reflecting the general cultural bias of the society, was more concerned with persuading the parties to make concessions and resolve the dispute amicably. Even where the rules of the penal code were relevant, as in the case of those providing for the punishment of defaulting debtors, the magistrate did not always apply them. Instead he sought to prevail on the creditor to accept less than the amount actually due or to make arrangements for the satisfaction of the debt by the payment of installments. Underlying this approach was the desire to promote the welfare of the people rather than to stick to the letter of the law.

Just as the magistrate's own attitude was not conducive to the development of a civil law, so also was the lack in China of a strong and independent legal profession. The official policy of all dynasties was to discourage the activities of legal specialists, unless such persons were themselves members of the government or administration. The state feared that private individuals who intermeddled in the legal process on behalf of others would contribute to the evil of false accusations, stir up litigation, and generally help families ruin themselves. Graphic pictures were drawn in official propaganda of the disasters befalling those who resorted to litigation. Lawyers were described politely as "litigation tricksters" or "pettifoggers" and less politely as tigers, wolves, or demons.

Legislation in Ming and Ch'ing times imposed severe punishments on persons convicted of helping others to make false accusations. The legislation conceded that the rustic and illiterate needed help to prepare their petitions, and it therefore provided that anyone who merely assisted such a person to bring a legitimate grievance before a magistrate was to be immune from punishment. But the helper must be careful to avoid contributing any suggestion of his own for the "improvement" of the case. Arguably there was a need to control the extortionate activities of persons who deliberately exploited others by getting them to indulge in costly litigations, the main object of which was to supply a profit for the "helper." Yet the law seems to have gone too far in subjecting to heavy punishment even legal specialists who might genuinely have been trying to help persons in trouble prepare their cases.[24] Although the law never succeeded in stamping out the class of litigation specialists, the occupation was risky, and there was no opportunity for the Chinese lawyer to emulate the Roman jurist or the English common lawyer in creating a body of civil law.

Two important collections of "legal customs" constitute major sources for the "unofficial law" of traditional China. One is the *Ming shang shih hsi kuan tiao ch'a pao kao lü* (Report Concerning the Investigation of Civil and Commercial Customs). This is a collection of "legal customs" drawn from a number of the Chinese provinces. The inspiration for its collection came with the "reform movement" in the closing years of the Ch'ing dynasty, but the main work of collection was done after the establishment of the Republic, the results not being published until 1930. The customary rules and practices presented in the collection are arranged by prefecture and province, and they have been classified by the compilers under three main heads: real rights and obligations, personal rights and obligations, and rights and obligations arising from marriage, adoption, or inheritance. Very little attention has been paid to the collection, and some important questions still require clarification. It is not clear what criterion of "legal" was adopted for the compilation, or whether all the customs recorded should properly be considered as forming part of the "unofficial law." Nor is the relationship between the customary and the statutory law clear, that is, the extent to which the one has influenced the other.[25]

The other collection relates only to Formosa (Taiwan) and was made on the instructions of the Japanese government after Japan had acquired the territory from China in 1895. It consists of a report written by a Japanese law professor in 1900 on the basis of researches completed prior to that time, an English version being issued in 1902.[26] This collection differs from the *Ming shang* in that it is more than a listing of a large variety of customs. The material has been analyzed by the reporter, and the legal institutions underlying the customs have been reconstituted. Only the law relating to land, its use, transactions involving it, and rights to water are fully discussed, but a useful summary of material relating to marriage, adoption, and succession is included in an appendix. On the relationship between the penal code and the customs followed by the people, the reporter concludes that, although the principles of the code were followed as a general guide, there were a number of customs, tolerated by the authorities, that infringed it.[27] Further, many customs dealt with matters not regulated by the penal code at all. An important datum found by the reporter was the reliance by the people on documents to record the incidents of an enormous variety of transactions arising from all aspects of daily life. He notes that these documents furnished a means by which the people secured a measure of protection for their rights in the face of a weak government and lack of judicial protection. Such documents constituted the basic source for the determination of the customs in use by the people.[28]

THE PENAL LAW

The centerpiece of the penal law is the "code of punishments" issued by each dynasty at its inception.[29] Although fragments of laws survive from the Ch'in, Han, and other pre-T'ang dynasties, the first code to have survived in its entirety was developed under the Sui and fully developed by the T'ang. This code provided the model for all the later traditional penal codes. From a comparison of the T'ang, Sung, Ming, and Ch'ing codes one is able to ascertain the remarkable continuity in the content of the penal law over a period of approximately thirteen centuries. Only the Mongolian dynasty of the Yüan failed to issue a penal code as such, but the collections of legal materials from that dynasty still show the strong influence of the T'ang code.

The penal codes contain only rules that prescribe punishments for specific offenses, rules that define generally the allocation of punishment, or those that establish principles of interpretation. Marinus Meijer has drawn attention to the concept of the "named offense." Each offense is given a specific name (*ming*) and allocated a specific punishment. The task of the magistrate or other official charged with enforcement of the code was to identify the proper "name" of the offense disclosed by the facts. Once this identity had been made, determination of the correct punishment automatically followed.[30]

The notion of punishment has dominated the Chinese conception of law since at least the epoch of the early Chou, around 1000 B.C. The earliest words for law in the sources express the fact of punishment. One of these, *hsing*, has a graph that contains the character for "knife."[31] Discussions by statesmen and literati on the role of law in government have always concentrated on two questions: to what extent should punishments be used to reinforce teaching, and, granted that rules imposing punishments are an indispensable part of government, what should be the correct quantum of punishment for any given offense? The latter question involved consideration in particular of the extent to which the punishments should be physical, requiring the death or mutilation of the offender, rather than exile or forced labor. These debates had in essence been settled by the time of the T'ang dynasty. It had become clear that the penal code was indispensable in government as a supplement to moral teaching. There was no serious dispute that the infliction of punishment by the state was necessary in order to secure good order and prevent the proliferation of evil. Yet punishments were still to be humane. The mutilating punishments that had characterized the earlier law and even been in use for a time under the Han were no longer to be used.[32] They were replaced with beatings or forced labor. The five regular punishments established by the T'ang code were in descending order of severity: death, life exile, penal servitude (forced labor), beating with the heavy stick, or beating with the light stick. They remained the regular punishments until the closing years of the Ch'ing, though under exceptional circumstances emperors might resort to other punishments.[33]

The penal codes were divided into a "General Principles" and a "Specific Offenses" section. Each dynasty retained the same basic content, though the Ming and Ch'ing codes introduced some variation in the classification of offenses.[34] The principal difference between the T'ang/Sung codes on the one hand and the Ming/Ch'ing codes on the other lay in their respective bulk and detail. The T'ang and Sung codes consisted of a number of articles (*lü*), many of which were adopted, sometimes without alteration, by the Ming and Ch'ing codes. A certain sacrosanctity attached to the *lü*. Once the articles of the code had been established at the beginning of the dynasty, there was a reluctance on the part of the founding emperor or his successors to change them. Certainly, the *lü* were revised from time to time and a few changes made, but generally in Ming and Ch'ing times there was a need for more frequent and more extensive additions to the code than were possible through the occasional revisions of the *lü*.[35] Consequently, the Ming, followed by the Ch'ing, started the practice of adding substatutes (*li*) to the code. The practice grew extensively under the Ch'ing, with the result that, by the end of the nineteenth century, the penal code had lost something of its internal coherence and become an unwieldy instrument, very difficult to use.

The principal function of the *li* was to allow the code to adapt to changing circumstances, to enable the penal code, as it were, to keep abreast of social problems. Most *li* originated in the following way. Sometimes legal cases arose in the provinces for which the local authorities were unable to find a provision in the code capable of covering the actual facts. One way of dealing with the matter was to propose a solution through the application by analogy of an existing provision. This was frequently done. But, where the matter was deemed to be of sufficient importance to warrant the establishing of a uniform rule to be followed for the future in every province, the provincial governor or the Board would ask the throne to consent to the enactment of a *li* for inclusion in the code. Normally, though by no means invariably, the throne would accede to the request. Alternatively, the governor of a province or other high-ranking official might detect a problem that in his opinion required the creation of a new offense. He would accordingly memorialize the throne. The emperor would refer the matter for consideration to the Board of Punishments or perhaps one of the other Boards, and again normally accept the Board's advice.[36]

Li tended to be more specific and detailed than *lü*. A *lü* might lay down in general terms how a particular situation was to be treated; *li* then dealt with more specific combinations of circumstances arising from that general situation, often repeating in their formulation the actual facts of the case that had given rise to them. We cite an example from the Ch'ing code. One *lü* established that, where A killed B in a fight, A was to be sentenced to strangulation after the assizes.[37] The same *lü* provided that, if A, B, and C plotted to beat D, and D was killed in the affray, then the person who initially broached the idea was to be sentenced to exile, and the person who inflicted the wound causing death was to be sentenced to strangulation after the assizes. These rules did not cover all the combinations of fact that could arise from the basic situation of a fight. Hence *li* were added to the *lü* to provide supplementary rules. Thus, if during a fight a gun was fired and someone was killed, then, even though there had been no intention to kill, the killing was to be treated as intentional, and the person who fired the gun was to be sentenced to beheading after the assizes.[38] Other *li* dealt with group attacks where it was not possible to identify one person as the "original plotter" or to determine which wound actually caused the victim's death or indeed which of the attackers inflicted which wounds. Detailed rules were established to apportion liability in such cases.[39] The general effect of the addition of *li* to the code by the eighteenth and nineteenth centuries is that most criminal cases were governed primarily by the application of *li* rather than *lü*. Indeed, under the Ch'ing, the *li* were given priority even over a contrary *lü* in the determination of a case.[40]

Explanatory commentaries of varying degrees of authority were added to the penal codes. The most authoritative were those approved by the throne for inclusion in the code. These often themselves contained rules not found in the articles or substatutes. The *shu-i* commentary of the T'ang code was of this kind, as was the "official" or "small" interlinear commentary of the Ming and Ch'ing codes, so called because it was written in smaller characters and inserted into the text of the articles.[41] Such official commentaries carried an authority equal to that of the articles or substatutes. There were also important private commentaries that publishers in Ming and Ch'ing times often added to their editions of the code. These commentaries were mainly explanatory and were clearly found useful by officials required to interpret and apply the code. Occasionally they might make suggestions for the handling of a particular situation, where no clear rule was to be found in the code. Such suggestions were often treated as authoritative propositions of law by provincial governors, a practice which the Board of Punishments itself discouraged.[42]

In theory the penal law was established by the emperor and applied by his officials. The latter were not considered to possess lawmaking powers themselves. Their task was to identify that article or sub-statute in the code precisely relevant to the facts before them. In such cases it was not necessary for the matter to be referred to the throne for a final decision, unless a capital sentence was involved. But what was to be done where no precisely relevant statutory rule could be found? The code itself provided for this situation. It recognized that it was not possible for the legislator to draft rules that might cover every eventuality in the future. Consequently, in Ming and Ch'ing law, should no precisely relevant rule be discoverable, the officials were empowered to suggest a rule from the code that might be applied by analogy with any appropriate increase or decrease in punishment. However, all proposals for the analogous application of a statute had to be referred to the throne for confirmation. In this way the emperor was able to keep a check on the way in which the law was being developed independently by his officials.[43]

Legal practice does not seem to have accorded entirely with theory. For example, in the field of homicide law, there are numerous cases in which a provincial governor or the Board of Punishments, in the absence of a clear statutory rule, will cite previous decisions of the Board that have dealt with the point at issue or at least refer to the fact that no such decisions are discoverable. Consequently, it seems as though decisions of the Board might function as "precedents" in the sense that they would be taken as providing authoritative guid-ance in a situation for which no unambiguous article or substatute could be invoked.[44]

3 The Conservative and Symbolic Spirit of the Law

In an essay on the life and work of the late Ch'ing scholar Wang Kuo-wei, Ching-I Tu has defined conservatism in words that aptly express the theme of this chapter:

> [T]he essence of conservatism is "preservation of the ancient moral traditions of humanity." A conservative has great respect for the wisdom of his ancestors and is somehow dubious of sweeping change. He regards society as "a spiritual reality, possessing an eternal life, but a delicate constitution: it cannot be scrapped and recast as if it were a machine." Most important is the conservative's belief that civilized society "requires order" and that "tradition and sound prejudice can provide checks upon man's anarchic impulse," especially in a revolutionary age.[1]

There are many aspects of the penal codes and of the legal process in general that stem from a concern for the "preservation of the ancient moral tradition of humanity" and from a "great respect for the wisdom of the ancestors." Equally, they reflect a concern for "order," the maintenance of social stability, and the rejection of anarchy.

In traditional China the "conservative spirit" had an effect on the law that to Western eyes appears quite exceptional. Not only were large sections of the substantive and procedural law retained more or less intact from the T'ang to the Ch'ing (a period of thirteen centuries), but many rules were retained long after they had ceased to have any connection with social reality. We give first some examples of substantive and procedural conservatism, then seek to identify in more detail the reason for the survival of these rules and institutions, and finally consider specifically what we term the "phenomenon of the nonenforceable."

CONSERVATISM IN SUBSTANCE

Organization of the Codes

Even the most cursory glance at the penal codes of the T'ang, Sung, Ming, and Ch'ing dynasties will reveal striking similarities in their structure and content. All the codes have the same basic organization with the material divided between "General Principles" and "Specific Offenses." Within these sections the treatment of topics follows roughly the same order, and the classification adopted for the enumeration of the offenses is largely the same. For example, the opening articles of the "General Principles" section in all the codes successively treat the five punishments, the ten abominations, and the persons entitled to the privilege of "deliberation." Within the "Specific Offenses" section the material is considered under a number of heads, with the Ming and Ch'ing codes still following the basic pattern of the T'ang code. The latter has the following subsections: offenses committed in connection with the imperial guard, offenses committed by officials in the exercise of their duties, offenses concerning relationships within the family (household and marriage), offenses concerning the management of state resources (stables and granaries), offenses concerning military matters, the most serious offenses against the state or the person (treason, homicide, theft, or kidnapping), offenses of assaults and false accusations, offenses of deceit and fraud, miscellaneous offenses covering inter alia breach of contract, illicit sexual intercourse, fires and damage to property, offenses of desertion or offenses committed in connection with the arrest of persons, and offenses committed in connection with the custody, treatment, or sentencing of offenders.

The Ming and Ch'ing codes, while retaining with modifications the T'ang classifications, have arranged all the material dealing with the specific offenses under six main heads derived from the spheres of competence of the six principal departments of government: those for the civil service, military affairs, ritual affairs, judicial affairs, financial affairs, and public works. Under the general head of "civil service laws" are grouped two sections, one retaining the T'ang title of "administrative regulations," the other entitled "public regulations." Under the general head of "financial laws" are seven sections concerning family and corvée, land and houses, marriage, granaries and storehouses, revenue and taxes, debts, and markets. Under the general head of "ritual laws" there are two sections, one on sacrifices, the other on etiquette. Under the general head of "military laws" are sections concerning the palace and imperial guard, the army, frontiers and ferries, stables and herds, and government couriers. Under the general head of "penal laws" are sections on brigandage and theft, homicide, fights and assaults, cursing and abuse, accusations and litigation, receipt of illicit goods, arrests and escapes, sentencing and imprisonment, and miscellaneous offenses.[2] Finally, under the general head of "public works laws" there are two sections, one pertaining to buildings and constructions, the other to river embankments.

The classification adopted in the T'ang code is the substratum on which the Ming and Ch'ing codes have been built. Essentially, there have been three changes. The T'ang categories have been perceived as covering too much material, and hence have been recast to yield a number of further categories. This process has necessitated a certain rearrangement of the T'ang articles. Most noticeable is the reallocation of many of the articles contained in the "miscellaneous offenses" subsection. At the same time, there has been a limited change in the content of the codes, some of the T'ang articles being suppressed and some new offenses being added.

Rebellion

Similarity of content extends not just to identity of substance, but even in some cases to the preservation by the later codes of the wording employed in the T'ang code. As illustrations may be selected three of the most important offenses in the code: rebellion, theft, and homicide. The first part of the T'ang article on rebellion (article 248) runs:

> All cases of plotting rebellion or great sedition, all those involved behead; their fathers and their sons aged sixteen or above all strangle; their sons aged fifteen or under, mothers, daugh-

ters, wives, and concubines [sons of wives and concubines being treated in the same way], grandfathers or grandsons in the male line, elder and younger brothers, elder and younger sisters, equally their personal retainers, lands and houses are all to be forfeit to the government. But men who are aged eighty or are incapacitated and women who are aged sixty or are disabled are to be exempt from forfeiture [the same is to apply in other articles where women are made jointly liable]. Their fathers' brothers and their brothers' sons are all to be exiled to 3,000 *li*, irrespective of whether they are on the same household register or not.

The portions in brackets give the interlinear official or "small" commentary. The corresponding section of the Ch'ing article runs:

All cases of plotting rebellion [to harm the state, that is, plotting to overthrow its guardian spirits] or great sedition [to harm the ruler, that is, plotting to destroy his temples, ancestral tombs, or palaces], where there is only a collective plot no distinction is to be made between principal and accessory [whether or not there have been acts to implement the plot], all involved are to be sentenced to death by slicing. The principal offenders' paternal grandfathers, fathers, sons, and grandsons, elder or younger brothers, or persons living in the same household [for example, nonmourning relatives of the same clan, maternal grandfather, wife's father, resident sons-in-law, or others], whether the surname is the same or not, or [one-year-mourning relatives of the principal offenders, namely] their paternal uncles or sons of their brothers, in the case of [males] aged sixteen or above, whether or not they are incapacitated or disabled, all are to be beheaded, in the case of [males] aged fifteen or below or [the principal offenders'] mothers, daughters, wives, concubines, elder or younger sisters, or the wives and concubines of their sons, all are to be given to meritorious officials as slaves. The property of the principal offenders is to be forfeit to the government.[3]

It can be seen that, although the Ch'ing article follows the same basic lines as the T'ang, there have been some changes. First, there is considerably more information given in the interlinear commentary as to the scope of the provision. Second, the punishments established by the Ch'ing code are markedly more severe than those of the T'ang. A larger group of relatives will suffer death. Even distant relatives or unrelated persons who happen to have lived in the same household as one of the principal offenders are to be executed. No mitigation is allowed on the grounds of age or infirmity. This reflects the greater concern with which the Ming[4] and the Ch'ing governments viewed treasonable activities, as well no doubt as their wish to emphasize the importance of the bond between ruler and subject, particularly the duty of loyalty owed by all to the throne.[5]

Theft

Where political or ethical considerations do not play so large a role as in the case of the duties of a subject to the throne, there may be no alteration at all in the original T'ang rule. A good illustration is provided by one of the articles on theft. All the codes contain a number of articles relating to theft. Of these most are concerned with the theft of specific kinds of property. Only one makes any attempt to define what constitutes theft, and that concentrates on the physical component, leaving the mental (the requirement of mens rea) to be understood. The T'ang version of the article states only, "Public appropriation and stealthy appropriation in all cases constitute theft." However, the interlinear commentary adds the following important information:

> In the case of things like utensils or ordinary articles it is necessary to move them. In the case of animals kept in enclosures or fettered it is necessary to move them from their usual place. As to the release of wild birds and beasts, here it is necessary to take special control of them, and then there is theft. If domestic animals [like cattle or horses] keep one another company and

follow their own kind, they are not to be added together [in calculating the penalty]. But if you then take and appropriate them
for yourself, or if you steal the mother and her offspring follows,
in these cases all are to be added together. (Article 300)

We may now compare the corresponding Ch'ing article. This states:

Public appropriation and stealthy appropriation in all cases
constitute theft ["public appropriation" means that the person
who commits theft takes the property openly, as by using violence to steal and rob; "stealthy appropriation" means to act
in secret, cover one's face, and then take the property, as by
secretly stealing, pulling out or groping for; all these cases have
the name of "theft"]. Utensils, money, silk [here as in other cases
it makes no difference whether the property is owned by the
government or a private individual], and the like, it is necessary
to move, and theft is constituted by the fact of moving [then it is
called "theft"]. In the case of articles like gold, jade, or precious
stones, it is enough [to be theft] if they have been concealed in
the hand, even if [in the place of the theft] they have not yet actually been taken away. As to timber, stone, or heavy implements
for which human force alone is insufficient, although they have
been moved from their original place, theft is not completed [it
is not permitted to treat the case as theft] until the object has
been placed on a means of transport. Horses, oxen, mules, and
the like must be brought from their enclosures; falcons, dogs,
and the like must be under the control and in the possession of
the taker, and then theft is completed [if one horse is stolen, and
then separately other horses follow it, it is not appropriate to
include the value of the latter in order to determine the penalty;
but if the mother is stolen and the foal follows, both are to be
included in the calculation of the penalty].[6]

Although the Ch'ing article looks longer than its T'ang counterpart,
it is in fact in all its essentials drawn from the T'ang code. The portions of the Ch'ing article that cannot be found in the T'ang article

are, with very minor variations in wording, taken from the explanatory commentary (*shu-i*) that follows the article in the T'ang code.
The Ch'ing article is a pastiche, put together from phrases extracted
from the T'ang article or its commentary.[7]

Homicide

With respect to the law of homicide, the basic structure is again
established by the T'ang code that distinguished between six kinds of
killing: premeditated murder where the intention to kill was formed
prior to the killing (*mou sha*), intentional murder where the intention to kill was formed only at the moment of the killing itself (*ku
sha*), mistaken killing where the intention was to kill A, but B was
killed in error (*wu sha*), killing in the course of a fight where the
original intention had merely been to injure (*tou sha*), killing in the
course of a dangerous sport or game (*hsi sha*), and accidental killing
where there had been an intention neither to kill nor to harm (*kuo-
shih sha*). These categories were adopted by the Ming/Ch'ing law.
Although some minor changes were made, the similarities are more
obvious than the differences.

As an illustration we may take the category of accidental killing.
Article 339 of the T'ang code states: "All cases of accidentally (*kuo
shih*) killing or injuring someone follow the manner in which the
death occurs and treat as redeemable." The interlinear commentary
adds, "This refers to what ear and eye do not reach, what thought and
care do not reach, for example, where several people lift an object too
heavy for their strength or climb a high place or traverse a dangerous
passage and one stumbles, or hunt wild beasts, and by mistake someone is killed." The *shu-i* commentary then adds the further examples
of throwing a brick or tile and not hearing or seeing anyone (illustrating the phrase "what the ear and eye do not reach"), and throwing
a tile or rock in a lonely place, where one would not expect people
to be, and by mistake killing someone (illustrating the phrase "what
thought and care do not reach").

In the Ch'ing code accidental killing is the third section of an article that also deals with killing in a game (*hsi sha*) and killing by mistake (*wu sha*). This section states:

> If someone is killed or injured accidentally (*kuo shih*) [this being much less serious than killing in a game], in each case the sentence is to be in conformity with (*chun*)[8] the punishment for killing or wounding in a fight, but, in accordance with the code, the payment of redemption is permitted, the money to be paid to the family [of the person killed or wounded]; ["accidental" means what ear and eye do not reach, what thought and care do not reach, as where one is shooting wild animals or for some reason is throwing bricks or tiles and unexpectedly kills someone, or is with others climbing a high or narrow place and one's foot slips involving others in the fall, or when one is navigating a boat driven by the wind, or is riding a horse which becomes frightened and runs off, or is driving a cart downhill and one's strength is insufficient to control it, or where with others one is lifting a heavy object but lacks the strength to sustain it and someone else is harmed; in all such cases in which from the beginning there has been no intention to harm, the sentence is to conform to the punishment for killing or injuring in a fight, but in accordance with the code payment of redemption is permitted, the money to be given to the family of the person killed or injured as a contribution to funeral or medical expenses.][9]

Although the treatment of accidental killing in the Ch'ing code is considerably more extensive than that in the T'ang, it adds nothing of substance. All the examples of accidental killing found in the T'ang code have been adopted by the Ch'ing, and some further cases have been added. Even the actual language of the T'ang code is largely followed. Two overt differences are the fact that the Ch'ing code states explicitly that the punishment is to be formally in conformity with that for killing in a fight, and the emphasis on the fact that there has never been any intention to harm. Certainly the second point and possibly also the first point were implicit in the T'ang treatment.

CONSERVATISM IN PROCEDURE

Many other examples of similarity or identity in content between the provisions of the T'ang and Ch'ing codes can be found.[10] The only further illustration we propose to cite at this stage concerns procedure rather than substance. Legal conservatism characterized not only the transmission of the substance of the law but also the constitution and procedures by which it was administered. An important example is supplied by the system of judicial review that operated from the T'ang to the Ch'ing.[11] Although some details were changed from time to time, the essentials of the system remained the same.

We give a brief description of the system as it obtained under the Ch'ing. In principle all criminal cases, whatever their gravity, were heard first in the court of the district in which the facts occurred (the place of the theft or homicide and so on). The magistrate investigated the facts, determined guilt or innocence, and then proposed the sentence for the offense as prescribed by the code. Should the sentence be merely a beating, the matter stopped there, and no further review occurred. Whenever a sentence of greater severity, ranging from penal servitude to death, was applicable, it was necessary to forward the case to the next superior court in the hierarchy, that of the prefect, for rehearing. The prefect's decision was final only in cases of penal servitude. Cases of exile or death were automatically reviewed by the provincial governor, who might give a final decision only in some exile cases. All homicide cases, whatever the punishment, and all cases attracting the death sentence were sent to the capital for review by the highest judicial tribunal, the Board of Punishments.[12] The Board might finally determine cases for which the punishment was exile, but all those for which the sentence was death were to be further considered by the emperor himself. No sentence of death could be implemented, except in certain extreme situations, without express imperial approval.[13]

CONFUCIAN RESPECT FOR THE PAST: THE RITES

What accounts for this remarkable adherence to the past displayed in both substance and procedure? At the risk of begging the question, we may invoke in the first place the generally conservative inclination of the Chinese people, in particular that of the educated elite. This might seem a trite and unhelpful observation. But in fact there was an aspect of Confucian training that paid a particular veneration to the past. Confucius himself stated that he was merely conserving and reestablishing the good customs of the past.[14] Appeal to the words and deeds not only of the early Chou rulers, regarded as models of the "sage king," but also of the very earliest mythical rulers of China, Yao and Shun, became a standard feature of Confucian rhetoric. Indeed, this recourse to the past as a means of managing the present was one of the characteristics of Confucian thought most strongly attacked by the Legalists.

It is perhaps not surprising that once Confucianism had become the dominant intellectual tradition in China and had provided the staple for the education of future officials, there should be a great reliance in administrative action on what had been done in the past, coupled with a reluctance to change well-tried procedures and rules. The Confucian respect for one's ancestors influenced rulers who were reluctant to depart from policies established by their fathers and grandfathers. A well-known example is that of the respect paid to the institutions established by Ming Tai-tsu, the founder of the Ming dynasty. He himself had ordered his descendants not to change them.[15] Respect for ancestors even extended to respect for previous dynasties, especially where they were regarded as models of successful government. It is interesting that the only dynasty not to have issued a penal code in the traditional form is the foreign Yüan, although some pressure was placed on the Mongolian rulers by their Chinese officials to remedy this omission.[16] On the other hand, the foreign dynasty of the Manchus (Ch'ing) deliberately adhered to the institutions of the Ming in order to make themselves as acceptable as possible to their Chinese subjects.

We may briefly recall here the discussion in chapter 2 of the difference in the Ming and Ch'ing penal codes between the articles (*lü*) and the substatutes (*li*). The former were regarded as unalterable, whereas the latter were more readily deleted from the code, added to it, or changed. A commentary on the Ch'ing code has this to say about the articles: "The articles (*lü*) are the rules of a dynasty which one ought respectfully to keep and to which one ought to conform. In effect the great principles and fundamental rules do not change in spite of the passage of the centuries."[17] The notion expressed here is that there is a duty on the part of all, including successive rulers, to respect the fundamental articles of the penal code either established by the founder of the dynasty or added by a later emperor.

No doubt most governments in any society, certainly any stable society, have a respect for the achievements of their predecessors and are reluctant to make changes in policies that have proved to be successful. No doubt also administrators everywhere are fond of acting in accordance with precedent and are reluctant to countenance change unless appropriate indicators can be found in the past. Nevertheless, the Chinese government and its officials for many centuries seem to have been more resistant to institutional change than has been the case in other societies. The points that follow do no more than flesh out these generalities.

Confucianism's respect for the past was visibly reflected in one aspect of its thinking, its emphasis on the rites, the casting of human behavior into ritually approved forms. This is most obvious in the elaborate rites marking the transitional stages of the human life cycle: birth, adulthood, marriage, and death. But it is also manifest in the conduct of ordinary daily life. Ritually correct forms of behavior had to be observed by children toward parents, wives toward husbands, ordinary people toward officials, and officials toward each other. Communication was neither spontaneous nor informal, but mediated through the observance of forms. These forms were not empty or arbitrary constructs unrelated to the essential problems of human intercourse. On the contrary, they were believed to reflect and reinforce the fundamental human duties. One of the most graphic examples is provided by the complex and elaborate rites to be performed on the death of a parent. The length of the period during which a parent was to be mourned (twenty-seven months), the kind of mourning costume to be worn, the obligations to give up office and abstain from participation in banquets or musical entertainments—all testify to the respect due from a child to a parent inherent in the parent-child relationship.[18]

Details of the rituals to be observed in the conduct of daily life were originally recorded in books written during the Han dynasty or earlier.[19] With the revival of Confucianism at the time of the Sung dynasty, the man who subsequently became the most influential of the Neo-Confucian thinkers, Chu Hsi, prepared a book of rituals for use in the family that had a profound impact on future generations.[20] Many editions and shortened versions of it appeared. So popular did it become that a French missionary in the 1720s reported that a copy was to be found in almost every household in China.[21] One reason for its popularity was that Chu Hsi had brought the rituals up to date by modifying them in accordance with actual practices of the times in order to make them more acceptable to the ordinary people, while at the same time purifying them of what he regarded as Buddhist or superstitious elements.

The Family Rituals contained detailed prescriptions for the performance of the main rites of passage. But it also had a prefatory chapter on general ritual, which discussed the behavior to be observed by members of a family toward each other in their daily life. In his preface Chu Hsi described the objectives of the rites:

> Ritual "has fundamental elements and elaborations." From the perspective of how ritual is carried out at home, the fundamental elements are to preserve status responsibilities and give concrete form to love and respect; the elaborations are the proprieties and specifications for capping, weddings, funerals, and ancestral rites. The fundamental elements are the daily courtesies of householders, the things they must not fail to perform even a single day. The elaborations serve further to regulate the beginning and ending of human affairs. Even though the elaborations are only performed at particular times and places, unless one discusses them clearly and practices them until they be-

come familiar, when the need arises one will not be able to do what is right and fitting. Thus one must also daily discuss and practice the elaborations.[22]

The whole purpose of the rituals, whether those used to mark rites of passage or those employed in daily life, was to imbue in people a concept of the proper way to behave, that is, the behavior enjoined on one by one's position in the family hierarchy. What is emphasized above all in the ritual is the respect due to senior relatives and to the ancestors who constituted the most senior relatives of all. Embedded in the rituals is a way of life handed down by the ancestors. Maintenance of that way is precisely the form in which the descendants manifest their respect and veneration for the past members of their line. It is this constant pattern of respect for the ancestors, expressed in and reinforced by the rites, that made the morality of traditional Chinese society so unchanging in its fundamentals.

The rites gave visual expression to the morality whose observance was deemed by Confucian orthodoxy to be essential for proper human society. The canons of moral behavior were stated in the same books that specified the rituals that expressed them. They were already in large part incorporated into the Han and other pre-T'ang codes, and they eventually formed an integral part of the T'ang code itself. Since the basic morality taught by Confucianism did not thereafter change in its essentials, and since, in addition, it was regarded by rulers as a strong bulwark of the state,[23] the same rules were adopted by the codes of all subsequent dynasties. We see this unalterable character of the basic morality and the law founded on it vividly illustrated in the concept of the "ten abominations" found in practically identical form in all the codes from the T'ang to the Ch'ing. Placed right at the beginning of the codes in the "General Principles" section, the ten abominations expressed the conduct most detested in Confucian thought. The abominations were concerned almost entirely with disloyalty to the emperor or official superiors and with lack of respect to parents or other senior relatives. Lack of respect was expressed in a wide spectrum of unacceptable conduct ranging from killing or injuring a senior relative to failure to observe the mourning rites on the death of a parent or paternal grandparent.[24]

Not only did the T'ang code represent the legal embodiment of the (unchanging) moral order, but it also achieved a level of technical excellence that made it a natural model for later ages. Experimentation with codification in China started in the sixth century B.C., if not earlier. By the time of the Sui/T'ang at the end of the seventh century A.D. there had been many centuries of trial and error in the drafting of codes. Many of the rules in the T'ang code undoubtedly had prototypes or equivalents in earlier codes, some perhaps being derived from legislation of the Ch'in kingdom and empire. But it was the Sui and T'ang legislators who succeeded in creating out of the mass of earlier material a well-constructed and workable code that carefully balanced offenses and punishments and distinguished the categories of offense with clarity and precision. Its adoption by later dynasties as well as its popularity in other countries of Southeast Asia owe as much to its intrinsic excellence as to veneration for the achievements of a great dynasty.

THE PHENOMENON OF THE NONENFORCEABLE

A particular aspect of Chinese legal conservatism requiring comment is what we have termed the "phenomenon of the nonenforceable." The codes contain a number of rules, often inherited from previous dynasties, which were either never enforceable or, since the time of their original adoption, had ceased to be enforceable. "Enforceable" in this context carries the connotation both of "recognized inability to enforce" and "lack of any desire to enforce." For example, the early T'ang emperors introduced rules into the code prohibiting private individuals from selling the land they farmed except under strictly defined circumstances. These rules were designed to put into effect a policy of land control that seems to have worked prior to the rebellion of An Lu-shan in the middle of the eighth century. The effect of that rebellion, although ultimately suppressed, was to cause such dislocation in the administration of the empire that the T'ang court never again managed to recover control of the whole. The rules on land allocation ceased to be effective not only in the parts of the empire over which central control had been effectively lost, but even in those where it was still retained. In other words, sale of land by private individuals had become the norm. Despite the discrepancy between legal rule and factual reality on this point, the Sung dynasty kept the T'ang rules in its code without any change. They remained part of the penal code and so technically in force until the end of the Sung, but they were not adopted by the Ming.[25]

A similar example of the sacrosanct character possessed by the rules of the T'ang code is supplied by the first and second of the five punishments: beating with the light stick and beating with the heavy stick. The T'ang rules provided that beatings with the light stick might be 10, 20, 30, 40, or 50 blows depending on the offense, and likewise that beatings with the heavy stick might be 60, 70, 80, 90, or 100 blows. Not only the T'ang but all successive penal codes retained this system. The Sung code reproduced the rules verbatim, and yet in practice the authorities adopted a totally different system, not only with respect to the rules on beatings but also with respect to those on penal servitude and exile also reproduced from the T'ang code.[26] The Ming code both adopted the T'ang rules and applied them as stated in the code. The same rules were inherited by the Ch'ing, but again with respect to beatings an important change was made in practice. The thickness of the stick with which the beatings were administered was increased. As a result the number of blows inflicted with each stick was significantly reduced. Where the code provided a punishment of 50 blows with the light stick, the number actually administered was 20; where it prescribed 100 blows with the heavy stick, the number actually administered was 40, with corresponding reductions in the other cases.[27]

A number of the rules on family relationships in the penal codes never seem to have been enforced. The codes had an elaborate set of rules governing the dissolution of marriage. The husband alone might repudiate his wife on one of the grounds stated in the code, and under certain circumstances, such as adultery by the husband with his mother-in-law, the marriage was required by law to come to an end.[28] In fact, these provisions largely seem to have been ignored. Where divorce did occur, it was normally achieved by consent of the families involved, a procedure itself sanctioned by the codes. Alternatively, the husband might simply send his wife back to her family, or she might choose to return, and that was the end of the matter.

Another rule prohibited marriage between persons of the same surname.[29] This also was disregarded in many parts of China, although in some areas it seems to have been enforced.[30] Even the Board of Punishments itself, when a marriage between persons of the same surname was brought to its attention, declined to treat the marriage as void. In 1789 a case arose in which a husband stabbed and killed his wife, who bore the same surname. The provincial authorities had proposed that the husband should be sentenced under the law on unrelated persons, since the marriage should be treated as void. The Board, however, rejected this approach and held that the offender should be sentenced under the law on beating and killing a wife. It said: "The law which annuls a marriage is based on the *li* which prohibits the taking of a person of the same surname as wife.[31] But since ignorant people are unaware of this prohibition, it often happens that in the isolated countryside, women of the same surname but of different *tsu* (clan) are taken as wives. Although the regulations set up in the law and *li* should not be disregarded simply because they are frequently violated on account of ignorance, it is still worse to disregard the husband-wife relationship because of a slight violation of the marriage law."[32]

The rules permitting only junior relatives of the same clan to be adopted as heirs also seem generally in practice to have been ignored or at least not strictly followed.[33] There may have been a preference for intraclan adoption, but if that, for some reason, was found to be difficult, a boy from another clan, perhaps linked by marriage with the clan of the adopter, might well be adopted.[34]

Some of the rules governing contractual relationships also do not seem to have been regularly enforced. The codes provided that, where a debt was not repaid on time, a punishment should be imposed on the debtor, the severity depending on the amount owed and the duration of the period of default.[35] Evidence from the nineteenth century shows that, when cases of debt came to court, the magistrate often attempted to settle the matter by a compromise, rather than through the imposition of the statutory punishment.[36] Nor do the rules prescribing a uniformity of weights and measures throughout China ever seem to have been more than a dead letter, although they appear in all the dynastic codes.

SYMBOLIC VALUES

All legal systems contain some rules that are obsolete or, for one reason or another, not enforced. But the extent of the phenomenon in the Chinese penal codes has led some scholars to find in it a fact that supports the conclusion that the penal law as a whole was intended to function as a model providing guides to conduct and not as a set of enforceable rules.[37] This conception of the penal law is unacceptable if taken in its literal sense, and, indeed, it appears to be absurd when we recollect the strictness with which large sections of the code (for example, those on homicide and theft) were applied. Nevertheless, there is embedded in the view of the penal codes as models a valuable insight that allows us to appreciate an important objective of the framers of the codes, namely, the expression of certain goals to which the ruler in particular and society as a whole should aspire.

We may distinguish between two rather different values that the codes were intended to express: that represented by the observance of the proper conduct deemed to be inherent in family relationships, and that represented by a proper concern for his people on the part of the emperor. The second of these values is the more embracing, because it includes the first, in that the emperor, as the individual on whom responsibility for the well-being of society ultimately rested, must be seen to take appropriate measures for the maintenance of proper conduct between family members. We should not, however, assume that every instance of a nonenforceable statutory provision is to be explained solely as an expression of one or the other of these values.

In some cases rules may have been introduced into the code with every intention that they be enforced. Initially, they may have been on the whole enforced and only have become unenforceable through the impact of changing social conditions. This appears to be what happened with respect to the T'ang/Sung rules prohibiting the alienation of land by private individuals. But the question still remains, why were these rules retained in the code for so long a period after they had become totally obsolete? It is doubtful whether the sole reason for their retention was the conviction that they expressed a fundamental value. We should not, however, discount altogether the possibility that the legislators looked upon the nonalienation of land as a factor of critical importance for the prosperity of the family and hence of the stability of society. A more influential factor may have been the conviction that the T'ang code should not again be altered once it had achieved its final form in 653 A.D.[38] Articles should not be deleted or added. The code had a status rather like that of the Confucian classics, constituting a work with which succeeding rulers and even dynasties should not have the temerity to tamper. As we have already noted, the land rules were not removed from the code until the major revision ordered by the founder of the Ming dynasty. At this time the gap between the position as stated in the rules and that as practiced by the people would have appeared so extreme that no good would have been seen as emerging from the continued preservation of the rules. It is also possible that the concept of nonalienation of land was itself no longer regarded as a sine qua non of a prosperous and stable society.

Many of the rules on family relationships, although not enforced, were retained in the codes on account of their "symbolic value." They expressed an ideal toward which society should aim, even if the realities of the time did not accord with that ideal. The rules imposing punishments for the breaking of engagements, marriage between persons of the same surname, or divorces that did not comply with the requirements of the code were not enforced by the authorities. Nor were the rules enforced requiring boys adopted as heirs to be chosen from junior members of the same clan. Although "family" cases were frequently brought before the magistrate's court,[39] they were not normally approached by the magistrate as matters calling for the strict application of the penal code; they were better treated by adjudication or mediation. Nor was the attitude of the provincial authorities always the same. Family rules were enforced in some parts of China but not in others.

The regulation of marriage and adoption is one of the most important concerns of the Confucian ritual classics. Both topics are treated in considerable detail, and the prescriptions contained in the classics form the basis for the rules found in the penal codes.[40] The legislators wished to state in the most emphatic way possible the content of the Confucian regulations governing the constitution of the family, a matter of direct concern to the ancestors themselves. By retaining the rules on marriage and adoption in the codes, even in the realization that actual practices were often contrary to those rules and that enforceability was not practicable, the Confucian government was affirming its central role in the complex of Confucian belief and expressing the idea that the behavior which it enjoined should be observed uniformly throughout the whole Chinese realm.

Other rules, inherited from earlier codes but not enforced during the Ming and Ch'ing dynasties, may be explained, at least in part, as expressions of the second value that we have identified, that of correct government on the part of the emperor. One example of such rules relates to the necessity for weights and measures used throughout the empire to be uniform.[41] This was a matter that had concerned writers on statecraft since antiquity. In the *Kuan-tzu*, an ancient collection of writings on government,[42] law, and economics, it is already said: "The intelligent ruler unifies weights and measures . . . and steadfastly maintains them."[43] The unification of weights and measures was an important duty of the "intelligent ruler" that became inseparably connected with the concept of ruling. One of the ways in which a ruler manifested his activity as ruler was to establish laws prescribing such uniformity. Whether or not they were observed was of secondary importance.[44]

Although the rules on payment of debts do not have the same standing in the canons of statecraft as weights and measures, they were presumably seen as an important part of the ruler's duty to ensure the prosperity of the people. Discouragement of debt should therefore feature in the penal codes as a sign that the ruler was concerned with the welfare of the people. At the same time, the formulation of the codes provided an emphatic statement of the necessity to repay what had been borrowed.

It is, of course, not just the "unenforceable" rules in the code that should be interpreted as statements of "symbolic value." The same may hold true of rules that were actually enforced. We know that the rules punishing adultery were enforced, at least where the matter came to the cognizance of the authorities. The erring woman's husband and his relatives might drag her and her lover to the magistrate's court for punishment.[45] These rules were intended to affirm the importance of the value of chastity in marriage.

We conclude that many of the rules contained in the penal codes can be interpreted on a "symbolic level." Their significance lies in the fact that they affirm the fundamental moral duties of the people and the fundamental responsibilities of the ruler in government. Often it is a rule's significance as an expression of a goal or value that explains its retention in the code despite the fact that it was never regularly enforced. Furthermore, we can see that the symbolic function of many rules, whether they belong to the class of the enforceable or not, provides a powerful reason for their retention in the codes of each successive dynasty and so helps to explain the conservative nature of the traditional penal law. Their retention is not dependent upon the degree to which they were actually enforced or to which they accorded with actual practice. Nevertheless, it by no means follows that the codes as a whole were not meant to be enforced or that their rules did not possess the character of law.

4 The Ethical Foundations of the Penal Law

LEGALIST AND CONFUCIAN PERSPECTIVES

We may investigate the ethical foundations of the penal law from two points of view. There is first the very fact of legislation itself and second the content of that legislation. Traditionally the fact of legislation itself has been considered a hallmark of Legalism. Confucius and his followers located the prime duty of the ruler in teaching and the setting of a good example, whereas the Legalists had stressed the duty of the ruler to enact and maintain harsh penal laws. Underlying this distinction is the difference in the basic objectives that the Confucianists and Legalists attributed to government. For the former it was the welfare of the people, as becomes plain from Mencius's famous debate with King Hui of Liang on the subject of "profit." When Mencius visited the king he was told, "You have come all this distance, thinking nothing of a thousand *li*.[1] You must surely have some way of profiting my state." Mencius's reply was, "Your majesty, what is the point of mentioning the word "profit"? All that matters is that there should be benevolence and righteousness."[2]

The Legalists, on the other hand, considered all that mattered was the strength of the state and the supremacy of the ruler. Classic statements of this position are found in the writings attributed to Lord Shang and Han Fei Tzu. For Lord Shang a ruler of a strong country had to promote war and agriculture through the infliction of heavy punishments and the occasional use of rewards. His views are well expressed in the following statements: "In a country that has supremacy, there are nine penalties as against one reward; in a strong country, there will be seven penalties to three rewards, and in a dismembered country, there will be five penalties to five rewards,"[3] and "Punishment produces force, force produces strength, strength produces awe, awe produces virtue. Virtue has its origin in punishments."[4] Han Fei Tzu, whilst not quite so draconian in his approach, also emphasized the need for the ruler to maintain his position of supremacy through the use of rewards and punishments. He said: "The way in which the intelligent ruler leads and governs his subjects is by means of two handles. These two handles are penalty and benevolence. What are penalty and benevolence? By penalty is meant capital punishment, and by benevolence is meant the giving of rewards. The subjects will stand in fear of punishment and will receive benefit from reward. Therefore, when the ruler uses penalty and benevolence, his multitude of subjects stand in fear of his majesty and rally round what is beneficial to them."[5]

However, it would be a mistake to press too far the Confucian and Legalist dichotomy between teaching and penal law. Confucians from an early time accepted the need for penal legislation. Hsün Tzu, perhaps the greatest of the early Confucian thinkers, had already achieved an amalgam of the positions adopted by the two schools.[6] In his discussion of royal government he advocated the administration of a system of penal justice by a ruler who was a man of virtue, a "gentleman." Only a ruler who fulfilled the model of the Confucian guidelines might properly operate a legal system. Hsün Tzu recognized that a central problem facing any ruler is that of "gaps in the law." What is to be done where the existing legal rules did not adequately provide for a given situation? The Confucian ruler would know the proper way to apply the rules and to extend them by analogy. Hsün Tzu concluded his discussion of the role of the ruler with the observation: "Hence, although there have been cases in which a good legal model nonetheless produced disorder, I have never heard of a case, from the most distant past to the present day, where there was a gentleman in charge of the government and chaos ensued."[7] Hsün Tzu thus saw the necessity for legislation, but emphasized equally the importance of virtue on the part of the ruler who was entrusted with the task of establishing and applying the laws. Confucian rulers from the time of the Han dynasty accepted this position. They recognized that penal laws were indispensable, but saw the whole edifice of the penal law as an instrument to assist in the protection, nourishment, and teaching of the people, not as a means of aggrandizing the state or securing their personal supremacy.

As an example we may cite the founder of the Ming dynasty, Ming Tai-tsu, known for his autocracy and the ferocity of his treatment of erring ministers and officials. He was expressly represented by his court as a ruler who was a teacher,[8] and he himself deliberately sought to revive the "good practices" of the past. In particular, he emphasized that primary importance in society should be attributed to *li-i*, the right way to behave as determined by one's status.[9] Law (*fa*) was necessary to ensure that the villainous elements of society did not disturb the moral order constituted by observance of *li-i*. The emperor described the relationship between *li* (propriety) and *fa* as similar to that between an outer garment and its inner lining, *fa* being in the background and reinforcing *li*.[10] In an essay on the art of government he stated: "So the Son of Heaven regulates with punishments and brings men to submit through the hierarchical distinctions. These he imposes and thereby makes his government visible, giving security to the people in a realm where benevolence and long life prevail."[11]

CONFUCIAN MORALITY

One of the principal objects of the penal law in traditional China was to secure the enforcement of fundamental Confucian morality. We may broadly and perhaps rather superficially divide the content of the codes into two bundles, one consisting of rules designed to enforce morality, the other of rules designed to provide for the good order and safety of the realm or the proper conduct of the administration. In the first bundle there clearly fall the rules on filial piety, marriage, adoption, and sexual relationships in general, and in the latter fall those on military matters, the control of prisoners, or the efficient running of the administration. Rules on treason, homicide, theft, or assault might be placed in either bundle. Indeed, one should not press the distinction between the classes of rules too far, since, as has already been noted in chapter 2, some rules which primarily seem to be concerned with administrative matters can also be viewed as measures for the "nourishment" of the people, flowing from the moral duty on the part of the emperor to care for his subjects.

The state did not concern itself so markedly with Confucian morality just out of a puritanical consideration for moral behavior as a good in itself. Rather, there was a conviction that maintenance of the Confucian moral prescriptions through the apparatus of the state was essential for the preservation of a civilized society. Only if members of families behaved toward each other in accordance with the Confucian rites could the Chinese society be distinguished from that of the inferior barbarian or foreign societies [12]—or even in the last resort from the animal world. But there was also a point of more practical importance to emperors and their advisers. Encouragement of the virtue of filial piety, of the general duty of respect and submission by a junior to a senior relative, helped to strengthen the related duty of respect and submission resting on subjects in relation to the emperor.

The codes dramatically signal their moral orientation by placing right at the beginning of the "General Principles" section a description of the offenses known as the "ten abominations." This term does not signify that the punishments for the offenses in question were to be exceptionally severe, but rather that the latter, although some attracted relatively light punishments, were to be regarded as the most abhorrent, those which most threatened the well-being of society. This point is vividly expressed in the official commentary of the Ch'ing code, which states that "persons guilty of any of the ten abominations destroy human bonds (*lun*), rebel against heaven (*t'ien*), go against reason (*li*), and violate justice (*i*)." [13] The abominations were all normally excluded from imperial amnesties, which were issued from time to time to remit or reduce the punishment of persons convicted of a wide range of offenses. [14]

At the head of the list stand those offenses which manifest disloyalty to the emperor, that is, rebellion, treason, and the like. [15] Any society, of course, will classify such offenses as amongst the most serious, because they are directed at the forcible destruction of the government or the subversion of the whole society. But in China there was the additional factor that loyalty to the emperor was explicitly identified in Confucian thinking as one of the "Three Bonds." The Ch'ing legal commentary even links revolt against the emperor with revolt against the "spirits" protecting the earth. How, it asks, will the spirits continue to act benevolently toward men if they plot to disturb the empire?[16] A further abomination, entitled "great irreverence," comprised various less serious offenses against the emperor, namely, theft of objects used by the emperor in the great state sacrifices, theft of the emperor's own possessions, or theft or forgery of the imperial seals. Even inadvertent offenses, where they concerned behavior potentially harmful to the emperor, were treated as a "great irreverence," such as mistakes in mixing the imperial medicine, preparing the imperial food, or constructing the imperial boats. The foundation of the offense in all these cases was disrespect to the emperor.[17]

Most of the remaining abominations are concerned with offenses against the family. These were "contumacy," defined as beating or plotting to kill a parent or paternal grandparent, or actually killing certain other close senior relatives;[18] "discord," defined as plotting to kill or selling any relatives within the normal circle of mourning relationships, or beating or bringing legal accusations against certain senior relatives;[19] "depravity," which included the killing of three members of one family who had not committed a capital offense, as well as certain "magical arts" (the making or keeping of a particularly feared poison called *ku* and sorcery in general);[20] "lack of filial piety," under which were subsumed many acts of disrespect toward parents or paternal grandparents, such as bringing legal accusations against them, cursing them, setting up a separate household during their lifetime, not supporting them, disobeying their orders, or neglecting the mourning requirements after their death;[21] and "incest," defined as sexual intercourse between certain categories of relatives.[22] Another of the abominations, termed "unrighteousness," in effect approximated certain nonfamily relationships to those that obtained within the family. Under this heading was brought the killing of one's department head, prefect, magistrate, or teacher.[23]

It is worth noting that several abominations specify acts committed by a wife against her husband or his senior relatives, but not acts committed by a wife against a husband. Thus, "contumacy" included

the killing by a wife of her husband or his parents or paternal grandparents, "discord" included the beating of a husband by his wife or
the lodging of a legal accusation against him, and "unrighteousness"
included the failure by the wife properly to mourn the death of her
husband.

The T'ang *shu-i* commentary states: "The ten abominations are the
most serious of those offenses that come within the five punishments.
They injure morality and destroy ceremony. They are specially placed
near the head of this chapter in order to serve as a clear warning."[24]
In effect, the abominations express what we have termed fundamental Confucian morality.

A wide range of other conduct, regarded from the Confucian perspective as immoral, though not of the same order of immorality as
the abominations, was also penalized by the codes. Prominent in this
"second order" category of the immoral stood a variety of infringe-
ments of the rules established for the proper regulation of the family.
These included the rules governing betrothals, the treatment of a wife
by her husband or vice versa, the circumstances under which a marriage might or must be dissolved, the taking of a boy in adoption as
the family heir, and the manner in which the family property should
be distributed upon the death of its head.[25]

Traditional Chinese society was never sexually permissive. Hence,
not only adultery but any kind of sexual relationship between unmarried persons was prohibited and punished. In Ch'ing times this
prohibition was extended to homosexual acts.[26] Sexual conduct is
everywhere regarded as a matter falling within the sphere of morality,
though societies differ enormously in their estimation of the kind
of sexual activity that is to be deemed "immoral" and even more in
their classification of that which should be illegal. Traditional China,
especially during the Ch'ing, treated any kind of sexual act outside
marriage as both immoral and illegal.

Nonsexual conduct of a kind regarded by most societies as immoral
was also punished. Apart from the obvious examples of arson, killing, injury, and theft, there was also damage to property, the abuse
or cursing of other people, and the practice of deceit, extortion, or
intimidation. Some of these offenses required intention for their com-

mission, and hence could clearly be denominated immoral, on the ground that the individual had deliberately chosen to behave in a way he knew infringed the conduct expected of a good person. But other offenses were punished despite the absence of intention in their commission. Thus, to varying degrees, unintentional killing, injury, or damage to property were all subjected by the code to a penal consequence.[27] Generally, one might argue here that factors other than the "moral" were taken into account by the legislators, such as the very fact that harm had been done. On the other hand, there may also have been a perception that the act causing harm, even if not intentional, was still immoral, since an individual who was paying sufficient attention to the propriety of his own conduct would not have placed himself in a situation that brought about loss or injury to another.

Certain other activities endemic in Chinese society were also the subject of legislative prohibition on the basis of the threat they posed to regular family life. Legislation, however, proved to be entirely ineffective in repressing them, and the rules by and large constitute another example of the unenforceable. The main example of antisocial activity is gambling. This was punished by all the codes from the T'ang to the Ch'ing. Under the Ch'ing punishments were imposed on those who gambled or operated a house for gambling. The stakes as well as the house were to be forfeit to the state. A commentary on the article states that those who take up the practice of gambling will eventually forget their trade and will neglect and abandon their families; they are comparable to evildoers and vagabonds who cause ruin to others.[28]

During the eighteenth and nineteenth centuries another destructive activity attracted the attention of the legislature. This was the smoking of opium. At various times the emperors sought to eradicate the practice by establishing laws that imposed heavy penalties on opium dealers and opium den operators and less severe penalties on smokers. Under legislation of 1830–31 even the parents of those who traded or smoked opium were to receive a beating of forty blows with the light stick, as prescribed for parents who could not prevent their children from stealing. As with gambling these legislative attempts at prohibition were totally ineffective. Enforcement was sporadic and on the whole unsuccessful.[29]

Many of the penal rules appear at first sight to be of a purely administrative character concerned with the regulation of state resources, the imposition and collection of taxes, the control of prisons, the conduct of military affairs, protection of the emperor, legal procedure, or the officials' performance of their duties. The presence of all these rules in the code can readily be explained in terms of a concern for good order and the stability of society. Yet, as has already been indicated in chapter 2, at least some of them, for example those concerned with the management of state granaries or the imposition of taxes, were also thought to be expressions of the emperor's concern for the welfare of his people. This concern itself derived from the Confucian conception of the ruler as one who should exercise restraint in the burdens that he placed on his subjects.

What is astonishing from a Western point of view is the variety and range of behavior to which penal sanctions are attached. One can understand the need to prohibit and punish the main forms of socially deviant behavior—killing, theft, and the like—and even perhaps certain kinds of sexual misconduct such as incest. More remarkable are the severe punishments established for what appear to be comparatively trivial misdemeanors such as unfilial behavior or breaches of the mourning regulations. For example, the Ch'ing code provided that a person who concealed the death of a parent or husband and did not go into mourning was to be punished with penal servitude for one year and sixty blows with the heavy stick. Removal of the formal mourning garments before the requisite period had elapsed and indulgence in pleasures such as the making of music or participation in banquets were to be punished with ninety blows with the heavy stick.[30] Under the T'ang code the punishments were even more severe. For example, a child or wife who concealed the death of a parent or husband was to be exiled to two thousand *li* or, if mourning was discontinued, to be sentenced to penal servitude for three years.[31]

The point, of course, is that in traditional China matters such as the mourning regulations were regarded as being of the utmost importance. They were a profound manifestation of respect for the relative who had died. Within the family context they constituted a visible sign of the relationship between the living and the dead, between the descendants and the ancestors. The death of the head of the household, for example, brought into being a complex set of rites of which mourning constituted an integral part. To judge from the space allocated to these rites in books such as Chu Hsi's Family Rituals, they were the most significant of all the rites.[32] Hence, it becomes understandable why the penal codes imposed punishments for breach of the mourning regulations.

The mourning rules constitute another case of "symbolic enactment." The penal rules expressed the importance attached by the state to the correct performance of the mourning rites, but do not appear actually to have been enforced through the infliction of the prescribed punishments. Rather, it seems that the state was willing to leave the matter within the jurisdiction of the individual's clan. When a member died, the clan was expected to see that the proper procedures were observed and to discipline any member who failed to comply. Many clans issued rules as to proper behavior for the guidance of clan members. Some of these compilations specified that a son should diligently perform the rites required by the death of a parent and prescribed a punishment for failure to comply.[33] Whether or not clans would have insisted on the strict maintenance of mourning evidenced by the wearing of mourning garments, abstention from undue pleasure, and the like is uncertain. But they would undoubtedly have expected members to perform at least part of the obligations required by the mourning rites. Exemplary performance was probably an important mark of respectability and social standing.

WERE LAW AND MORALITY INSEPARABLE?

The extent to which the penal codes prescribed punishments for conduct that infringed Confucian morality has led some writers to unwarranted conclusions. Statements can be found to the effect that in traditional China law and morality were coextensive, with the implication that the whole sphere of the moral was reinforced by penal sanctions.[34] Such statements apparently derive support from the famous catchall article found in the penal codes, which directed that conduct which ought not to be done was to be punished with eighty blows with the heavy stick if the matter was serious, and forty blows with the light stick if the matter was light.[35] It has been alleged that the effect of this article was to instruct district magistrates to punish any immoral conduct with a beating.[36] It is not impossible that the article might have been given this interpretation. Equally, it is conceivable that on occasion it might have been used by a magistrate to punish conduct he deemed to be immoral. Nevertheless, so far as can be determined from decisions of the Board of Punishments, it does not in practice, at least during the Ch'ing, appear to have been used as a blanket instrument for the enforcement of moral conduct as such. It was frequently invoked to punish persons who had been involved in the facts leading to a homicide, but had not committed an offense separately identified by the code. Other examples of the article's use may be cited from the cases translated by Bodde and Morris.

Where a son had committed a capital offense and his father in anger had beaten him to death, then secretly buried his body, he was held to be liable not for the death but for the secret burial. This constituted an act "which ought not to be done" punishable under the article with eighty blows with the heavy stick.[37] Clerks in a government office who had failed to notice that one of their number had neglected to stamp a document with the official seal as required by law were sentenced to forty blows with the light stick on the grounds of "what ought not to be done."[38] Rural persons were prohibited from buying more than a certain quantity of rice in Peking. When an official in a district outside the capital bought more than the permitted quantity to feed his soldiers who were engaged in public construction, it was held that he should be sentenced to a beating of forty blows under the article on "what ought not to be done."[39] The Board observed in this case that, although the official had in fact acted for the public good, he had nevertheless broken the law restricting the amount of rice to be taken from the capital "so that it would be impolitic to grant complete exemption of penalty." Where a magistrate in violation of the law on state sacrifices was carried in heavy rain through a gate in the local Confucian temple, the chair bearers were sentenced to eighty blows under the article.[40] In another case it was held that, where a husband after his wife's death raised a concubine to the position of wife, he should be sentenced to eighty blows under the article.[41]

No final conclusion on the sphere of operation of the catchall article can be established until a wider range of case material has been studied. Yet the strictly limited investigation that we have so far conducted[42] suggests that the word "ought" in the article should not be understood as having a purely moral reference. The available evidence shows that the article was frequently invoked to punish persons who had in some ancillary way contributed to the commission by another of a specific crime or whose conduct was sufficiently analogous to an existing offense to warrant the imposition of a penalty. One does not know the extent to which magistrates indiscriminately resorted to the article to impose summary punishments for all manner of conduct that they disliked. Such cases would never have gone beyond the magistrate's court and so never have been recorded by the Board.

NEO-CONFUCIANISM

We have already argued that one of the principal reasons for the "conservatism" exhibited by the traditional penal codes is the fact that the Confucian morality that they enshrined did not fundamentally change from the Han to the Ch'ing. This is particularly apparent in the rules concerning the constitution and maintenance of the family. The ritual books whose content had become settled by the end of the Han dynasty at the latest defined the essential requirements for the validity of a marriage, the circumstances under which it might be dissolved, the methods for securing the continuance of a family through adoption where no male heir had been born, and the treatment of the dead members of the family who had now become "ancestors." These books as well as many other Confucian writings constantly emphasized the duties and virtues that inspired the rules for mar-

riage, adoption, and death, especially those embodied in the concepts
of filial piety and the chastity of women.

Although the fundamental principles of Confucian morality did not
change in the period under discussion, it would be a mistake to assume that no change at all took place in the emphasis given to certain
aspects of them. From the time of the Sung dynasty, a stricter attitude
began to be taken to the implementation of some of the basic Confucian duties. This change is associated with the rise of the school
of Neo-Confucianism under the Sung, which developed through the
efforts of orthodox scholars to combat what they saw as the per-
nicious influence of alien doctrines, especially those of Buddhism
which had become popular under the T'ang. Neo-Confucian scholars, apart from spending much time in the discussion of metaphysical
questions, wished to restate the fundamental Confucian moral doctrines and reassert the importance of the rites associated with them.
We have already noted one of the most influential products of the
school, the Family Rituals of Chu Hsi. Perhaps as a consequence of
the need to restate and reassert, the new formulation of moral doctrine betrayed a degree of puritanism and emphasis on the fulfillment
of duty that to some extent altered the balance of the fundamental
human relationships.

The Three Bonds, those between ruler and subject, father and son,
and husband and wife had originally been conceived as entailing
mutual obligations. The subject was to be loyal to the ruler, but the
latter was to treat his ministers with respect and listen to their remonstrances. The son was to be filial, but the father was to love and
protect him. The wife was to obey, but the husband was to respect her
position as wife. Neo-Confucian writings still pay attention to the
reciprocal aspect of these relationships, but, at the same time, there
arose a tendency to stress the duties of the inferior in the relationship. Of prime importance was the loyalty of the subject or minister,
the duty of respect for parents, and the duty of the wife to be submissive and chaste.[43] The wife's duty of chastity was treated merely
as part of a duty resting on all women, whether married or not, to
be chaste. Consequently, the emphasis was on chastity as a form of
behavior incumbent upon women in general, not just upon wives.

The Neo-Confucian emphasis on the filial piety of sons and the chastity of wives and daughters had an effect on the law. This became particularly apparent during the Ch'ing dynasty when the punishment of behavior deemed to be unfilial or unchaste was taken to extraordinary lengths. We may cite first the changes in the law of rape made by the Ch'ing in 1646 shortly after the establishment of the dynasty. Rape had always been treated as a serious offense, and the Ch'ing did not basically lessen its gravity. But certain modifications were introduced that, on the one hand, made it very difficult for the actual offense of rape, as distinct from some lesser offense, to be constituted and, on the other, treated the previous sexual conduct of the woman as a reason for mitigation in favor of the offender.[44]

As a result of the Ch'ing changes, rape could be substantiated only if the woman offered forcible resistance for the whole duration of the act. Should she initially resist, but then, overcome by the strength of the rapist, passively submit, she was deemed to have consented to the act of intercourse. The nature of the offense now changed. It ceased to be rape and became one of illicit sexual intercourse by consent in which not only was the punishment of the man greatly reduced but the woman herself incurred a punishment. This particular change could conceivably be attributed to the desire on the part of the legislators that the proof of rape, given the fact that it entailed a capital sentence, should be absolutely incontrovertible.[45] However, it has been plausibly argued that a more compelling factor was the value that had come to be placed on the woman's maintenance of her chastity. In line with the dictum of the Sung philosopher Cheng I that it was preferable for a woman to die from starvation than to remarry after her husband's death, it was held preferable for a woman to struggle to the end when her chastity was threatened, even though that struggle should result in her death.[46] That this interpretation is correct is suggested by the other concomitant change in the law. Where a man saw a woman having intercourse with another man and subsequently proceeded to rape her, he was not to be convicted of the offense of rape because she had already committed the offense of illicit sexual intercourse. He was to be punished only with a beating in accordance with the law on enticing a woman to have intercourse.[47]

Ch'ing substatutes made the prior sexual history of the rape victim a factor in determining the rapist's punishment. A substatute on gang rape had originally provided that the ringleader was to be sentenced to immediate beheading where the woman was "good" but that the punishment should be reduced to deportation to a distant frontier region where the victim was known to be "unchaste." The punishment of the others who had participated in the rape was also to be reduced in this case, from strangulation after the assizes to exile to three thousand *li*. In 1814 this clause was removed from the substatute on gang rape and made into an independent substatute with some modification in the punishment. Where the victim had been guilty of illicit sexual intercourse, the ringleader was to be sent to Manchuria as a slave to the soldiers, and those who had joined in the rape were to be exiled to three thousand *li*.[48]

In Ch'ing times the legal obligations placed on a child, deduced from the value of filial piety, were taken to what M. J. Meijer has described as totally unrealistic and unacceptable lengths. Such a process he ascribes to the tendency of the Neo-Confucian legislators to ignore the normal expectations of actual living in favor of an impracticable ideology.[49] A striking illustration of this tendency is supplied by the legislation that made a child liable for the suicide of a parent, where that suicide could be attributed, even in the loosest possible way, to unfilial conduct. The Ming code had already provided that a child who had caused the suicide of a parent or paternal grandparent through intimidation and pressure (*wei-pi*) should be beheaded.[50] In the light of the Chinese conception of the family and the requirements of filial piety, this was not an unreasonable provision, since it was based on the fact of actual intimidation. However, in 1772 the wording of the legislation was changed. The offense was reconstituted to cover any case in which a child through unfilial (*pu hsiao*) conduct brought about the suicide of a parent or paternal grandparent.[51] This provision was interpreted by the Board of Punishments in a very broad manner. The result was that any child who had acted in such a way as to cause a parent in a fit of anger to commit suicide, no matter how trivial the "cause," was to be sentenced to death.

The attitude of the Board is well demonstrated in a case of 1821. By a trivial act a son had managed to anger his mother who, in a fit of insanity provoked by her anger, had taken poison and killed herself. The provincial governor had proposed that the death sentence should be reduced to exile on the grounds of the victim's insanity. The Board refused to accept this and sent the case back to the province for further consideration. In the course of its opinion it observed:

> The relationship between a son and his parent is associated with a pleasant countenance and a happy appearance. It is altogether impossible for a son to upbraid his parents. Only among the stupid people[52] it is believed that they have simply been unable to comply with their parents' instructions, even when their parents, outraged at their disobedience, have committed suicide. . . . That is why when we evaluate the circumstances in these cases we let the law take its full course in order that a sense of moral obligation be firmly implanted into those people's minds. Consequently cases of disobedience have always been handled without any reduction of punishment for considerations of leniency.[53]

Another instructive example derived from the obligations comprised in the concept of filial piety is supplied by the history of the legislation on the accidental killing by a child of a parent. This had always been regarded as a grave matter, but there is a significant difference in the way the offense is treated in T'ang and Ming times as compared with Ch'ing. In the earlier dynasties the son who accidentally caused the death of a parent was to receive a noncapital sentence, that of exile to three thousand *li*.[54] The original standpoint of the Ch'ing code was the same.[55] But, during the eighteenth and nineteenth centuries, the legislators began to pursue a stricter policy. Although their attitude fluctuated, the general trend was to impose a capital sentence on a child who had accidentally killed a parent. Even the way in which the matter was handled procedurally is illuminating.

In 1763 a case arose in which a woman fired a gun at a thief and by mistake wounded her stepmother, who died. The throne responded to a memorial from the Board of Punishments by increasing the punishment from exile to immediate strangulation. This decision led to a change in the law governing slaves or wives who had accidentally killed their masters or husbands; in both cases, the punishment was increased to immediate strangulation. It appears that this punishment was established by substatute for all three cases (child, slave, wife) in 1766. In 1799 in a case in which a wife had accidentally killed her husband, the Board recommended that for such cases as well as those in which a child or slave had accidentally killed a parent or master, the original punishment established by the article (exile) should be followed. In the following year in a case in which a son had accidentally killed his father, the Board reversed again. It regarded the circumstances as less serious than those of the 1763 case in which a woman had mistakenly shot and killed her stepmother, but still thought the immediate imposition of a sentence of exile as prescribed by the code to be inappropriate. Hence, it recommended that the son should be sentenced to immediate strangulation as prescribed by the substatute, but that a petition to the throne should be permitted, requesting a reduction of the punishment to exile. By 1806 it was considered that a final sentence to exile was still too lenient. Accordingly the substatute on a child, slave, or wife accidentally killing a parent, master, or husband was altered to bring it into conformity with a general substatute on mitigating circumstances in cases involving mourning relationships. As a result, the child, slave, or wife was still to be sentenced initially in immediate strangulation, but, once the fact that the killing had been truly accidental had been confirmed by the highest judicial bodies (the Board of Punishments, Censorate, and Court of Revision), the sentence was to be reduced to strangulation after the assizes. Finally, in 1843 a clause treating in the same way daughters-in-law who accidentally killed their husband's parents or paternal grandparents was added to the substatute.[56]

Two points arising from this elaborate sequence of changes are worth stressing. First, the Board was anxious that children, slaves, and wives should all be treated in the same way when they had accidentally killed a parent, master, or husband. This indicates that they were all regarded as the same sort of "inferior" in the family structure. Second, there was a reluctance on the part of the authorities to dispense with the requirement that the formal sentence for the accidental killing of a parent, master, or husband should be immediate strangulation. Although a procedure was instituted under which the sentence was reduced eventually to strangulation after the assizes (with the possibility of commutation to a noncapital sentence), the nominal sentence had to remain more severe in order to express the gravity with which the very fact that the "inferior" in the relationships of parent and child, master and slave, husband and wife had killed the "superior" was viewed. It is this kind of approach which arguably reflects the Neo-Confucian abhorrence of any act by which a junior in the family brought harm to a senior.[57]

We should reiterate the point, by way of conclusion, that the penal codes were concerned not to enforce morality as such, but to ensure that the subjects of the emperor complied with the behavior inherent in the fundamental human roles expressed in the Three Bonds. All dynasties made central to their penal policy a regard for the moral duties flowing from the relationship between ruler and subject, father and son, and husband and wife. What tended to alter was the precise evaluation attributed by the legislators to these duties. We have argued that, particularly under the influence of Neo-Confucianism, during the Ming and Ch'ing dynasties a greater emphasis came to be placed on the duties of those occupying the inferior position in the relationship, namely, the duty of loyalty on the part of the subject, the duty of obedience on the part of the son, and the duty of chastity on the part of the wife (understood generally as a duty resting on all women). The law, even prior to the advent of Neo-Confucianism, was always concerned with the enforcement of these duties. Those rules which we have described as being merely or largely of "symbolic" significance, in that they expressed moral desiderata but were not intended regularly to be enforced, concerned matters more peripheral to the maintenance of the fundamental human relationships than the core duties.

5 The Fundamental Family Roles

The slightest acquaintance with the penal codes reveals the fact that the principle of equality before the law did not operate in traditional China. The subjects of the emperor were not treated alike by the law. For any given offense one person might be punished more heavily—sometimes significantly more—than another person who to all appearances had committed the same offense. In fact, the offenses were not regarded as the same because the relationship between the offender and the victim in the two cases was different. One factor that determined the punishment was the status of the offender in relation to the victim. At the broadest level this involved consideration of which was "senior" and which "junior," as measured by the family, class, or administrative hierarchies constituting traditional Chinese society. Within the family the principle operated that a relative of a higher generation was senior to a relative of a lower generation irrespective of age, whereas within the same generation seniority was determined by age. The exception was constituted by the relationship of husband and wife in which the husband always counted as the senior for certain purposes. Within the administrative and military structure seniority was determined by a complex system of ranks and official positions. Under the class system graduates and officials counted as senior in respect of the bulk of the population who did not hold a degree or office. Ordinary people counted as senior with respect to slaves or others holding mean occupations.

When a criminal case came before the court, the first thing the magistrate ascertained was the precise family relationship (if any) existing between offender and victim. In most cases questions of status concerned family relationship. But other relationships could be relevant such as those between a free person and a slave or between two officials or an official and a commoner. The magistrate trying the case had to determine which rule of the penal code was applicable to the precise relationship in which victim and offender stood. These rules were elaborated in great deal to cover many possible variations in status. The general principle applied was that a senior who committed an offense against a junior was punished less severely than a junior who committed the same offense against a senior. The greater the disparity in status, the more or less severe the punishment. We may ask, what accounts for this perspective, which was maintained by all the Chinese codes until the fall of the Ch'ing, and which appears so contrary to Western conceptions of justice?

The underlying thought, antecedent to Confucius but adopted by Confucian orthodoxy, may be represented very simply as follows.[1] All phenomena in the universe, including men and women, have their appointed role or course. The sun, the moon, the stars, the seasons all have appropriate ways in which to behave, just as there are appropriate ways for men and women to behave. Chinese thinking does not make a distinction that Western philosophy has largely accepted as fundamental, that between the descriptive and the prescriptive or the "is" and the "ought." Description of the way in which natural phenomena regularly behave is at the same time a statement of the way in which they ought to behave. Put another way, each object has its own nature, which determines for it the way in which it is to behave. This applies to men and animals as well as to inanimate phenomena. Just as it is the nature of the sun to move across the sky from east to west, so it is the nature of humans to behave in certain ways.

We now have to consider the relation of the elements of "objects" of the universe to one another. The universe as a whole will only function properly or harmoniously when each of its constituents behaves according to its natural role. For example, there will only be prosperity on earth if the seasons occur in their regular sequence and perform their normal functions in the production of crops. Reflection on the elements of the universe and the relationship in which they stand to one another reveals that some are to be seen as "superior" and some as "inferior." Most obviously, perhaps, the sky is regarded as "superior" to the earth over which it stands, and the sun, which occupies the sky in the day, is regarded as "superior" to the moon, which occupies it at night. Hence, the harmonious working of the universe requires the maintenance of the distinction between "superior" and "inferior" in the sense that each component of the relationship behaves in the manner appropriate to it. The moon must not compete with the sun for possession of the sky during the day.

This point becomes more obvious and in practice more important when we consider human relationships. The very fact of being a human in itself entails a certain form of behavior that marks off the human from the merely animal. Human society in its proper sense is constituted when its individual members each behave according to his or her proper nature. The kind of behavior appropriate to any particular person is determined by his or her place in the family and social structure. A society only functions properly when its members behave in accordance with the roles that they occupy within it. The most important of these roles are those constituted by the relationship between ruler and subject, father and son, husband and wife, and elder and younger brother. We may recall here the oft quoted cryptic reply of Confucius to an enquiry concerning the correct principles of government, which runs literally "ruler ruler, minister minister, father father, son son."[2] What these words mean is that the ruler should behave toward his ministers and subjects as a proper ruler should, ministers and subjects should behave toward their ruler as proper ministers and subjects, a father should be a proper father to his son, and a son a proper son to his father. Embedded in the notion of "proper" is a complex set of obligations.

The primary family and social roles involve interacting behavior. The behavior of the ruler impinges on that of the subject and vice versa, the same applying with respect to the behavior of father and son, husband and wife, and elder and younger brother. The problem thus arises: how are such interacting sets of behavior to be "harmonious," so enabling the fundamental social and family roles to work constructively without friction. The answer is supplied by the principle of hierarchy. In each of the primary relationships one is to be ranked as "superior" and one as "inferior."[3] Harmony is secured through the exercise of kindness, protection, and benevolence by the superior and of respect and submission by the inferior. The proper maintenance of the family and social hierarchy entails harmony in society, achieved through the harmonious working of its fundamental relationships.[4]

The crucial ideas of "hierarchy" and "harmony" can be extended beyond the basic social and family relationships to encompass more generally those characterized by the interaction of persons with "higher" and "lower" abilities. Those who possess higher abilities will rank as superior with respect to those who possess lower. This is the basis of the distinction frequently drawn in Confucian writings between the "superior" and the "little" person, where the underlying principle of distinction is drawn from education and the cultivation of the mind. We have here the thought that explains the distinction in traditional Chinese society between the official or graduate and the person who has never attained a degree or never become an official. It explains the class differentiation in traditional society not only between official and nonofficial, but also between free and slave or mean person.

Emperors, embracing orthodox Confucian thought, stressed the importance of the twin notions of hierarchy and harmony for the good government of the state. Instructive in this regard is the attitude of Ming Tai-tsu, who rose from peasant origins to overthrow the Yüan dynasty and found the Ming. He was particularly interested in resurrecting the ideals of antiquity, ascribing the fall of the Yüan to its failure to honor them. On one occasion he observed that *li* (ritual, propriety, maintenance of social roles) and *fa* (the penal law) together constituted the norms of the state by which "men's ambitions are settled and superior and inferior are harmonized."[5] On another he said, "There is no greater purpose for *li* than distinguishing the noble from the base and clarifying the gradations of power." He also explained his view of government as follows: "So the Son of Heaven regulates with punishments and brings men to submit through the hierarchical distinctions. These he imposes and thereby makes his government visible, giving security to the people in a realm where benevolence and long life prevail."[6]

The "hierarchical distinctions" embedded in Confucian thought to which Ming Tai-tsu referred had a decisive influence not only on the content of the rules of the penal codes but also on the way those rules were interpreted and applied by the Board of Punishments in the eighteenth and nineteenth centuries. We shall consider the material in two sections. The rest of this chapter will examine the impact on the law of the fundamental family relationships. Chapter 6 will look at political relationships and class distinctions.

FAMILY RELATIONSHIPS

As we have seen, Confucian thought during the Ming and Ch'ing periods made the concepts of the Five Relationships and the Three Bonds central to its ethical and political philosophy.[7] The Five Relationships were those between ruler and subject, father and son, husband and wife, younger and elder brother, and friend and friend, whereas the Three Bonds singled out the first three of these as possessing the greatest significance for the family and society. Both concepts have earlier antecedents. Confucius himself had stressed the relationships of ruler and subject and father and son. Mencius had already alluded to the Five Relationships when he cited their maintenance as that which prevented man from sinking to the level of the animals.[8] They are described in the following terms: "love between father and son, duty between ruler and subject, distinction between husband and wife, precedence of the young over the old, and faith between friends."[9]

It is also worth noting that the emphasis in political thinking on some of these fundamental relationships antedates even Confucius by several centuries. In the *K'ang kao*, the earliest Chinese document on law and justice, King Wu impresses upon the young prince Feng that unfilial and unbrotherly behavior is more to be detested than robbery and murder. If those who do not respect their fathers or elder brothers are not treated as offenders, "the norms given by Heaven to our people will be greatly brought into disorder. I say may you speedily follow Wen Wang's [rules of] punishments, and punish these without pardon.[10] One has here the earliest evidence of a ruler's insistence that the penal laws be used to enforce the primary social bonds, denominated by King Wu as those between father and son and between elder and younger brother.

Of the Five Relationships, all except that between friend and friend had an important impact on the law. The significance of the relationship between elder and younger brother lay in the fact that it came to be understood as expressing not just a strict fraternal relationship but one between senior and junior relatives in general. The formulation in Mencius already goes beyond a relationship that exists purely between brothers. The rules of the penal codes focus on either the specific relationship between parent and child or husband and wife or with that between the more general class of senior and junior relatives. The parent and child relationship, which the law conceives in the strictest terms, comprises also that between paternal grandparent and grandchild. The role of a woman depended fundamentally on whether she was married or not. Before marriage she counted as a "child," and her most important relationship was with her own parents. After marriage she counted as a "wife" and "daughter-in-law," and her most important relationship was now with her husband and his parents or paternal grandparents. Since in traditional Chinese society all women were destined for marriage at an early age either as wife or concubine, the parent-child relationship was concerned primarily with the relationship between sons and their parents or with that between women and their parents-in-law.

The relationship that presented the greatest problem for the law was that between senior and junior relatives. The reason was that, while rules could readily be drafted to deal with the relationship between parent and child or husband and wife, the same was not true of that between senior and junior relatives. "Senior" and "junior" in this context covered a potentially inexhaustible range of persons, especially if one took into account matrilineal and affinal as well as patrilineal connections. Social mores already dictated that juniors should respect and obey seniors. The problem for the law was to determine how far the social recognition of a senior-junior relationship should be given penal enforcement. To what extent should the law define and make enforceable the obligations arising from family relationships, where "family" was given the broadest possible interpretation?

The solution was found in the mourning prescriptions explained in the ritual books. Persons were required to mourn for varying periods upon the death of certain relatives. The length and depth of mourning were determined by two principal factors: the closeness of the relationship and the status position that mourner and deceased occupied with respect to each other. A junior was required to mourn longer for a senior than a senior for a junior. Five degrees of mourning were normally recognized, each entailing the overt demonstration of grief through the wearing of distinctive clothing. The periods of mourning attached to these degrees were three years, one year, nine months, five months, and three months. Whereas a large number of patrilineal relatives were held to fall within the circle of mourning, only relatively few matrilineal or affinal relatives were included.

Some examples may make the principles clear. A son mourned for a parent for three years, whereas a parent mourned for a son for one year. The closeness of the relationship was the same, but the parent was of the senior generation. A wife mourned for her husband for three years, whereas the husband mourned only one year for his wife. As between nephew and paternal uncle, each mourned the other for one year, the distinction between "senior" and "junior" here being disregarded. Brothers, irrespective of seniority, mourned each other for one year. Where a daughter died unmarried, her parents mourned for her for one year; if she was married, the period was reduced to nine months. For a sister-in-law or a maternal uncle or aunt, the mourning period was five months, as it was for maternal grandparents. The largest mourning category comprised relatives who mourned for three months, as for the son of a paternal aunt or maternal uncle, the wife's parents, or a son-in-law.[11]

The penal codes took the five degrees of mourning as the basis for the imposition of legal liability in respect of dealings between relatives. Persons who were related but did not fall within at least the fifth degree of mourning (that for three months) were treated by the law as unrelated. This had the further consequence that their respective status positions were also ignored. Only in the case of the emperor was an exceptionally wider category of relatives given legal recognition, in the context of those entitled to the privilege of deliberation or of liability for beating or killing.[12] In working out the rules imposing liability, the penal codes took into account both the period of mourning and the status position. In principle it was a more serious matter to commit an offense against a relative for whom one mourned for one year or nine months than against one for whom one mourned for three months. Often the period of mourning itself already reflected the status position, in the sense that normally the senior in the relationship mourned the junior for a shorter period than the junior mourned the senior. But sometimes this was not the case, as in the relationship of nephew and paternal uncle, where each mourned the other for one year. Although the period of mourning was the same, it was still a more serious offense for the junior in the relationship, the nephew, to injure the senior, the uncle, than vice versa.

Normally the rules were framed in terms of the degrees of mourning with the simple addition of the characters for "senior" or "junior" referable to both generation and age. For example, a rule might state that, where a junior accidentally killed a senior to whom he stood in a mourning relationship of one year, the punishment was to be x, whereas it was to be y if the mourning relationship was only three months. However, occasionally the rules will particularize the kind of seniority that is relevant by distinguishing between persons of a higher generation and persons who are of the same generation but older. Or they may draw a specific distinction between patrilineal relatives and matrilineal or affinal relatives.

The family relationships with which we are concerned, those of father and son, husband and wife, and senior and junior relative, were conceived in the earlier Confucian thought as involving reciprocal obligations. The junior in the relationship was obligated to respect and obey the senior, but the senior was obligated to show kindness and benevolence to the junior. Furthermore, in the case of the husband and wife relationship there was an emphasis on the different function that each possessed in the family. This is graphically recalled in an injunction found in one of the early books of clan rules: "No hen should herald the dawn lest misfortune follow."[13] The role of the wife was strictly to be within the inner apartments. She was not to take charge of "outside" affairs. In the penal codes, especially those of the Ming and Ch'ing dynasties, it was not the reciprocity of obligation that came to the fore, but rather the obligation of respect and submission resting on the junior. This is shown partly in the range of offenses, as demonstrated in the ten abominations, which in the family context dealt with failure on the part of a junior to show proper respect to a senior, and partly in the fact that the punishment for a junior who offended against a senior was often very much more severe, especially in the context of the parent and child relationship, than that for a senior who committed a like offense against a junior.

In Ming and Ch'ing times, especially the latter, we see an increase in the range of offenses it was possible for a junior to commit against a senior. This is particularly striking in the lengths to which the law went in punishing lack of filial piety. At the same time the discrepancy in punishment of seniors and juniors, at least for some offenses, became more marked. The strengthening of the legal position of the senior vis-à-vis the junior, including that of the husband vis-à-vis the wife, reflects a change in the concept of the nature of the basic relationship. Emphasis on the reciprocity of obligation diminished. What came to be stressed was the duty of respect and submission resting on the junior.

Partly responsible for this change in attitude is what has been termed the increasing moral puritanism of Neo-Confucian thought, which placed the greatest weight on the values of filial piety and chastity.[14] The child must in all circumstances be obedient and respectful, and the wife must in all circumstances be chaste and dutiful. One should not exaggerate this one-sided perspective, since we find statements in the writings of the most influential Neo-Confucians, such as Chu Hsi, that express the reciprocal nature of the fundamental human relationships.[15] Nevertheless, it does seem to be the case that Neo-Confucianism in its attempt to restore the influence of Confucian doctrine in the face of inroads by Buddhism stated the importance of the values of filial piety and chastity in stronger terms than earlier Confucianism.

However, the mere fact that these values were given a prominent focus in Neo-Confucian literature would not of itself have ensured changes in the law. It is true that some of the most powerful and authoritarian rulers, such as Ming Tai-tsu or K'ang-hsi, were attracted to Confucianism. But in part the attraction lay in the political use to which they could put the Confucian moral doctrines. They believed that harmony in the home maintained through observance of the "hierarchical distinctions" would ensure harmony and good order in the state as a whole. In particular, they saw an attractive parallel between the concepts of filial piety and loyalty to the throne. Consequently, the Ming and Ch'ing rulers found it politically expedient as well as morally necessary to strengthen through penal sanctions the duty of respect and submission owed by juniors to seniors.

We now proceed to consider how the penal codes themselves and the supreme judicial bodies sought to secure the implementation of the behavior associated with the central family roles. As examples we take the most important of the family relationships: those between parent and child and between husband and wife. It will be of particular interest to compare the treatment in the T'ang code with that of the Ming and Ch'ing codes. The former reflects early Confucian thinking as it had developed throughout the Han period, whereas the latter show the influence of Confucian teaching as redefined by the Neo-Confucians. It will also be of interest to consider the attitude of the Board of Punishments to these relationships as revealed by decisions of the eighteenth and nineteenth centuries.

PARENT AND CHILD

The most marked phenomenon in law is that a parent was treated with extreme leniency for harm or injury inflicted on a child, even where the harm was deliberately inflicted, whereas a child was treated with great severity in respect of any harm caused a parent, even through an inadvertent act. The later law, indeed, took the liability of the child for harm inflicted or brought on a parent to an extreme. A very wide concept of causation was adopted in this connection. Provided the harm suffered by the parent could be traced to an act of the child, then even though there had been no intention to harm and even though the act was not the direct cause of the harm, there was likely to be liability. As we have already noted, it was particularly the Ming and Ch'ing law, under Neo-Confucian influence, that treated as absolute the duty on the part of the child, derived from the concept of filial piety, to cause no harm or distress to a parent.

To illustrate the above propositions, we take first the rules in the penal codes on filicide and parricide. The deliberate killing of a parent by a child was considered in all codes as one of the gravest offenses and punished with the most severe of the punishments prescribed by law. On the other hand, the deliberate killing of a child by a parent saw a degree of fluctuation. In T'ang law (article 329) the punishment was two or two and a half years penal servitude, depending on whether a sharp-bladed weapon had been used or not.[16] In Ming and Ching law, for the case of the deliberate killing of a son, the punishment was reduced to sixty blows with the heavy stick and penal servitude for one year.[17] Likewise, where the son had disobeyed instructions and was beaten so severely by his father that he died, the T'ang punishment was penal servitude for one year or one and a half years, depending on whether a sharp-bladed implement had been used (article 329). But the punishment in Ming and Ch'ing law was reduced in all cases merely to one hundred blows with the heavy stick.[18] Where the father had accidentally killed the son, all law codes held him immune from punishment. The position was very different where the son had accidentally killed his father. The T'ang and Ming law imposed a punishment of exile to three thousand *li*, whereas the Ch'ing law, as we have seen, made the punishment capital.[19]

We have already noted the introduction under the Ming of the liability of the son for the suicide of a parent and the way in which this liability was extended under the Ch'ing.[20] Decisions of the Board of Punishment show that in late Ch'ing law, even where a parent or parent-in-law had been accidentally killed, as distinct from committing suicide, the child was still to be sentenced to a severe punishment should the accident be attributable to that child's behavior. Several cases decided by the Board around the middle of the nineteenth century well illustrate its approach.

In a case forwarded from the province of Shensi in 1838, a daughter-in-law had prepared food that was not properly cooked. In anger, Tu, her father-in-law, rushed to beat her, lost his footing, fell, and received injuries from which he died. The provincial authorities had proposed a sentence of immediate strangulation with a special petition to the throne stating the extenuating circumstances, as prescribed by the substatute on wives accidentally killing their husbands' parents.[21] The Board rejected the recommendation on the grounds that in this case Tu had fallen through his own act and had not actually been killed by his daughter-in-law. It found that the previous practice in cases of this kind had been to apply by analogy the substatute on sons disobeying orders and so driving their parents to commit suicide.[22] Consequently, the daughter-in-law should be sentenced to strangulation after the assizes as prescribed by this substatute.[23]

In a Soochow case of 1845, Mrs. Ch'en was washing clothes at the well when her father-in-law called out for food. He was ill, his voice was weak, and she did not hear him. In anger, he rushed out to beat her, fell, and received injuries from which he died. The provincial authorities, on the grounds that Mrs. Ch'en had had no intention of disobeying her father-in-law's orders, recommended that the capital punishment normally to be imposed should be reduced by one degree to exile. The Board accepted this recommendation, possibly because Mrs. Ch'en had not in any way acted improperly, as compared with Mrs. Tu in the previous case, who had aroused her father-in-law's anger by not cooking his food properly. However, when the case was referred to the throne, the emperor stated that, since the obligations derived from human relationships (lun chi) had been broken, there should be no reduction in sentence allowed. Yet, since the offender was a woman, she should be permitted to redeem her capital punishment.[24] The report is particularly interesting because it shows that an offender might in the end escape without physical punishment. We see again the phenomenon in which the formal sentence must express the full disapproval of the law, and yet a way was found to prevent its actual implementation.

The following facts were raised in a Chehkiang case of 1847. Chu was scolding his younger brother when their mother called on him to desist. He did not hear, and she came to intervene, but slipped and fell. As a result an old illness revived and she died. The Board noted that this was a case in which there had been neither defiance of parental instructions nor a suicide committed in anger. The appropriate punishment was therefore exile, being a reduction of one degree of the punishment of strangulation prescribed by the substatute on the suicide of a parent. Here the Board's recommendation was confirmed by the throne.[25]

In the context of sons held liable for the suicide of a parent, we may note an even more extreme piece of legislation introduced by the Ming and adopted by the Ch'ing. It was provided that, where a son was too poor to provide proper support for a parent, and in consequence the latter took his or her own life, the son was to be sentenced to exile.[26] The strictness with which this rule was applied, at least by the nineteenth century, can be seen from a decision of the Board of Punishments given in 1821.[27] A stepmother had committed suicide because her two stepsons had been unable to make a living and so provide the resources with which to support her. In fact, one of the stepsons suffered from a physical handicap, being lame, although he could still walk. The Board refused to treat the lameness as a mitigating circumstance, and confirmed the sentence of exile that had been passed on the two stepsons by the provincial authorities. It accepted that in the villages many people found it difficult to earn enough to keep their own families and even more difficult to acquire a surplus with which to support their parents. Nevertheless, it asserted that there was an absolute duty on sons to be more diligent and to ensure that they acquired adequate resources for the support of their parents, where the latter were in need of help. In the course of its opinion the Board observed: "When we investigate the original meaning of the substatute, it is that filial piety is the most important of our duties. A son serves his parents from morning to night and is never allowed any disrespect or carelessness in speech or behavior."[28] One has a good example here of the way in which adherence to Confucian orthodoxy prevailed over common sense and social reality.

Decisions of the Board on other aspects of the law of homicide also illustrate the way in which the concept of filial piety might influence the final disposition of a case. In 1811 Mrs. Huang, in disgust at her son's failure to observe her instructions, plotted to kill him by poisoning his wine. Huang himself, not knowing the wine was poisoned, exchanged it for some food with two other persons, a husband and wife. They drank the wine and in consequence died. The Board had some difficulty in determining the appropriate sentence for Mrs. Huang. In the end it sentenced her to exile and permitted redemption by payment of money. What is of interest here is the Board's treatment of the offending son who, to all appearances, could not be held responsible for the death of the persons who had drunk the wine poisoned by his mother. Yet the Board found that, as a result of his conduct in disobeying his mother, not only had two lives been lost but his mother had committed an offense entailing the punishment of exile. The cause of these misfortunes lay in the fact that Huang had not been a filial son. Hence, the punishment of exile as prescribed by the substatute on unfilial sons was in the circumstances of the case too lenient. Accordingly, Huang should be sentenced to deportation to the "outer regions" as a slave to the colonists.[29]

Sometimes a son was placed in an impossible dilemma. Filial obedience required him to honor a parent's instructions. But what was he to do when those instructions were to help the parent commit suicide? In 1829 the following facts were presented to the Board. Mrs. Jao had borrowed money from a relative of her husband and had been unable to repay when requested. In consequence there had been a quarrel in which she had been struck and humiliated. Resolving to poison herself in such a way as to implicate her creditor in her death, she ordered her son to obtain some arsenic. He remonstrated with her and without success sought to dissuade her from her design. In the end he procured the poison, hoping by obedience to his mother's orders to prevent further trouble, and he continued to remonstrate with her. However, Mrs. Jao suddenly swallowed the poison and died.

Despite the fact that Jao had had no intention of harming his mother, the provincial authorities held that he should be sentenced to death by slicing in accordance with the article on plotting to kill a parent. The Board, although emphasizing the points that the son had acted under pressure, that he had had no alternative but to obey his mother, and that he had at no time any intention of harming her, nevertheless merely reduced the punishment to immediate beheading, a sentence with which the emperor concurred.[30]

In another case the throne was more compassionate. Pao, who lived with his widowed mother and his small son by his deceased wife, with his mother's consent, took as his second wife a woman subject to fits of insanity. After a while his mother found the situation at home intolerable and declared she wished to take her own life. Pao frequently exhorted her to remain calm, but in the end said that he would kill himself at the same time. Later, when Mrs. Pao had taken her grandson to the edge of a river, Pao in alarm followed them. Upon his mother declaring that she wished to jump into the river, he implored her not to kill herself. She took no notice, but reminded him of his decision to die with her. Accordingly, he submitted when she took the ends of his belt and tied one around her waist and the other around her grandson's waist. All three then jumped into the river. Pao alone was rescued, his mother and son having drowned. When these facts were referred to the Board in 1816, it found that there was no clear text in the code under which they might be brought. However, since Pao had not managed to prevent his mother from killing herself, an infringement of the obligations imposed by the fundamental human relationships (lun chi) had occurred. Leniency was not in order; a sentence of immediate beheading should be recommended, and the emperor's decision awaited. Pao's wife, whose conduct had been the cause of the tragedy, should be confined in prison.

The emperor held that, since the case involved the fundamental human relationships, the judicial authorities had been correct in treating the matter sternly and recommending a capital punishment. However, the facts should be carefully scrutinized in order to determine what should be the just sentence. They disclosed that Pao, in fact, had not been unfilial. He had tried to dissuade his mother from jumping into the river, and then, when his attempt proved unsuccessful, he had resolved to die with her. No offense was thereby committed. Consequently, Pao should not be executed, but should be immediately released so that he might thereafter care for his mother's grave. On the other hand, Pao's wife had caused the loss of two lives by her mad conduct. She should accordingly be formally sentenced to beheading after the assizes, but have the sentence commuted to permanent imprisonment.[31] We notice here that, although the son was not punished, it was still a person in the position of a child, Mrs. Pao's daughter-in-law, who was held to be the cause of her mother-in-law's death and subjected to a severe punishment, even though she had not been responsible for her actions.

Some of the cases discussed above justify the severity of the punishment imposed on the son or daughter-in-law, whose behavior had been instrumental in causing the death of a parent or parent-in-law, by citing "the obligations entailed by human relationships" (lun chi). This expression refers to the obligations that arise under the relationships comprised within the Five Relationships and the Three Bonds. In the cases under consideration, the particular obligation is the respect and care that a son or daughter-in-law owes to a parent or parent-in-law. It is this which accounts for both the severity of the statutory rules and the strictness with which they are applied by the Board and the throne. In effect, any act or omission by the child that starts a chain of events culminating in the death of a parent counts as a failure to show the requisite care and hence calls for exemplary punishment. At the same time, the Board and the throne do attempt to evaluate the precise circumstances in each case to determine whether there are any mitigating factors. Such factors, if found, will not exempt the child from punishment, but will at least secure a reduction of the sentence from capital to noncapital.

Before we leave the topic of filial piety, we may note that it underlies a number of specific offenses in the code that will not be examined here in detail. In summary form, these are the beating, cursing, or accusing to the court of a parent or paternal grandparent, maintaining a separate household during the lifetime of parents, marrying during mourning for parents or while they are in prison, or generally failing to carry out the mourning rites properly. Nearly all these offenses, as has already been noted in chapter 4, fall within the ten abominations. In addition, the codes contain a general article punishing unfilial acts. The T'ang code had provided that, where a child disobeyed the instructions of a parent or paternal grandparent or failed to provide them with support, the punishment was to be two years penal servitude, provided the parent or grandparent lodged a formal complaint with the authorities. The text of the article and the *shu-i* commentary made it clear that the instructions must be such as were possible for the child to obey, and liability for failure of support was conditional upon the possession of adequate resources.[32] This article was adopted by the Ming and Ch'ing codes with the modification that the punishment was reduced to one hundred blows with the heavy stick.[33] The reason was not that unfilial acts were treated with greater leniency during these dynasties (the reverse was the case), but that the article was interpreted as covering merely minor or trivial acts of disobedience.[34]

Toward serious acts of disobedience the Ch'ing law took a harsher stance than had the T'ang. A substatute enacted by the Ch'ing in 1777, probably endorsing earlier practice, provided that, in the case of repeated acts of disobedience or grave insubordinate behavior, a parent or paternal grandparent might ask the authorities to banish the erring son for life to one of the malarial regions of China. If the daughter-in-law was included in the complaint, she was to accompany her husband and settle in the place of exile.[35] Another substatute provided that, even where an amnesty permitted the exiled son to return home or to have his sentence reduced to penal servitude, he was to have the benefit of the amnesty only if the offended parent or paternal grandparent had consented.[36]

Although these laws were intended to encourage sons in the virtue of filial piety, one can see that they might readily become an instrument of oppression in the hands of a tyrannical parent. The very fact of a complaint to the authorities might well be in itself sufficient to secure the exile of the son. However, it does seem that magistrates did not leave the decision entirely in the hands of the angry parent. In one case a mother-in-law, angry at the fact that her daughter-in-law had disobeyed an order, went to the magistrate and requested that she be sent into exile. The Board of Punishments (it seems) was asked whether the magistrate should simply accede to the complainant's request. The answer was that he should not. He should investigate the matter to determine how serious the disobedience had been. Where, as in the instant case, there had merely been an isolated act, the appropriate punishment was one hundred blows with the heavy stick under the article on sons disobeying the instructions of their parents. The offender, being a woman, might redeem the beating.[37]

A Ming substatute, adopted by the Ch'ing code,[38] provides inter alia that, where a stepmother accused her stepson of being unfilial, the neighbors and relatives were to be interrogated in order to determine the truth. Does this imply that an accusation by the real mother or father would not have been subject to the same scrutiny? A substatute of 1823[39] distinguished between the real parents and the principal wife (in relation to the son of a concubine), stepmother, or adoptive parent. In the first case, once the magistrate had satisfied himself as to the facts alleged by the complainant, a fresh investigation was not necessary. A report was sent to the prefect for examination, then forwarded to the governor for transmission to the Board, who determined the actual place of exile. But, in the second case, there was to be a fresh investigation of the allegation by the higher tribunal. Sometimes the Board itself uses language which suggests that, once a son has offended his parents so seriously that they lodge a formal complaint, the court will follow the parents' wishes in ordering a punishment of beating or exile.[40] In practice, the position may have been that the choice was left to the parents only where the son had been incorrigibly disobedient.

We cite one further example to show the lengths to which the Ch'ing legislators took the obligation of filial respect and submission. A substatute of 1830 provided that, where there had been a genuine case of attempted rape by a father-in-law, clearly proved by trustworthy evidence, and the daughter-in-law, in resisting the attempt, driven by the emergency of the situation, at that time had struck him a blow from which he died, the trial court was still to pass the prescribed sentence of death by slicing. But the Board was to state the facts in a report to the throne and request that consideration be given to a reduction of punishment to beheading after the assizes.[41]

A very different aspect of filial piety was also subject to regulation by the penal codes. This relates to the adoption of an heir. An important duty resting on the heads of family was the need to ensure that the ancestors were adequately supplied in the future with sacrifices. Hence, if no son was born to a wife or concubine, it was necessary to adopt a male child as heir. Because the purpose of the adoption was primarily to ensure the continuance of the family line for the benefit of the ancestors, the boy selected as heir had to be drawn from a very restricted class of persons. In a much quoted passage from the *Tso-chuan* (a classic pre-Ch'in work on the history of the Chinese states) it is said: "The spirits [of the dead] do not enjoy the sacrifices of those who are not of their kindred, and . . . people only sacrifice to those who were of the same ancestry as themselves."[42] Hence, to satisfy the ancestors, the person adopted as heir had to be drawn from the same clan as the adopter. The great Neo-Confucian philosopher Chu Hsi echoed the same sentiment when he remarked of divergent practices: "The setting up of heirs of a different surname is indeed an abuse on the part of our contemporaries and is nowadays difficult to correct after it has happened."[43]

The Confucian attitude to adoption as the means of preserving sacrifices to the ancestors explains the rule found in all the penal codes that the child adopted as heir must belong to the same clan as the adopter, and further he must belong to the correct (junior) generation. Punishments were imposed for disobedience, and any adoption contrary to the law was to be undone.[44] In point of fact, these rules were frequently not observed in practice, and their infringement did not attract prosecution. Nevertheless, the formal law remained as the endorsement by the state of the correct ritual position, as defined by orthodox Confucianism.

HUSBAND AND WIFE

For much of her life a woman was subjected to a double set of restrictions imposed on her conduct by morality and law.[45] These derived from her dual role as daughter-in-law and wife, the former being arguably the more significant at least during the lifetime of her parents-in-law. Even as a widow she might be subjected to considerable pressure or ill treatment from her husband's family or her own relatives in order to induce her to remarry. In this section we shall concentrate on the relationship between the wife and her husband.

The law found itself in something of a dilemma with respect to the way in which it should view the relationship of husband and wife. The wife, as distinct from the concubine, was an integral part of the family. Marriage itself was described by Mencius as the most important human relationship.[46] From one point of view the wife was recognized as her husband's equal. She was in full charge of the domestic arrangements, of the "inner apartments," she was the mother of the heir and hence had a crucial role with respect to the continuation of the family line, and she joined with her husband in the worship of the ancestors. Yet, from another point of view, she was rated as the "junior" in the relationship in which her husband counted as "senior." We will consider here three aspects of the relationship between husband and wife: the rules defining their respective obligations arising under the marriage, the legal treatment of offenses committed by either spouse against the other, and the weight given by the law to the preservation by the wife of her chastity.[47]

In traditional China the marriage of a boy and girl was not a matter left to their individual initiative and choice. It was the parents or other close senior relatives who determined whom a child should marry, the preferred procedure being for the conduct of negotiations through a go-between. Once the betrothal was made, the two families already incurred certain liabilities. This is one respect in which the law of the later dynasties treated the parties more equally than that of the earlier. In T'ang law, should the girl's family break the engagement, the person in charge of the marriage (for example, her father or paternal grandfather) was to be sentenced to sixty blows with the

heavy stick, and the marriage was still to take place. On the other
hand, should the boy's family refuse to complete the marriage, there
was no punishment, and the marriage was not required to take place,
the family merely forfeiting the betrothal gifts.[48] In Ming and Ch'ing
law both families, in the event of a broken engagement, were to be
treated in the same fashion. The person in charge of the marriage,
whether on the boy's or the girl's side, was to be sentenced to fifty
blows with the light stick, and the marriage was still to take place.[49]
One may infer from these and other rules that a significant social
shift in the position of women had occurred.[50] In the context of betrothal they were to be valued in the same way as men, it being no
more serious for the girl's family to break the engagement than the
boy's.

Although the rules of the penal codes were not strictly enforced
with respect to broken engagements, litigation arising from alleged
breaches of marriage contracts was frequent. In his guide for magistrates, the Ch'ing official Huang Liu-hung notes the problems arising
from informal engagements concluded by parents at feasts, sometimes even before the child has been born. His advice is that an
engagement properly contracted through a go-between, followed by
the acceptance of betrothal gifts, should be upheld "to preserve the
proper social relations in the community." In other cases, where the
engagement was less formal, the boy and girl should themselves be
summoned to the court and asked whether they wished to marry. The
magistrate should then respect their wishes. This advice is of particular interest because it shows that, unless the engagement had been
contracted in the proper ritual form, the law would take account of
the wishes of the boy and girl themselves, as distinct from those of
their parents.[51]

The relationship between husband and wife was described by the
expression *en i* on which M. J. Meijer has commented: "The relationship between husband and wife was based on the principle of 'favours
and obligations' (*enyi*). The favours coming from the husband, the
obligations from the wife."[52] The penal codes gave effect to the obligations of the wife in the rules on divorce, but they did not altogether
ignore the obligations of the husband. They did not require the hus-

band to treat the wife with kindness, but they did require that in certain essential ways he should respect her position. Thus, it was an offense for the husband to take a second wife while still married to the first, although he might take one or more concubines. T'ang law imposed a punishment of penal servitude for one year, whereas Ming and Ch'ing law required a beating of ninety blows with the heavy stick. All codes provided that the second marriage was to be undone.[53] The point is that husband and wife were regarded as two halves of a whole, as equals, or, in the words of the T'ang *shu-i* commentary, as the sun and the moon.[54] The taking of a concubine did not threaten the wife's position of equality, since the former ranked as inferior to the latter in the family hierarchy. But the taking of another woman as wife did threaten that position and hence the foundation of the family itself. Furthermore, all the codes contained provisions designed to prevent a diminution in the wife's legal position. Her husband was punished if he sought to reduce her to the status of a concubine (two years penal servitude in T'ang law and a beating of one hundred blows with the heavy stick in Ming and Ch'ing law), and she was to be restored to her position as wife.[55] The codes were concerned to ensure the maintenance of the proper hierarchy within the family through protection of the wife's status.

It is in the rules relating to dissolution of the marriage that we find a clear statement of the duties expected of a wife. The codes, following the prescriptions contained in the Confucian ritual books, permitted the husband to divorce his wife on any of the following grounds: failure to bear an heir (by the time she was fifty), shameless behavior, not serving the husband's parents, talking too much, theft, jealousy, and incurable illness. A wife proved herself to be unworthy and so deserving of repudiation if she failed to provide for the continuance of the family through the birth of a male heir, if she was unfilial toward her husband's parents, if she caused trouble in the family, or if she indulged in certain flagrant kinds of misconduct. Punishments were to be imposed on husbands who repudiated their wives for a reason not recognized by the law (penal servitude for one and a half years in T'ang law and eighty blows with the heavy stick in Ming and Ch'ing law), but, significantly, the marriage was to remain dissolved.[56] Although these rules do not appear actually to have been enforced by the authorities, they retain importance as a solemn statement of the proper behavior to be expected from a wife.[57]

The wife in principle could not unilaterally repudiate her husband.[58] Yet the codes, in a surprising contrast with Anglo-American law until very recent times, all recognized divorce by mutual consent.[59] Further, again echoing the fundamental Confucian conception of marriage, the codes took an approach that appears alien to Western thinking. It was provided that, on the commission of certain acts either by the husband and wife or by their relatives, the marriage was to be forthwith dissolved, irrespective of the actual wishes of the parties. Basically these acts were those the commission of which was held to be incompatible with the continued existence of the marriage. They "broke the bond" (chueh i) between husband and wife, leaving no recourse but separation. Examples were the beating by the husband of the wife's parents or paternal grandparents, or the cursing or beating by the wife of the husband's parents or paternal grandparents, or adultery committed by the wife with three month or closer mourning relatives of the husband, or adultery committed by the husband with the wife's mother, or the breaking out of a violent quarrel with resulting deaths between close relatives of the husband and wife.[60] These examples, not an exhaustive list, already indicate that the range of acts committed by the wife that entailed "breaking of the bond" was broader than the corresponding range committed by the husband.

In T'ang law the rule was strict. The commission of any act by which the marriage bond was broken entailed dissolution of the marriage. According to article 190, either spouse who refused to separate was to be sentenced to penal servitude for one year. In Ming and Ch'ing law the severity of the law was somewhat relaxed. The punishment for failure to separate was lighter (eighty blows with the heavy stick), and in some cases the parties were given a choice as to whether the marriage should continue or not. The wounding of the husband by the wife or vice versa, although an act "breaking the bond," did not necessarily entail separation, whereas the act of the husband in forcing his wife to commit adultery or giving her in pledge to another "broke the bond" and necessarily entailed separation.[61]

Although from one point of view husband and wife were regarded as equals, from another their relationship was one of subordination in which the husband counted as senior and the wife as junior. This aspect predominated in the legal treatment of offenses committed by husband and wife against each other. As in the case of the other family relationships, we take our examples from the law of homicide.[62] In T'ang law a wife who plotted to kill her husband or his parents or paternal grandparents was to be sentenced to beheading, irrespective of whether the plot had been carried out (article 253). She was to suffer the same punishment if she intentionally killed him or struck him a blow from which he died. If she accidentally killed him, she was to be sentenced to three years penal servitude (article 326). By contrast, where the husband plotted to kill his wife, he was to be sentenced to beheading only if the plot was successful. If he merely managed to wound her, the sentence was to be exile, and if she was not even wounded, it was to be penal servitude (articles 253 and 325). For striking his wife a blow from which she died, the punishment was to be strangulation, but in the case of accidental killing, there was to be no liability at all (article 326).

In Ming and Ch'ing law for the premeditated killing of the husband or his parents or paternal grandparents, the wife was to be put to death by slicing. If she had planned the death but been unable to carry it out successfully, she was to be sentenced to immediate beheading.[63] For the intentional killing of her husband she was to be sentenced to death by slicing, and for striking her husband a blow from which he died she was to be sentenced to immediate beheading.[64] For the accidental killing of her husband the punishment was originally penal servitude for three years. In 1744 it was increased to exile, and in 1763 it became immediate strangulation. In 1766 the law was settled on the basis that the wife should be treated in the same way as the child who had accidentally killed a parent, giving her the benefit of the special procedure by which the sentence was reduced to strangulation after the assizes.[65] By contrast, for the premeditated or intentional killing of his wife the husband was to be sentenced to strangulation after the assizes. The same sentence was to apply where he struck her a blow from which she died. For the accidental killing of a wife there was to be no liability.[66]

What is of interest is that the Ch'ing law of homicide treated the wife in relation to her husband in the same way as a son in relation to his parents. The same tendency can also be seen in the very harsh treatment of a wife to whom responsibility for her husband's suicide could be attributed. A substatute of 1783[67] provided that, where a wife oppressed and drove her husband to suicide, she was to be sentenced to immediate strangulation. The sentence was reduced to strangulation after the assizes where there was no evidence of real oppression but where the husband had hastily taken his life after some trivial quarrel.[68] On the other hand, where a wife committed suicide as a result of ill treatment by her husband, there was normally no liability. Only where he had inflicted on her a physical injury of some substance, and she then in consequence had committed suicide, was he to be sentenced to the very light punishment of eighty blows with the heavy stick.[69]

Although the law was concerned generally with giving effect to the principal obligations entailed by the relationship between husband and wife, it placed particular emphasis on one of the obligations resting on the wife, that of maintaining her chastity. This was an obligation that in Confucian, especially Neo-Confucian, thought constituted a lifelong commitment of fidelity to her husband. We read in the T'ang *shu-i* commentary: "she should remain faithful until buried in the same grave."[70] Strictly construed, the obligation of fidelity meant not only that a wife should refrain from sexual intercourse or dalliance with other men while her husband was alive, but that she should not remarry after his death, no matter how young or destitute she was at that time. Indeed, a really noble woman would never marry, should the groom to whom she had been betrothed die before the marriage had been consummated.[71] While the law did not seek to enforce the duty of fidelity and chastity in all its aspects, it did concern itself particularly with the sexual conduct of the wife while the marriage lasted and with certain problems that arose through pressure placed on a widow to remarry.

Both husband and wife committed an offense if they had sexual intercourse with another person. This was part of the general prohibition against sexual permissiveness.[72] Such rules in fact were not normally enforced. Their function in the code was again to constitute a solemn statement of the wickedness of indiscriminate sexual activity outside marriage. But in one respect the laws concerning adultery were rigorously enforced, and it is notable that they bore with particular severity on the unchaste wife. These were the rules concerned with deaths occurring on account of adultery. That such deaths were of frequent occurrence is evidenced by the very large number of legal cases arising from them that are reported in the standard collections.

The Ming and Ch'ing rules on adultery in some respects show a marked difference from the T'ang. In particular they strengthened the legal position of the husband vis-à-vis his adulterous wife. Under T'ang law the husband was not entitled to kill his wife when he caught her in the act of adultery. Ming and Ch'ing law, on the other hand, adopted a provision first introduced under the Yüan, according to which a husband was to be immune from punishment where he caught his wife and her lover in the act of intercourse and killed them both on the spot.[73] Should he have killed only his wife at that time, the lover having succeeded in making his escape, he was to receive the very modest punishment of eighty blows with the heavy stick.[74] The standpoint of the law is that the husband had acted on the spur of the moment, "overcome with righteous anger," and hence had committed a justifiable homicide. The reasons for the legislative introduction of such exemption from liability, or the reduction of liability to the minimum, appear to have been mixed.[75] However, one factor that almost certainly influenced the Confucian legislators was the conviction that a wife who had been unchaste to the point of actual sexual intercourse with a man not her husband deserved no sympathy or protection. Should her own husband have killed her in flagrante delicto, not only was there no need for a life to be given in requital but no punishment at all, or just a very light one, was the appropriate response.

In another respect, too, the law treated the adulterous wife with exceptional severity. Should her lover have killed her husband, then she, even though unaware of the circumstances, was still to be sentenced to strangulation after the assizes, on the grounds that her husband's death had been caused by her adultery. This was the rule in the T'ang code as well as in the Ming and Ch'ing.[76] Yet, in the converse situation, where she had killed her husband, her lover, provided he was unaware of the circumstances, was to be punished only for the offense of illicit sexual intercourse, even though the death of the husband had been prompted by the adulterous relationship. Two decisions of the Board of Punishments make the attitude of the law clear.

In a case of 1792 from Kuangsi, the Board had to consider the complex set of rules specifying the precise circumstances under which the wife was to be liable, where her lover had quarrelled with and killed her husband. Should she not at the time have shouted for help, or afterwards made no attempt to inform the authorities or help them to identify the lover, she deserved, in the Board's view, the punishment of strangulation after the assizes. The Board pointed out that she had already lost her chastity, the relationship of *en i* with her husband had been destroyed, and the law could not be lenient.[77] In a Kiangsi case of 1765, the Board in a memorial to the throne noted that the rules concerning the liability of the wife, where the lover had killed her husband, differed from those concerning the liability of the adulterer, where the wife had killed her husband, precisely because of the importance of the relationship of *en i* between husband and wife and the lack of any particular relationship of status (*ming fen*) between the husband and the lover.[78]

Where her husband had died, the widow, especially if still young, was often in an awkward position. She might wish to keep her chastity, remain loyal to her deceased husband, and not remarry. On the other hand, her husband's family might place considerable pressure on her to remarry, since on remarriage the property she had inherited from her husband would revert to them.[79] Her own relatives, should there be lacking relatives of appropriate seniority of her husband, also had an interest in securing her remarriage, since they might then obtain a substantial betrothal gift. The law, with its interest in the enforcement of fundamental family morality, did not go as far as to prohibit widows altogether from remarrying. But it did impose some restrictions. In particular, it was an offense for a widow to remarry during the three-year period prescribed by the rites for the mourning of her husband, punished in T'ang law by penal servitude for three years (article 179) and in Ming and Ch'ing law by one hundred blows with the heavy stick.[80]

As to the case where the widow had been compelled against her will to remarry, the T'ang code provided that, where any relative other than the woman's own parents or paternal grandparents had exercised compulsion, a punishment of penal servitude for one year, reduced to a beating of ninety blows with the heavy stick in the case of other close agnatic seniors, was to be imposed, and the marriage was to be undone.[81] The implication is that the widow might be compelled to remarry by her parents or paternal grandparents, suggesting that in T'ang times the duty of filial obedience outweighed the duty to maintain chastity. The Ming position was broadly the same, with somewhat lighter punishments.[82]

Under the Ch'ing important changes were made. In the first place, the exception in favor of parents or paternal grandparents was removed. The code provided that either the paternal grandparents or the parents of the widow or the paternal grandparents or parents of her deceased husband were to be punished with eighty blows with the heavy stick, should they have compelled her to remarry. The punishments for other relatives exercising pressure were heavier. In the second place, the legal consequences of the forced marriage were made to depend on whether it had been completed or not. If it had, the marriage was to stand, but the betrothal presents were forfeit to the state. If it had not, the widow was to return to the home of her former husband, and the betrothal presents were to be returned to the giver.[83] To some extent in the thinking of the Ch'ing legislators the value of chastity outweighed that of filial obedience. But even the former gave way to the value represented by the relationship between husband and wife. Once this had been established, it should not lightly be undone.[84]

The rules discussed above contemplate that the widow, although subject to compulsion, has not resorted to the drastic step of taking her own life. But widows were sometimes so concerned to protect their chastity that, rather than submit to the compulsion placed on them by their husband's relatives or their own relatives to remarry, they chose to commit suicide. How was the law to respond? The law in fact encouraged and protected the chastity of widows in a double way. Those who had committed suicide, when forced by their husband's family or their own to remarry, were to be given public marks of honor by the state. According to the laws of the Ch'ing dynasty, for example, "In case a chaste widow has perished because her family compelled her to remarry, public marks of distinction shall be accorded her in accordance with the existing ordinance."[85] These marks of distinction might be a testimonial of merit from the emperor or the right to have the name of the widow inscribed on a commemorative arch.[86]

The persons who had driven the widow to suicide were to receive heavy punishments. A substatute, which appears to have originated in the Ming, states in its final consolidated form that, where her parents or paternal grandparents or those of her husband forced a widow to remarry and she in consequence put an end to her life, whether the marriage had actually been completed or not, those responsible were to be sentenced to one hundred blows with the heavy stick and penal servitude for three years. For other relatives exercising pressure, the punishments were greater.[87] Of particular interest is the severity of the punishment imposed on the widow's parents or paternal grandparents. We have already noted that even for the intentional killing of a child the punishment in Ch'ing law was only sixty blows with the heavy stick and penal servitude for one year. The much more severe sentence imposed in the case where the widow, forced to remarry, took her own life is explicable only on the basis of the weight now given by the law to the wish of the daughter or daughter-in-law to preserve her chastity in fidelity to her deceased husband.

It is probable that the cult of the chaste widow that flourished in the Ming and Ch'ing period among all classes of person owed much to Neo-Confucian teaching. We may recall the famous dictum of the

Sung Neo-Confucian Ch'eng I that it was preferable for a widow to starve to death than to forfeit her chastity by remarriage.[88] Certainly, the evidence appears to suggest that, prior to the time at which Neo-Confucianism became orthodox, the public and official attitude to remarriage was less hostile than it later became.[89]

The complex of rules in the penal codes relating to marriage reflects the hierarchical structure of society in two ways. There is first the point that the marriage itself was arranged by senior relatives of the bride and groom, normally their parents or paternal grandparents. Even after the marriage, the husband's parents or paternal grandparents continued to play an important role. The wife in the typical marriage came to live with her parents-in-law and in effect occupied the position of a daughter to them. She was required to show submissiveness and respect, a grave failure in this duty being a cause for repudiation. Should the husband die, either his senior relatives or those of the widow might exert pressure on her to remarry. The law was thus required to determine which, if any, of such relatives might legitimately compel remarriage, and what should be the consequences if the widow preferred death.

Second, the fact that in the context of the specific relationship between husband and wife the latter ranked as junior affected the content of the law in several distinct ways. Particularly in the earlier law, the wife and her relatives were at a disadvantage with respect to the rules governing the breaking of an engagement or the dissolution of a marriage. In principle, only the husband might end the marriage through unilateral repudiation. Wrongs committed by the wife against the husband were punished more severely than those committed by the husband against the wife. The duties resting on a wife with respect to her husband were more stringent than those of a husband with respect to his wife. The husband was required by law to maintain his wife in her position as his equal; he might neither reduce her to the level of a concubine nor take a second wife (as distinct from a concubine) during the subsistence of the marriage. On the other hand, the wife might be divorced if she failed in any of the various duties incumbent upon her. Of particular importance here, especially in the later law, was her duty to be chaste, that is, faithful to her husband. Not only did her unfaithfulness constitute grounds for repudiation, whereas unfaithfulness by a husband did not permit repudiation by his wife, but, should she be caught by her husband in flagrante delicto, she might be killed at that time with impunity.

6 The Fundamental Social and Political Relationships

We discuss in this chapter the legal effect given to hierarchical relationships other than those found in the family itself. Of particular importance in this context is one of the Five Relationships and Three Bonds, understood here in the broad sense of the relationship between ruler and subject, rather than in the narrow sense of ruler and minister. The relationship between ruler and subject may itself be considered under two heads: that between the ruler and those of his subjects who occupied an official position in the administration, and that between the ruler and the totality of his subjects (including officials in their private capacity). Apart from the relationship between ruler and subject, we have also to consider two basic social divisions, that between the officials or graduates and the ordinary people, and that between free persons and those of servile or mean status. Both these divisions are echoed in, and have been influenced by, the old Confucian distinction between the "noble" and the "base" or the "superior" and the "inferior" man. Essentially the distinction in Confucian terms was based on the possession and cultivation of superior ability, recognized particularly in intellectual achievement as revealed in knowledge of the rites and the Confucian classics. Officials and graduates were certified through the examination system as possessing this knowledge; other persons were not. Further, those of servile or mean status were debarred even from the opportunity of acquiring a formal education and so entering the privileged class, since they were not allowed to enter for the examinations.

MINISTER/OFFICIAL AND RULER

Officials in the later dynasties were persons who had successfully passed through the examination system and been appointed by the emperor to a regular civil service post, for example, to a position as district magistrate, prefect, governor, or holder of one of the high offices of state in the capital. Whereas only the high officers of state might properly be called "ministers," all officials might reach such a position, and any might be summoned to give advice to the emperor. In the Confucian configuration of the relationship between ruler and minister or official, the ruler was always the superior and the official the inferior. But the way in which the obligations arising under the relationship were interpreted appears to have changed over the course of time. The early Confucian view had been that the minister owed loyalty to the ruler but was expected to remonstrate when the latter wished to act in a manner that did not coincide with propriety. On the other hand, the ruler was required to treat his ministers with respect and listen carefully to their advice. In effect the ministers were regarded as participating with the emperor in the government of the state.[1] There had probably always been a tendency on the part of at least some rulers to place the greatest weight on the loyalty owed by a minister or official, to expect a submissive response to imperial orders, and to tolerate only a limited degree of dissent. Such an attitude seems to have intensified in the Ming and Ch'ing periods.[2] The position of the minister or official in relation to the ruler came to be depreciated. Rather than being seen as one who shared in the ruler's responsibility to govern, the official came to be treated more as a servant of the emperor. From Sung times the Neo-Confucian statesmen emphasized the duty on the part of the minister to obey, though admittedly some Neo-Confucian philosophers still held to be important the right of the minister to remonstrate with and criticize the ruler. Indeed, even the most autocratic rulers accepted in theory the right of the minister to criticize. Ming Tai-tsu insisted that the duty of a loyal minister lay in remonstrating with his ruler whom he knew to be acting wrongly.[3]

Against this changing conception of the relationship between ruler

and minister or official, we may consider the special position of
the official in relation to criminal liability. Early Confucian thought
already held that the penal law should discriminate in favor of officials with respect to the imposition of punishment. A much quoted
dictum contained in the *Li chi* (Book of Rites) stated: "*Li* (the rites)
do not extend down to the common people; punishments do not extend up to the officials."[4] The sentiment expressed in this dictum was
never literally applied. Officials were punished by their ruler, sometimes savagely. Nevertheless, the fact remains that in the T'ang and
even earlier codes an elaborate system of privilege was instituted for
the benefit of officials. We do not propose here to describe the very
complex provisions in detail,[5] but some general points may usefully
be made.

In T'ang law the extent of the privileges enjoyed by nobles, officials,
or their families depended primarily on two factors: the degree of
blood relationship, if any, with the imperial family, and the particular
rank of the noble or official. There were five possible privileges: deliberation, petition, reduction of punishment, monetary redemption,
and surrender of office. Deliberation and petition gave consideration
to those entitled to the privilege in the event they committed a capital
offense. The effect of the special procedures, which differed according
to the nature of the privilege, was to leave the decision as to whether
the death penalty should be exacted in the hands of the emperor. The
expectation was that, in view of the standing of the offender, clemency would be exercised and the death sentence commuted to exile
or a lesser punishment. The third privilege permitted an automatic
reduction by one degree in the normal punishment for a noncapital
offense. For example, if the normal punishment was three years of
penal servitude, exercise of the privilege entitled the offender to a
reduction to two and a half years of penal servitude. The fourth and
fifth privileges were linked. For noncapital cases an office held by
the offender could be surrendered as a substitution for punishment
according to a prescribed scale. Where the surrender of all available
offices was insufficient to cancel the total amount of punishment, any
balance could be redeemed by the payment of copper. Equally, where

the offense was too trivial to require surrender of office, the regular punishment might be redeemed by payment of copper.

The persons entitled to one or more of these privileges, collectively regarded, were relatives of the imperial family, the corpus of regular officials, certain other categories of distinguished person, and, importantly, relatives of those primarily entitled to a privilege. The distribution of privileges worked roughly as follows. Relatives of the emperor or empress,[6] the highest officials, and the other most distinguished persons in the state were entitled to deliberation as well as to the lesser privileges. Somewhat less senior officials were entitled to petition, less senior still to reduction of punishment by one degree, and so on.

The treatment of the relatives of those primarily entitled to privilege is interesting. In general, close relatives of a noble or official were themselves entitled to "protection" through the very fact of the relationship. The principle adopted by the T'ang code was that the close relatives of a person entitled to a particular privilege were to be entitled to the privilege immediately below. For example, the grandsons in the male line of a person entitled to deliberation, as well as the relatives for whom he mourned for one year, were entitled not to deliberation but to petition and the remaining lower privileges (article 9). Again, the paternal grandparents, parents, brothers, sisters, wives, sons, and grandsons in the male line of a person entitled to petition were entitled to reduction of punishment by one degree and the remaining lower privileges (article 10).

Privilege did not give immunity from ordinary punishment in respect of all offenses. Care was taken to exclude the most serious offenses from the ambit of privilege, the principle being, the higher the degree of privilege, the less the range of excluded offenses. Thus, those entitled to deliberation could not plead the privilege if they were accused of having committed one of the ten abominations (article 8), and those entitled to petition could not plead the privilege if they were accused of having committed one of the ten abominations, or of having killed a person, or of having committed certain (other) offenses, or of having taken bribes to subvert the law within their areas of jurisdiction (article 9). One may note particularly that, except for those entitled to deliberation, any official who took bribes and acted corruptly in the exercise of his official duties could not shelter behind privilege in order to escape the full punishment for his offense.

T'ang law did, therefore, introduce certain safeguards to minimize the possibility of an abuse by officials of their privileged position. Nevertheless, the fact remains that the ambit of privilege was wide. For many offenses officials might escape the normal punishment through a combination of surrender of office and payment of copper. How was this justified in contemporary conceptions of the role of the official? The main idea, perhaps, was that, since officials were associated with the emperor in the government of the state, they should not be subject to the normal processes of the law. The emperor was himself "above the law," and while his ministers and officials could not be placed in the same position, they could be granted some degree of immunity from the ordinary operation of the law. In effect, the precise degree of immunity was related to the closeness of the official to the emperor. Those most closely associated with the emperor in the government received the highest level of privilege. A practical consideration also probably entered into this idea. To expose relatives of the emperor or those in whom he confided the greatest trust to the ordinary legal processes and punishments would have damaged the standing of the government with the public as a whole and risked bringing into disrepute the whole system of administration with the emperor at its head.

Some evidence from the time of the Han dynasty suggests that the relationship between the emperor and his officials was the governing consideration in the grant of privileges to the latter. In the *Li chi*, immediately after the statement that punishment does not extend to the officials, it is said, "Men who have suffered punishment should not be by the side of the ruler." There seems to be implicit here the thought that those associated with the ruler should not be objects of punishment, at least in the ordinary sense of "punishment." In 176 B.C. the Confucian scholar Chia I sent a memorial to the then Han emperor remonstrating against the practice of subjecting high officials to the degrading and humiliating processes of the ordinary law. Among the points he made was this: "The reason why the favorite ministers of the Ruler do not have punishments of mutilation or execution inflicted on their person is because the Ruler is respected. Such are the means to remove beforehand any (show of) disrespect from the Ruler, and, by showing deference to the great ministers, to strengthen their virtuous resolve." He also said: "So the reason why anciently the Rules of Ceremonious Behaviour did not extend to the commoners, and why the mutilating punishments were not applied to the Grandees, was in order to stimulate the virtuous behaviour of the favored ministers."[7] Chia I's general argument is that the ruler by a proper treatment of his ministers, even where they had committed offenses, ensured respect for himself, and at the same time encouraged his officials in their task of promoting good in the state.

We may also adduce a further consideration. Officials belonged by definition to the class of the "superior man" or the "gentleman." It was this class especially that was expected to model its behaviour on the rites and generally conduct itself in accordance with the rules of propriety. For such persons the disgrace and shame that would be entailed by the discovery that they had committed an offense may have been deemed in themselves a sufficient punishment, especially where disgrace was made visibly evident through the loss of office. The possibility of such disgrace may have been considered the main deterrent in securing the proper performance by officials of their duties. Should they commit an offense, subjection to the normal punishments, in addition to the disgrace, may have been regarded as excessive. The theme that officials would be more responsive to good treatment than to humiliating punishments also occurs in Chia I's memorial. He says: "If the Ruler Above treats his great ministers as he would treat horses or dogs, they will of course act like horses and dogs; if he treats them like government convicts (labourers), they will naturally act like convicts."[8]

Under the Sung the T'ang system was retained, the sphere of privilege accorded to officials and their families even being slightly extended.[9] The Ming and Ch'ing dynasties saw a number of important changes. Of the five T'ang privileges only deliberation and petition were formally retained by the Ming and Ch'ing codes, and these were not exactly the same as they had been under the T'ang. Deliberation was strengthened. It might now be invoked for any offense, whether capital or not, except those falling under the ten abominations. Furthermore, imperial permission was required before the authorities could even take cognisance of the offense; if they were permitted to conduct a preliminary investigation, they again had to request imperial permission before making a full investigation of the offense and the grounds permitting the exercise of privilege, and finally they must await the imperial determination of the sentence.[10] Deliberation was confined to imperial relatives, officials of the highest rank, and a few other persons of great eminence or extreme worth.[11] Petition was also extended. In its final form, established by the 1725–27 revision of the Ch'ing code, its effect was that no offense, other than a light fault, committed by an official of any rank might be investigated without permission from the throne. Nor might any proposed sentence be implemented without express imperial permission.[12]

Thus, Ming and Ch'ing law conferred on all officials a procedural privilege that removed them, where they had committed an offense, from subjection to the ordinary legal process. It also radically overhauled the system of punishment. A much greater use was made of administrative punishments than in earlier times. The rules were complicated and frequently changed. We note here only the main features of the late Ch'ing law. Where the official had committed a "public offense," that is, one committed in the exercise of his duties without ulterior motive or private profit, for which the punishment prescribed by the code was a beating, this was to be commuted to loss of salary, reduction in rank, or transfer to another post.[13] For "private offenses," that is, those committed for private profit, punishable by a beating, commutation to loss of salary, reduction in rank, transfer, or dismissal from office was permitted.[14] For more serious public or private offenses, the official was to be sentenced to the punishment prescribed by the code, but implementation required express imperial authorization.

While the punishment for relatively light private or public offenses was commuted into a variety of administrative sanctions, the articles of the Ming and Ch'ing codes contemplated that for more serious matters the official would remain liable to the punishment prescribed for the specific offense that he had committed. However, substatutes provided that, in cases where the punishment for the offense was penal servitude, exile, or, as for certain offenses, only nominally death, he might be permitted to redeem the punishment. The privilege of redemption was readily available under the Ming, but the Ch'ing significantly restricted its scope. In the first place, it was not to be allowed where the official had been corrupt and accepted bribes or had profited personally from state funds. In the second place, redemption ceased to be a matter of right. The chance to redeem might be granted by the emperor after consultation with the Board of Punishments. At no time could the punishment be redeemed for really serious offenses, such as homicide, rape, forcible theft, or those falling within the ten abominations.[15]

An important gloss has to be added to the above account of official privilege. Not all the laws conferring privileges on officials were applied in practice, at least in the late Ch'ing period. The Yung-cheng emperor, for example, at the time of the 1725–27 revision of the penal code wished to delete altogether the article on deliberation. He was persuaded to retain it, but issued an edict in 1728, affirming that it was not the practice of the dynasty to apply the law on deliberation, since it conflicted with the principles of justice and fairness. He also observed that it was necessary to punish the offenses of high officials with particular severity, in order to encourage them to provide a proper model for their inferiors.[16] In other words, the emperor was advocating a policy that resembled that of equality before the law in the sense that high officials should not be singled out for special treatment. While it is doubtful whether this was ever completely achieved,[17] it does seem as though the Ch'ing emperors made some attempt to control the more undesirable consequences of privilege. In particular, they tried to exclude the possibility of redemption in the case of offenses marked by corruption and to remove the *right* to redeem in the case of other offenses, leaving the matter to the discretion of the throne. These moves may be associated with a changing conception in the role of the official. Officials were still entitled to respect as servants of the emperor, but it was precisely the fact that they were regarded as servants and not as associates that contributed to the policy of curtailment of privilege.

RULER AND SUBJECT

The way in which Confucian thinking understood the relationship between the ruler and the people at large also seems to have undergone changes in emphasis. Confucius's own formulation, in its highly elliptic way, had stressed the obligations of the ruler just as much as those of the subject.[18] Mencius had suggested that the subject's duty of loyalty was discharged where the ruler no longer behaved as a ruler should, but had turned into an oppressive tyrant.[19] There is implicit in this conception the notion that the relationship between ruler and subject was not immutable. Improper behavior by the ruler might entail its dissolution. Later thinking does not seem to have contemplated this possibility, and placed the emphasis rather on the duty of the subject than that of the ruler. The Sung statesman Ssu-ma Kuang held that "the positions of the sovereign and the subject are as immutable as those of heaven and earth," and the Neo-Confucian philosopher Ch'eng Hao observed: "The relations of sovereign-and-subject and of father-and-son belong to the eternal principle of the cosmos from which there is no escape between heaven and earth."[20] What may also have influenced such thinking is the gradual adoption by the Confucians of ideas drawn from the thinking of the Legalists on "the elevation of the ruler."[21]

Neo-Confucian thinkers and statesmen looked at the ruler-subject relationship primarily from the point of view of the duties of the subject. This did not mean that rulers regarded themselves as devoid of obligation. Most saw their task as that of promoting the welfare of the people. But they did not see themselves as accountable to the people. The ruler was the intermediary between the people and heaven. It was to heaven that he was accountable, and it was heaven who might

withdraw the mandate from a tyrannical and oppressive dynasty.[22]
The ruler's attitude toward the people was that of a vastly superior
being who, through acts of benevolence and kindness, sought to improve their lot and secure their happiness. In return, the absolute duty
of the people was that of loyalty characterized by submission and obedience. Neo-Confucian orthodoxy, as in the quotation from Ch'eng
Hao, made a strong association between the duty of the son to be
filial and the duty of the subject to be filial.[23]

Legal recognition of the subjects' duty of loyalty is found primarily
in the offenses of rebellion, great sedition, and treason that head the
list of the ten abominations. These offenses in all dynasties attracted
the harshest punishments, but one can detect an increase in the
severity of the rules adopted by the Ming and Ch'ing legislators.[24] In
T'ang law, for example, rebellion, defined as plotting to endanger the
state, attracted the following punishments: those who had engaged
in the plot were to be beheaded, the father and sons aged 16 or above
of the principal offenders were to be strangled, their sons aged 15
or below, mother, daughters (neither married nor engaged), wife and
concubines (whether their own or their sons), paternal grandfather,
grandsons by sons, and brothers and sisters were all to be forfeit to
the state as slaves. Their paternal uncles and nephews in the male
line were to be exiled to three thousand *li*.[25] The *shu-i* commentary
stresses the position of the ruler as the father of his people: "The
king occupies the most honourable position and receives heaven's
decrees. Like heaven and earth, he acts to shelter and support, thus
serving as the father and mother of the masses. As his children, as his
subjects they must be loyal and filial. However, should they dare to
cherish wickedness and have rebellious hearts, they will run counter
to heaven's constancy and violate human principle."[26]

When we compare the Ming and Ch'ing law, we see that the severity
of the punishment for rebellion has been significantly increased. Not
only is the death penalty extended to a wider class of persons, but the
range of relatives selected for punishment is greater. Those involved
in the plot are to be put to death by slicing. The paternal grandfather,
fathers, sons, grandsons in the male line, brothers, and other males

living in the same household, whether of the same surname or not,[27] paternal uncles and nephews in the male line, if aged 16 or above, are to be beheaded. Males falling within the above description, if aged 15 or below, the mother, sisters, daughters (unless married or engaged), wife and concubines of the principal offenders as well as those of their sons are to be given as slaves to deserving officials.[28]

Late Ch'ing law took a somewhat more lenient attitude by decreasing the number of relatives exposed to the death penalty. A substatute, introduced in 1801 and subsequently revised on a number of occasions, in its final form provided that the sons and grandsons of the principal offenders, where it was clear that they had no knowledge of the facts, were to be castrated and given as slaves to the officials and soldiers of the newly acquired frontier regions. Other male relatives not involved in the plot were to be enslaved but not castrated.[29] Although the male relatives of the plotters now escaped death, they were to be subject to a mutilation that had not been part of the regular legal system since the Han dynasty.[30]

The explanatory article to the Ch'ing article states that the atrocity of the act of plotting rebellion is extreme, and hence the punishment is the most terrible. The breach of duty on the part of the subject is in fact a revolt against heaven itself, and no indulgence or laxity is possible.[31] The severity of the Ming and Ch'ing rules may be explicable in part simply through a natural desire on the part of rulers to safeguard their position with all the means at their disposal, including the use of the most draconian punishments. Yet, it also seems likely that the stronger conception of loyalty induced by the Neo-Confucian analysis of the relationship between ruler and subject played a part. The failure to show loyalty was so fundamental a breach of the individual's natural duty that only the severest possible punishment constituted an adequate response, a position reflected in the Ch'ing commentary. One may readily see a parallel between the treatment in Ming and Ch'ing law of the disloyal subject and the unfilial son.[32]

SOCIAL CLASSES

All societies, except perhaps the simplest, have classes that determine an individual's social if not legal status. Social classes vary according to the degree of fluidity that obtains between their boundaries, according to the criteria that determine their composition (birth, wealth, occupation), and according to the legal incidents attached to membership. Traditional China until the end of the Ch'ing possessed a class system with aspects both of rigidity and fluidity. It was rigid in the sense that there was a fixed distinction between free persons and persons of servile or mean status. Those classified as slaves or as belonging to a caste practicing one of the "mean occupations" were barred from attaining membership of the class of free persons, except under some special dispensation. On the other hand, the system was fluid in the sense that any (male) member of the free class might aspire to becoming an official. The criteria for membership of a class were birth or education. Birth determined whether one was a slave, a member of a mean caste, or a free person. Education, understood in the sense of success in the state examinations, permitted free persons, if male, to join the official class. Of course, it was true in China, as elsewhere, that persons born into upper-class or wealthy families had a better chance of competing in the taxing educational *cursus honorum* than those born into a family of ordinary, poor people.[33]

The late Ch'ing class system can be delimited in somewhat fuller fashion as follows. In descending order of superiority the main classes were officials and ex-officials, graduates (those who had progressed some way along the educational ladder but had not yet been appointed to an official post), the ordinary free people, the mean people (those following one of the base occupations such as music or prostitution), and slaves. In addition there was a social and legal division between the class of the conquerors (Manchu) and the conquered (the Chinese), just as in the earlier Yüan dynasty there had been such a distinction between the Mongol conquerors and their Chinese subjects.[34] This system of classes reflects the fundamental distinction drawn in Confucian thinking between the "noble" and the "base," a distinction which can be applied in a relative fashion to the actual class structure. For example, officials counted as "noble" in relation to the rest of the population, ordinary free people from this perspective falling within the "base" category. Yet, from the perspective of the relationship between the servile and the free, the former counted as "base" and the latter as "noble."

The essential feature of Confucius's own thinking, accepted by his followers, was that the distinction between the "noble" and the "base" should be grounded not upon birth but upon personal achievement as demonstrated through cultivation of the mind and knowledge of propriety.[35] This conception passed into orthodox thinking and was accepted by the ruling dynasties as one of the foundations of society. Mental cultivation and knowledge of propriety were held to be demonstrated by success in the examinations set and controlled by the state.[36] Only those who had successfully completed a series of examinations designed to reveal a detailed knowledge of the Confucian canon might be elevated to the status of an official. This was always the essential requirement for the acquisition of official status, even though the system was sometimes abused and the purchase of degrees permitted. On the whole there was a successful implementation in traditional China of the Confucian principle that the route to office and high status lay in education.[37] In Confucian theory slaves or mean persons had demonstrated by their conduct that they were not worthy of aspiring to higher status, a disability that was held to be hereditary.

The penal codes reinforced the social divisions in a number of different ways. They provided sanctions for the rules determining the outward signs marking the status constituted by membership of a class, such as the clothing, housing, or grave monuments to which an individual was entitled. They sought to prevent contamination of the "noble" by the "base," on the one hand, by excluding slaves or those of mean occupation from access to the examinations and, on the other, by a series of marriage prohibitions. In a different way they reinforced the distinction between "noble" and "base" through the privileges conferred on officials and graduates. Finally, where a member of a lower class committed an offense against a member of a higher, the general principle adopted was that the punishment should be more severe than in the reverse situation. We will consider these matters under the following heads: sumptuary laws, marriage prohibitions, privileges and restrictions, and offenses.

Sumptuary Laws

A good introduction to this topic is provided by the views of the founding Ming emperor, Ming Tai-tsu, who was particularly concerned with the maintenance of status distinctions in society. After the barbarisms introduced by the Mongols he sought to return to strict Confucian propriety. In a set of regulations introduced in 1370 he observed that it was necessary "to differentiate noble from base, and clearly exhibit rank and authority." In 1391 he stated: "There is no greater purpose for *li* (rites/propriety) than distinguishing the noble from the base and clarifying the gradations of power." Ming regulations provided that the official elite should return to T'ang fashions for their hairstyles and dress, that ordinary people should have a lower living standard than officials, that the rank of an official determined the kind of clothing, house, transport, and utensils to which he was entitled, and that local officials were to travel within their districts by carriage rather than on horseback in order to impress the people with their authority.[38]

Both the Ming and the Ch'ing penal codes contained detailed rules on these matters. An article, identical in each code, provided that there ought to be differences in the dwellings, food, carriages, and furniture of officials and ordinary persons. Within the class of officials there were to be further differences according to the rank of each. An official who used an object to which he was not entitled was to be removed from office and sentenced to one hundred blows with the heavy stick; where an ordinary person committed a like offense, the head of the family was to be sentenced to fifty blows with the light stick. The workman who had supplied the object was also to be sentenced to fifty blows. The punishment was to be one hundred blows and penal servitude for three years if a person used silks and brocades bearing emblems reserved for the emperor or empress.[39] The explana-

tory commentary of the Ch'ing code notes that, in determining the
dwelling, clothing, and so on to which a person was entitled, the law
followed the degree of "being noble" or "being base" or "being senior"
or "being junior," in order to establish his authority and power.[40] This
echoes exactly the thought of the Ming founder. The substatutes regulated in great detail the exact kind of dwelling, clothing, carriage,
utensil, and tomb appropriate to each class of individual.[41]

Marriage Prohibitions

The T'ang code prohibited a slave from taking a free woman as his
wife.[42] Punishments were imposed on the slave or the person responsible (penal servitude for one year and a half) and the person responsible for the girl's marriage (penal servitude for one year), and the marriage was to be undone. The *shu-i* commentary explains that people
who marry must be of equal status and that the difference between
"free" and "base" precludes the possibility of a match.[43] Other persons who, although not actually slaves, were of servile status were
also forbidden to marry free persons. While the code does not seem to
contemplate the possibility that a free male might take a slave wife,
it does prohibit the marriage between a free male and a woman of
servile status.[44]

The Ming and Ch'ing codes contain an article prohibiting a slave
from taking a free person as wife similar to the T'ang, except that the
punishments are lighter.[45] The Ch'ing commentary makes the same
point as the T'ang, namely, that a marriage between the "noble" and
the "base" is not proper.[46] However, with respect to a free man taking
a woman of servile status as his wife, these codes contain provisions
relating only to officials. They are forbidden from marrying prosti-
tutes or singing girls.[47] It does not seem that in Ming and Ch'ing law
a male commoner was prohibited from marrying a female slave or
prostitute. On the whole, therefore, it appears that the later law was
somewhat less concerned than the earlier with the need to enforce a
strict separation between the servile and the free class.

Privileges and Restrictions

We have already discussed in this chapter the privileges accorded officials. Here we need to add only some words concerning graduates,
taking our illustrations from the Ch'ing period. Graduates were given
certain privileges in connection with the legal process and the imposition of punishment. Once an individual had passed the examinations that entitled him to be a member of a government school and
proceed to further studies in order to qualify for appointment as an
official, he became known as a *sheng-yüan,* a term often translated as
"licentiate." The *sheng-yüan* immediately acquired a more elevated
status in society, being entitled to wear a special uniform and to receive marks of respect from ordinary commoners.[48] An attribute of
his new status was that he could not be treated by the authorities as
though he were still an ordinary person. He was given something of
the privilege pertaining to an official.

According to a substatute of 1767, which had antecedents,[49] where
a *sheng-yüan* had committed an offense entailing the punishment of
penal servitude, exile, or death, the local magistrate was to report to
the head of the offender's academic institution requesting his degradation and to immediately begin investigating the case. According to
Boulais, if the academy had ultimately refused to degrade the graduate
or ratify the judgment of the magistrate, the latter had to dismiss the
case or appeal to the emperor. The substatute further provided that,
where the offense was light, meriting only an official reprimand, this
was to be administered in conjunction with the offender's local academic superior. Boulais cites a decree of the Chien-lung emperor to
the effect that the magistrate and the academic superior were to meet
in a special hall to censure the graduate and administer a beating.[50]

Graduates who had obtained one of the higher degrees (*chu-jen* or
chin-shih) were no longer subject to the jurisdiction of the academic
authorities, but fell under the supervision of the provincial governor.
No offense could be investigated by the local magistrate without prior
authorization from the governor.[51]

Under the general redemption law applying to officials, all grades of graduate were allowed to pay money to redeem the punishment for any offense entailing ninety blows with the heavy stick or less. Where the offense entailed one hundred blows with the heavy stick, punishment was redeemed not by payment of money but by degradation.[52]

Generally, therefore, we may say that graduates partook of the privileges accorded to officials in two ways. Where they had committed an offense, jurisdiction was not entirely in the hands of the local magistrate. Approval for the implementation of the sentence or the conduct of the proceedings had to be obtained from the academic authorities or the provincial governor, depending on the rank of the graduate. Further, graduates were not subjected to the humiliating punishment of flogging, but might redeem it through payment or removal of their status.

In contrast to the privileges enjoyed by graduates and officials, slaves and followers of mean occupations were subjected to restrictions that precluded them from improving their status. Neither class of person was allowed to participate in the examinations or acquire any public dignity. The class of "mean person" was extensive, comprising at various times during the Ch'ing artists, musicians, beggars, fishermen, runners, constables, and equivalent employees in the government offices. One or another of these occupations was occasionally removed from the "mean" category by imperial order during the Ch'ing,[53] but at any given time a significant number of persons were excluded from the right to participate in the examinations. Since slaves and the followers of mean occupations were looked upon as belonging to hereditary castes, these restrictions applied also to descendants. Even where a slave had been manumitted, the rule established by the Ch'ing was that access to the examinations should not be permitted until the third generation following manumission; that is, the grandson of the manumitted slave was the first member of the family to be allowed to become an examination candidate. Severe restrictions were also placed on the descendants of persons who had been removed from the mean category.[54] The thought underlying these rules seems to have been that only after the lapse of a number of generations from loss of slave or mean status could the family be considered sufficiently "purified" to permit the possibility of entry into the official class.

Offenses

The codes treat offenses committed between members of different social classes in a discriminatory fashion. This was most obvious in connection with slaves in relation to their masters and the latter's relatives, as well as in relation to the free population as a whole, but there was also a certain discrimination in favor of officials in relation to ordinary people. We shall cite a few examples, largely from the Ming and Ch'ing law concerning homicide.

The Ming and Ch'ing codes provided that, should an ordinary person beat the magistrate or prefect under whose jurisdiction he was, a certain scale of punishments should apply that was more severe than the punishment inflicted for a like assault on another commoner. Where the official died as a result of the blows, the punishment was to be beheading after the assizes instead of the normal strangulation after the assizes. The commentaries explain the increase in punishment on the grounds of the special bond between the people and their magistrate or prefect created by the government (as distinct from the bond created by heaven characteristic of blood relationships).[55] Should an ordinary person strike and kill an official other than one under whose jurisdiction he fell, the case was to be treated as though the official were a commoner. But, in the case of blows not resulting in death, again a special scale of punishment was to be applied, its severity depending on the rank of the official. The commentary explains that the duty (*i*) toward officials who were not directly in a position of authority over an individual was less stringent than in the case of those who were.[56] It was the precise evaluation by the legislators of the content of this duty in different relationships that yielded the very detailed rules which varied the punishments according to the respective status and rank of official and commoner. The same consideration governed the treatment of offenses committed by junior officials against their superiors.[57] On the other hand, where an official beat and killed an ordinary person under his jurisdiction or an official subordinate, there was no decrease in the punishment that would normally be applied.

Slaves (nu-pei), or as they are sometimes termed in the literature "serfs" or "bondsmen," were treated in the codes along with another class of family employee called "hired workman" (ku-kung). There is, however, a very important difference between these two classes of underling. In respect to persons outside the family that owned them, slaves were still treated as "inferior," whereas hired workmen were treated as ordinary free people. It was only in respect to the family that employed him that a hired workman was treated as "inferior," and then not to the same degree as the slave. The reason for the difference is that all relationships within the household were conceived in kinship terms. Slaves and hired workmen who lived with the family were treated as though they were junior members. But, in relation to strangers, hired workmen counted as equal, whereas slaves were still classified as "inferior."

The general principle applied to the treatment of offenses between slaves and free persons is that the slave was to be punished one degree more and the free person one degree less for the same offense.[58] In the case of homicide the principle was applied only in part. Where a slave beat and killed or intentionally killed a free person, in both cases the punishment in Ch'ing law was to be beheading after the assizes; in the reverse situation the punishment for the free person in both cases was to be strangulation after the assizes. The effect is that in the case of beating and killing, but not intentional killing, the punishment of the slave was increased from strangulation to beheading, whereas in the case of intentional killing, but not beating and killing, the punishment of the free person was reduced from beheading to strangulation.[59]

One article of the code specifically deals with and prohibits sexual intercourse between slave and free. Where a male slave had intercourse with the wife or daughter of a free person, the punishment for both was to be one degree higher than that for the case where the parties were both free. On the other hand, should a free male have sexual intercourse with another person's female slave, the punishment for both was one degree less than that for the case where both were free.[60] The Ch'ing commentary explains the rules on the grounds of the relationship of "superiority" and "inferiority" between the "free" and the "base." In the first case, the slave exceeded his status and the woman debased herself, hence the increase in punishment. In the second case, the punishment was less, because the free man had lowered himself to the position of the slave.[61]

In the context of the family the discrepancy in punishment is much greater. We will again confine our illustrations to the law of homicide, noting the differences between the T'ang and the Ming/Ch'ing law. In T'ang law, where a slave struck his master a blow from which he died, the punishment was to be beheading. In this respect there was no difference from the case in which a slave had struck and killed a free person.[62] On the other hand, should the master beat and kill the slave or even kill him intentionally, the punishment was to be one hundred blows with the heavy stick if the slave had committed an offense and penal servitude for one year if no offense had been committed.[63] For the accidental killing by the master of his own slave there was no liability,[64] whereas a slave who accidentally killed his master was to be sentenced to strangulation.[65]

Ming and Ch'ing law normally distinguished between the slave and the hired workman. Yet, for plotting to kill the family head or a relative for whom he mourned for three months or more, both slave and hired workman were to be treated in the same way as a son or grandson.[66] Where a slave beat and killed or intentionally killed the family head, the punishment was to be death by slicing. If the killing was accidental, the punishment provided by the articles of the codes was strangulation after the assizes,[67] increased by substatute to immediate strangulation coupled with the benefit of a special report to the throne of extenuating circumstances.[68] The punishments for the killing by the family head (or a year-of-mourning relative or maternal grandparent) were the same as under the T'ang: one hundred blows if the slave had committed an offense, penal servitude for one year if he had not. For hired workmen there was a slight variation. Should he have intentionally killed the family head, he was to be put to death by slicing. For beating and killing he was to be sentenced to immediate beheading.[69] For accidental killing he served three years in prison. In the reverse situation the family head was to be sentenced to strangulation after the assizes for the intentional killing of a hired workman, to one hundred blows and penal servitude for three years where he had beaten and killed him, and to no punishment for an accidental killing.

These rules appear to be clear and readily capable of application. In fact, when cases of homicide involving persons alleged to be slaves came before the courts, it was often difficult to determine the true status of the offender, and on this point depended the correct identification of the punishment. Ch'ing legal commentaries defined "slaves" as the children of persons who had been enslaved on the grounds of incrimination in an offense such as rebellion committed by a relative.[70] One would have to add here also persons who had received the punishment of enslavement for an offense that they had personally committed.[71] Hired workmen were defined as free persons who have for a temporary and defined period hired out their services to a master. It is their occupation not their person which is "base."[72] From other sources we know that hired workmen were often debtors who had pledged themselves to their creditors for a certain period to work off the debt.[73]

As so defined the two categories of slave and hired workman were easily distinguishable. However, the problem was that many persons on account of debt or for some other reason entered into a relationship of subordination with another on conditions that might leave unclear both the extent of the subordination and the time for which it was to endure. Their services might have been acquired by a "contract of sale." Were such persons to be regarded as slaves? Much depended on the type of contract, and in particular whether it was registered with the authorities as involving a change of status for the individual bought from "free" to "slave." Where the contract was not so registered, the individual was not regarded as a slave unless he had served the master for over three years or had been provided with a wife by his master.[74]

7 Moral Values and the Law

We have seen that many rules of the penal codes were designed to enforce the kind of conduct held by Confucian orthodoxy to be essential for the maintenance and proper functioning of the central family and social relationships, particularly those designated under the head of the "Three Bonds." With respect to some matters falling within this area the law was particularly strict and sternly enforced; with respect to others it seems rather to have had a symbolic force. There are also certain values not specifically linked to family, political, or social roles that had a considerable effect on the law. These are respect for life, benevolence or humanity (*jen*), repentance, and sexual restraint.

Repentance and humanity were closely embedded in Confucian thinking, and indeed were among its most striking facets. Respect for life and sexual restraint were not so clearly confined to the spectrum of Confucian thought; they appear to draw upon wider considerations of the kind of value that society should seek to implement. Aspects of the value represented by sexual restraint were certainly strongly endorsed by Confucian orthodoxy. We have already seen that the requirement of female chastity was a hallmark of Neo-Confucian thought. But the Ch'ing law also sought, although to a lesser extent, to promote male chastity, which does not appear to have been a specific feature of Confucian moral thought. Respect for life was characteristic of Buddhist as well as Confucian thought, and Buddhism had been influential in China from the time of the Han dynasty.[1]

THE VALUE OF LIFE

Although "life" in this context means not just the life of a human but also that of an animal, by far the greater emphasis is placed, as one might expect, on human life.[2] The law pays explicit respect to the value of human life in two contrasting but complementary ways. Where one person caused the death of another, the loss of life by the victim in principle called for the loss of life by the killer in requital. On the other hand, the life of the killer also had a value. The law took great care before putting an end to it, utilizing various devices to prevent too rigorous an implementation of the principle of requital. We shall consider first the principle of requital, the qualifications to which it was subjected, and then the ways in which the law demonstrated care for the life of the killer.

From the point of view of the formal sentence, in cases of homicide the principle of requital was strictly applied. Where one person had directly caused the death of another, the sentence for the offender was to be capital. This was so even where the death had resulted from pure accident.[3] By this means the law manifested the importance of the principle that for the loss of a life there must be exacted another life in compensation.[4] However, in some cases, such as that of the pure accident, it was held to be unjust that the "offender" should actually be put to death. Therefore, the formal sentence also provided that the punishment of strangulation should be commuted to the payment of a sum of money to the family of the victim. In other cases, too, there was a mechanism of review that permitted commutation of the death penalty, where extenuating circumstances were present.

The principle that the life of the killer should be exacted by the law in requital for the life of the victim applied on the assumption that the value of the two lives was equal. This was not always the case. The most obvious example is supplied by family relationships as expressed in the mourning regulations. The life of a junior was always regarded as of less value than the life of a senior. Hence the killing of a senior by a junior was always in principle punished by the imposition of a capital sentence, whereas the same did not hold true for the killing of a junior by a senior. Determination of the punishment depended on the mourning relationship involved. In some cases, such as that of parent and child, even the premeditated or deliberate killing of the junior by the senior was not treated by the law as a capital offense.[5]

Strictly, the principle of requital demanded an equivalence between the lives lost and the lives taken by the law. This was not always possible, although the law sometimes went to considerable lengths to secure a balance between the number of victims and the number of those to be sentenced to death in requital. Where one person had brought about the death of two or more persons, the normal response of the law was to impose an increased punishment on the offender, extending in some cases to the punishment of his close relatives. All the penal codes contained an article establishing a particularly severe punishment for the deliberate killing of three persons in one family, none of whom had committed a capital offense. In its Ch'ing form the article provided that the killer was himself to be put to death by slicing, his property was to be given to the family of those killed, and his wife and sons were to be exiled to two thousand *li*.[6] Ch'ing substatutes added many further rules dealing with a variety of situations in which more than one person had been killed. One, for example, provided that, where three or more persons in a family had been killed in a fight, the killer was to be sentenced to immediate beheading. Should two lives in one family, or three not in one family, have been lost, he was to be sentenced to immediate strangulation.[7] This may be contrasted with the normal rule on killing in a fight (*tou sha*), which prescribed the punishment of strangulation after the assizes, there being a good chance of reprieve in the autumn review.

The law was concerned not just with the fact that there should be adequate requital but also with the fact that the loss of life demanded by the law should not be excessive. Two statutory rules introduced in Ming or Ch'ing times may be cited as illustrations. A substatute of 1740/1814 provided that, where two families (here designated as A and B) engaged in a fight and one life was lost on each side, if the killer in family A belonged to the same clan as, and stood in a mourning relationship to, the victim in family A, and likewise if the killer in family B was a clan mourning relative of the victim in his family, both killers should escape death and be sentenced to exile.[8] The thought behind this concession was stated by the Board of Punishments in a decision of 1751.[9] The death in the fight of one member of each family provided in the circumstances of the case sufficient requital, each death compensating for the other. The law should not exact two more lives, since then the families together would have lost four lives, a circumstance meriting pity.[10]

Another substatute, originating under the Ming, dealt with the situation in which several persons had formed a plot to beat another. The penal codes had provided in this case that, should the victim of the beating die, the person who struck the fatal blow was to be sentenced to strangulation, and the person who initiated the plot should be exiled.[11] The substatute now provided that, should the "original plotter" die of illness while in jail or awaiting trial or sentence,[12] the person who struck the fatal blow was to have his capital sentence commuted to exile.[13] The Board explained the rationale in a discussion of the substatute in 1791.[14] It quoted a juristic commentary to the effect that it was inequitable for the loss of one life to require in requital the loss of two lives, and it expressed its support for this proposition.[15]

A case of 1799 from Chekiang illustrates the application of the last-mentioned substatute. The Board had to consider a situation in which the following deaths had occurred in a conflict between two groups, the first represented by Wang, Tan, and Ch'en, the second by Hsia, Yu, and some others. Hsia inflicted a mortal wound on Wang, Tan inflicted a mortal wound on Hsia, and Ch'en inflicted a mortal wound on Yu. Wang, Hsia, and Yu all subsequently died from their wounds. The provincial authorities had proposed that both Ch'en and Tan should be sentenced to strangulation after the assizes under the ordinary rule on killing in a fight (tou sha). The Board considered that Tan's sentence should be reduced to exile. It argued that Hsia's life could be taken as given in requital for Wang's.[16] If Tan also were to be sentenced to the loss of his life in requital, the result would be that two lives (those of Wang and Tan) would be given for the loss of one (Hsia). There would thus be a lack of harmony between the facts and the law. Hence the substatute on the original plotter dying of illness in jail should be applied by analogy.[17] The death of Wang (the original plotter) provided sufficient requital for the death of Hsia, and Tan's punishment as the person who had inflicted the mortal wound should accordingly be reduced to exile.[18]

In certain circumstances it was deemed equitable that two or more lives should be given in requital for the loss of one life. Thus, where several persons had plotted to kill another, the Ch'ing code provided that the person who instituted the plot should be sentenced to beheading after the assizes and that all those who had actively contributed to the death should be sentenced to strangulation after the assizes.[19] It is clear under this article that several persons might be condemned to lose their lives in requital for the death of a single victim. The explanatory commentary of the code makes precisely this point, and observes that both the facts and the law justify this result, since the original plotter was the source of the evil and the others had participated in it.[20]

The Board not infrequently instanced the importance of human life when maintaining a particular interpretation of the law or arguing for a stronger penalty than that proposed by the provincial authorities. Thus, in a case of 1761 from Kiangsi, Ting was engaged in sexual intercourse with the wife of a distant relative when another person entered the room on an errand. In his surprise Ting leapt up, his fingers pressing into the woman's stomach and causing an injury from which she later died. The provincial authorities treated the death as arising from an accident, and hence proposed that Ting should pay the appropriate redemption, but the Board considered this approach to be too lenient. It warned against the tendency to treat any unintentional killing as accidental. Where the parties were face to face, and the act resulting in death could be considered as falling within the contemplation of the offender, the case must be treated as one of killing in a fight (*tou sha*), and the latter must be sentenced to die in requital. In reaching this conclusion the Board stressed that a person's life (referring here to the victim) was an important matter.[21]

In a Fengtien case of 1824, the following facts were submitted to the Board. Yin was traveling with his wife and her sister. The party stopped overnight at an inn, where Yin heard something that made him think his wife was about to abscond. Overcome with anger, he rushed to her room to stab her. Instead, by mistake he seized his wife's sister in the dark and stabbed her to death. Realizing his mistake, he then turned upon and killed his wife. Under the code the punishment for the intentional killing of one's wife was strangulation after the assizes,[22] but for the intentional killing of an unrelated person the sentence was beheading after the assizes.[23] The problem before the court was to decide which rule was to be applied where a person treated as unrelated to the offender was killed in mistake for his wife. The military authorities who first heard the case thought that there was room for pity, since the sister had been killed in mistake for the wife, and they proposed a sentence of strangulation after the assizes in respect of both killings. The Board held that this was wrong and that Yin should be sentenced to beheading after the assizes in respect of the killing of his wife's sister. It argued that it was not possible to be lenient where through a mistake an innocent person had cruelly been made to lose her life before its natural end.[24]

An interesting case was submitted from the province of Szechuan in 1779. Two nine-year-old boys had quarrelled. One struck the other, causing him to fall over and receive injuries from which he died. The province proposed a sentence of strangulation after the assizes in accordance with the law on killing in a fight (tou sha), but cited the general rule of the code according to which homicide cases involving children aged ten or under were to be referred to the throne for special consideration.[25] The case was so referred, but the throne held that the special procedure was applicable only where the victim had been somewhat older than the killer. Where they were of the same age, there was no room for leniency and the sentence should still be capital, though it might subsequently be commuted at the autumn review. In commenting on the imperial edict the Board noted the importance to be attached to human life as a factor militating against leniency.[26]

Cases involving multiple killings caused the Board and the throne particular difficulty with regard to the correct application of the principle of requital. In a Shantung case of 1815 Su had ejected his tenant farmer, Wei, from his land and house. Wei thereupon formed a plot to kill Su and his whole family, involving in the plot his own adopted son and Su's hired workman, Li. The part of Wei's son had been to persuade Li to open the door of Su's house, thus enabling Wei himself to enter and kill Su together with four other members of his family. He had already killed another relative of Su. Wei was captured by other relatives of Su and beaten to death. The question before the courts was the appropriate punishment for Li and Wei's adopted son. There was no dispute that Wei himself, despite his death, should still be sentenced to death by slicing, his body disinterred, and the punishment inflicted on it. With respect to Li and Wei's adopted son, the provincial authorities had proposed the punishment of exile under the law on plotting to kill, participating in the plot, but not actively contributing to the death of the victim. The Board held that the proposed punishment was too light. It pointed out that, although it was Wei who had actually stabbed to death Su and his family, this would not have been possible without the concerted efforts of his son and Li in opening the door. Accordingly, they should be treated as having actively contributed to the killing and sentenced to immediate beheading as accessories under the article on killing three persons in one family. In reaching this conclusion the Board stressed that there was no adequate loss of life in requital were only Wei to be executed. Such a result would be insufficient to deter the wicked or to provide a proper redress for the wrong done.[27]

In a Kwangtung case of 1833, Ch'en led a band of people to attack another group, as a result of which thirteen people in fleeing from the attack fell into a river and drowned. The provincial authorities proposed that Ch'en as principal should be sentenced to immediate strangulation under the substatute on killing three or more persons not in one family.[28] However, Ch'en had already died in jail. For the other members of the band a sentence of exile was proposed. The Board held this to be too lenient. It stressed that in cases where many lives had been lost it was essential to ensure that for each life lost one was given in requital. In the present case, on the provincial recommendation, there was not even one life truly given in requital. This was very much to neglect the importance that should be attributed to human life. Accordingly, the case was remitted to the province for further consideration.[29]

Sometimes the throne itself intervened. In a Shansi case of 1828 the Board reviewed the changes that had occurred in the law on the joint liability of the wife and sons of a man who had killed several members of one family. It noted that in 1776 a recommendation had been made by the Board for the enactment of a substatute to the effect that, where someone had killed four or more persons in one family with the result that the family line was extinguished, the sons of the killer, irrespective of age, were to be sentenced to immediate beheading. In 1779 a case arose in which a person had killed four members of one family. In accordance with the new substatute the Board had proposed that the killer be sentenced to death by slicing and his four sons to immediate beheading. The throne, however, replied that the number of persons whose lives would be lost in requital now exceeded the number of lives lost in the killing. Therefore, only three sons should be executed, the youngest being reprieved. This achieved a balance between the lives lost and those forfeited in requital.[30]

The principle that a person who had brought about the death of another should forfeit his own life in compensation applied only where the death had been directly caused by the act of the offender. In cases of indirect causation a noncapital sentence was imposed, its severity depending on the nature of the causal link between act and death. Where that link was close, although still "indirect," the punishment was likely to be exile; where it was more remote, the punishment was likely to be less severe. Two examples of this way of thinking may be cited from Ch'ing law. Where the victim had been wounded in a fight and died sometime later as a result of "wind" that had entered the wound, the offender was to be sentenced to exile and not strangulation.[31] Here the link between initial act and death was regarded as reasonably close. On the other hand, where one person had oppressed another to such an extent that the latter had committed suicide, the punishment established by the code was light, being a beating of one hundred blows with the heavy stick.[32] Here the causal link was regarded as slight, since the victim had deliberately chosen to bring about his own death. Under certain circumstances, such as oppression of another on account of theft or fornication, or where family relationships were involved, the punishment was much higher.[33]

It was not only to the life of the victim that the law attributed value. Even though under the principle of requital the life of the killer was forfeit, the greatest care was taken in determining not only whether the alleged offender had committed the offense but also whether any mitigating circumstances might justify a reduction of the capital sentence to exile.[34] The sentiment underlying this approach, frequently expressed in opinions of the late Ch'ing Board of Punishments, was also firmly endorsed by the throne. The founding emperor of the T'ang dynasty ordered in 631 A.D. that a sentence of death should be enacted only after repeated memorials to the throne had each received an affirmative reply, and he declared, "Once the sentence has been executed, a man cannot again come to life."[35] Many centuries later the K'ang-hsi emperor, third of the Ch'ing dynasty, known for his devotion to Confucian studies, expressed the same thought and noted that nothing caused him more distaste than the final ratification of a death sentence.[36]

The procedure for hearing capital cases was expressly intended to provide the maximum possible care in determining the facts and identifying the correct punishment. In all dynasties, although details might vary, a capital case had to proceed through the main levels of the administrative and judicial hierarchy. It was first heard by the magistrate of the district in which the offense was committed. He investigated the facts and, if satisfied as to the guilt of the accused, proposed a sentence. The case was then sent for rehearing by the superior tribunal of the prefect or provincial governor. The accused and witnesses were all reexamined to determine whether the magistrate had conducted an adequate investigation. If his finding was affirmed, the case was then forwarded to the capital (in later dynasties usually just the documents) for scrutiny by the central judicial agencies and ultimately by the emperor himself. At the highest level the greatest care was still taken to see that the correct facts had been unearthed. In the Ch'ing period the Board of Punishments was constantly alive to the dangers of collusion, deceit, and prevarication on the part of the accused and witnesses and to the risk that the lower tribunals had not been successful in unraveling the truth. As soon as the depositions of the accused or witnesses revealed discrepancies or appeared contrary to reason and common sense, the case was remitted to the originating province for a fresh investigation. This scrupulous regard for the ascertainment of the facts reflects the Board's general concern both that there should be a proper requital for the life lost and that the offender should not suffer an injustice.

As a particular example of the care taken in handling capital cases we cite the procedure adopted during the Ch'ing once the case had reached the Board of Punishments. For a few such cases the appropriate sentence was immediate strangulation or beheading (or death by slicing). Once the confirmatory imperial edict had been obtained, the sentence was executed in the culprit's own province. Most capital cases, however, attracted a sentence in the form of "beheading after the assizes" or "strangulation after the assizes." Where such a sentence was imposed, a further review of the case had to be conducted by the provincial authorities and personnel of the central judicial agencies. This lengthy period of review culminated in elaborate ceremonies held in Peking in the autumn at which the cases were classified essentially into two groups: those where the death sentence was verified, and those where extenuating circumstances had been found, warranting postponement of the penalty and eventual commutation to exile.

The list containing the verified death sentences was submitted to the emperor for a final scrutiny. He examined the list and put a hook against the name of each offender who was actually to be executed. It used to be thought that the emperor acted at random in distributing his hooks and that whether an offender was to be put to death or to receive a further chance of life was a matter of luck.[37] Now it is clear that, with the advice of his closest ministers, the emperor personally examined the merits of the cases presented to him. The K'ang-hsi emperor has left a vivid account of the anxiety that "giving the hook" occasioned him and the care that he exercised in determining whether the facts of any particular case disclosed grounds for pity.[38]

There is thus ample evidence to demonstrate the concern of the throne and its officials for the importance of human life. What is more surprising is to find concern evidenced in the codes for the life of the main species of domestic animal whose services were utilized by man. The codes prohibited the killing not just of a neighbor's beast of burden (cow, ox, horse, or mule) but even of one's own.[39] According to the Ch'ing legal commentary the reason is the gratitude that man owes these animals for the contribution of their labor to his service.[40] Is this thought purely Confucian, or does it reflect also Buddhist influence? One cannot be sure, but it is interesting that Chinese Buddhists expressed concern for the sanctity of animal life. In the late Ming, the Buddhist monk Chu-hung wrote an "Essay on Nonkilling" in which he presented a number of arguments against the killing of any animal, not just domestic beasts of burden.[41]

Another consideration may also have underlain the prohibition on the killing of beasts of burden. This was derived from their importance to the economy of the peasant household. Without a ploughing ox the household might not be able to survive economically. Nevertheless, there must have been a temptation in hard times for the owner to kill his ox to save the cost of feeding or to obtain the value of the carcass. When the Neo-Confucian philosopher Chu Hsi, during his period of office as prefect of Chang-chou, included in a proclamation to the population of his prefecture the injunction to see that no one killed his ploughing ox, he was probably activated more by a concern for the well-being of the household than by specific gratitude to the animal.[42]

JEN: BENEVOLENCE OR HUMANITY

"*Jen*," a term usually rendered in English as "humanity" or "benevolence," was one of the fundamental Confucian virtues. Already mentioned frequently by Confucius and Mencius, it was adopted by the Neo-Confucians as the cornerstone of their philosophical system. We cannot trace here the various ramifications of its meaning or examine in detail the historical development of the notion. Rather, we restrict ourselves to some remarks on the relationship between *jen* and government and to the identification of those areas of the penal law that were thought particularly to incorporate the spirit of *jen*. In his study of the evolution of the term's meaning, Wing-tsit Chan observes that in pre-Confucian texts *jen* most frequently expresses the notion of the kindness of a ruler toward his subjects.[43] Although *jen* in Confucian writing takes on the character of a more general virtue, more or less coextensive with "goodness," it is the notion of benevolence on the part of the ruler, the humane regard that he has for the welfare of his subjects, that seems to express the meaning of *jen* in the legal commentaries of the Ch'ing period.

Some Sung Neo-Confucian philosophers and statesmen had in their formal lectures to the throne stressed the duty of *jen* on the part of the emperor. For example, Fan Ch'ung-yen (1027–1101) made the following remarks in his lectures: "The basis of the state lies in the ruler, and the basis of rulership lies in the mind-and-heart. The learning of the ruler should be directed at rectifying his mind-and-heart, making his intentions sincere, taking humaneness as the basic substance, and not letting heterodox and superficial notions gain entry. Only thus will the issuing of orders and promulgation of decrees serve the welfare of the state and dynasty."[44] While part of the import of the reference to "humaneness" may be that the emperor in his personal life should exhibit such particular Confucian virtues as filial piety and propriety, there is also a reference to his role as ruler. He should treat the people with "humaneness" and base his legislation on a regard for their welfare.

A conspicuous general example of the role of *jen* in government is provided by the imperial use of amnesties.[45] In all dynasties, with varying degrees of frequency, amnesties were issued under which offenders, except those condemned for the most serious offenses such as the ten abominations, were reprieved from punishment or granted a reduction in their sentence. Although there were good practical reasons for issuing amnesties, such as the need to free space in overcrowded jails, an important consideration was the emperor's self-perception and his reputation with the people as the fount of benevolence. He was the originator and enforcer of stern punishments, but he was also the dispenser of kindness and mercy. It is the latter aspect which was demonstrated in the imperial grant of amnesties. The exercise of benevolence implied in the grant of an amnesty is clearly stated in a T'ang example from the year 736 A.D. The emperor prefaced his decree with the words: "We in our thoughts on the roots of good government consider that teaching is primary and punishment is secondary. And yet convicts who suffer the hardships of being transported and those who have become involved in crimes are still numerous. Sometimes they are held in jails for years. Now [this problem] is spreading like a fog. How can I forget to have a natural pity for them? Moreover I am concerned that those who enforce the law are not careful [and that] among those who are punished some are not deserving of punishment. If I do not investigate this how can I be said to be possessed of mercy?"[46]

We now turn to the influence that *jen* has had on the rules of the penal code, though we do not claim to offer an exhaustive account. One important complex of rules rests fundamentally on the idea of compassion for those who cannot be treated as possessing the full strength and capacity of the adult male. These are the rules contained in all the codes that confer privileges on the young, the old, the disabled, and women. Here we summarize only the main effects of these rules.[47] Persons under 16 or over 70 were not subject to the normal punishments, the general principle being that the younger or older an individual was, the greater the degree of leniency with which he or she was treated by the law. Those aged between 70 and 79 or between 15 and 11 were allowed to redeem punishment by payment of money except in the case of capital offenses. Those aged between 80 and 89 or between 10 and 8 were broadly given immunity from punishment for noncapital offenses, and in capital cases they were allowed to petition the throne for clemency. Those aged 90 and above or 7 and below were altogether immune from punishment even in capital cases, except that the later law (Ming/Ch'ing) still held the elderly liable for rebellion, irrespective of age.

The disabled were granted privileges according to a similar principle: the greater the degree of disability, the greater the leniency extended by the law. Those held to be merely disabled (*fei-chi*), as where they lacked the use of one limb, were treated in the same way as those aged between 70 and 79; those held to be incapacitated (*tu-chi*), as where they lacked the use of two limbs, were treated in the same way as persons aged between 80 and 89. In the later codes disability was confined to the physical, but in T'ang law it also included degrees of mental deficiency.⁴⁸

The source of these rules lies in the old Confucian ritual books that speak of respect for the old and compassion for the young.⁴⁹ The T'ang *shu-i* commentary itself cites pity as the basis for the lenient treatment accorded the young, the old, and the disabled.⁵⁰ Respect for the old, indulgence for the young, and pity for the disabled are reasons cited in the Ming or Ch'ing legal commentaries.⁵¹ A Ch'ing commentary also cites this complex of rules as an example of "grace" or "favor" (*en*) accorded by the law.⁵²

The word *"jen"* does not appear at all in the T'ang commentary. In the Ming and Ch'ing commentaries it is used only in the context of a particular variant of the rules according privileges to the young, old, or disabled. Where an offense had been committed before a person reached the age of 70 or became disabled, but was discovered only after that age or state of affairs had occurred, the offender was still to be entitled to the appropriate leniency in the determination of the punishment. Similarly, where an offense had been committed during a person's youth, but was discovered only after adulthood, the appropriate privilege was still to be extended. These concessions are described as exhibiting "the height of *jen.*"⁵³ The implication of this language is that, while the whole complex of rules rests on *jen*, that concept is taken to its extreme in the leniency still granted an offender, despite the fact that there had been no entitlement to privilege at the time when the offense was committed or when it was discovered.

Women were also granted some privileges. In T'ang law the leniency extended to a woman was limited. For offenses entailing death, penal servitude, or beating there was to be no mitigation of punishment. Only in the case of exile did the law make a concession, on the grounds that it was inappropriate for a woman to be sent into exile alone. The punishment of exile was converted into a beating together with labor in her home locality for three years.⁵⁴ In Ming and Ch'ing law considerably more favorable treatment was extended to women.

Under a variety of provisions they were permitted to redeem themselves by payment of money from the ordinary punishment prescribed
for all offenses except the most serious. Among the latter were included illicit sexual intercourse (reflecting the importance of the concept of chastity), theft, and failure to show filial piety.[55]

Whereas none of the legal commentaries specifically mention *jen*
as the source of the legal privileges accorded women, an opinion of
the Board of Punishments delivered in 1871 does invoke *jen* in this
context. Problems had arisen because officials' wives had abused their
position. A number of these women had adopted the practice of treating their maid servants so cruelly that they died. When the matter
came to court, they were able to redeem themselves from punishment by the payment of money. A censor now requested that in such
cases the head of the household should be held personally responsible.
In commenting on his memorial the Board observed: "This provision allowing female offenders to buy themselves free was originally
meant as a token of benevolence (*jen*) bestowed beyond the strict rules
of the law, but now it had suddenly become the road to avoid punishment altogether so that there was only an offense in name but no
punishment in fact."[56] This remark evidences a perception on the part
of the officials that the right to redeem punishment allowed a woman
was ultimately derived from the concept of *jen*. Imperial benevolence
permitted a mitigation of the strict law in their case.

The word "*jen*" occurs in the Ch'ing commentaries with respect
to one of the special privileges allowed a woman. The code provided
that a pregnant woman might not be subjected to torture (normally a
beating) until a period of one hundred days had elapsed after the birth
of the child. Nor, where she had been condemned to death, might
the sentence be executed until one hundred days after the birth.[57] The
commentary notes that the protection granted to the fetus prior to
birth and to the young child in the first hundred days of its life, when
it might still be suckled by its mother, again manifested "the height
of *jen*."[58]

Where an offender was the only adult son in a family and the
offense, even though capital, was not one of the most serious, that is,
was not the kind of offense excluded from the operation of the ordi-

nary amnesties, he might be reprieved and allowed to return home. This privilege was granted where his parents were old or destitute and required his support, or where he was the only surviving member of the family competent to undertake the sacrifices to the ancestors. Known in all codes,[59] the concession appears part of the complex of rules designed to foster filial piety. A Ch'ing commentary describes this rule as a particular "grace" or "favor" (en) accorded by the law.[60] The same language is used in a memorial of the Board of Punishments forwarded to the throne in 1745.[61] Although the language of *jen* is not used in these sources, from other decisions of the Board it is apparent that such "grace" was regarded as an example of the general "benevolence" or "humanity" of the ruler, by which under appropriate circumstances the rigor of the ordinary law was mitigated. In a Szechuan case of 1826, the Board observed: "It should be pointed out that the practice of allowing criminals to remain at home to care for their parents originated as an extralegal (*wai fa*) manifestation of kindness (*jen*),[62] designed to provide comfort for the parents during their declining years. It was not intended to be a loophole for escaping punishment."[63]

From time to time the Ch'ing commentaries describe other rules found in the penal code as exhibiting "the height of *jen*." So described[64] is the rule by which the grading of the most serious punishments (exile and death) was operated in favor of the offender. There were two degrees of death (beheading and strangulation) and three degrees of exile (that to three thousand, twenty-five hundred, or two thousand *li*). When a rule provided that for a specific offense there was to be an increase of one degree, each of the two degrees of death and three degrees of exile was given separate effect, but when the rule provided for a decrease of one degree, the two death penalties and the three kinds of exile were each treated as constituting one degree. Thus, when a rule provided that the punishment was to be one degree less than that for an offense entailing the punishment of beheading, the appropriate punishment was exile to three thousand *li* and not strangulation; when it provided for the punishment to be one degree less than that for an offense entailing the punishment of exile to three thousand *li*, the appropriate punishment was penal servitude for three years and not exile to twenty-five hundred *li*.

Rather astonishingly the very harsh rule punishing a large group of the relatives of persons convicted of rebellion is also said to combine "the height of *jen*" with great severity. The reference to *jen* is to the fact that certain relatives were still excluded from the range of punishment, namely, sons who had previously been given in adoption to another family and daughters who had already been married. Further, sons aged fifteen or under, although still punished, were at least spared from death.[65]

Sometimes one finds another use of *jen* in the Ch'ing legal commentaries. It expresses a justification for a particular rule in terms of the lack of "humanity" displayed by the offender. Here the reference is not to the "benevolence" displayed by a superior (the ruler) to his inferiors (the subjects) but to a failure to observe the obligations owed to other people or even animals, derived from man's characteristic as a humane being. Thus, an article of the code punishes with a beating children who failed to care for their parents when they were aged eighty or above or were infirm.[66] The commentary gives one common instance of such neglect. Officials who refused to leave office in order to care for their parents are described as not acting in accordance with *jen*.[67] Again, the commentary to the article that forbids the killing of one's own beast of burden justifies the rule on the grounds that the killing of animals who have served man was not in accordance with *jen*.[68]

Possibly the two uses of *jen* (that exercised by the ruler toward his subjects in the making or application of the laws and that to be exhibited by man in his dealing with other living creatures) can be brought together in the following way. The ruler displayed his "benevolence" toward his subjects by displaying humanity in his dealings with them and by ensuring that they behaved with "humanity" in their dealings with one another.

REPENTANCE AND CONFESSION

The penal codes all contain rules that, under certain conditions, accord offenders who have genuinely repented of their offenses complete or partial exemption from punishment.[69] These rules stem from the Confucian conception of punishment as appropriate for the correction of the incorrigibly wicked. Where the offender had himself repented and resolved to reform, punishment was unnecessary. Confucius's observation in the Analects that "to err and not reform may indeed be called error"[70] forms the basis of the T'ang *shu-i* commentary that explains the thinking behind the rules.[71] Repentance must be genuine. The law took sincerity to be demonstrated when the offender had voluntarily confessed to the authorities before the offense in question had been brought to their attention. However, even should repentance not have been entirely "pure," as where, for motives of self-interest, an offender confessed after hearing that another person was about to inform the authorities or that the latter were commencing an investigation, he was still to be entitled to a reduction of two degrees in the punishment that would normally be applicable.

The law introduced an important safeguard that protected the victim. It allowed the offender to benefit from his confession only where the harmful consequences of his offense could be completely undone. This consideration imported two important qualifications into the rules permitting exemption from punishment. Where the offense had concerned property, any goods that the offender had unlawfully acquired must be returned to the owner. On the other hand, if the consequences of the offense were irreversible, as where someone had been wounded or killed, the offender was not allowed an exemption from or mitigation of punishment, even though he had voluntarily confessed.[72] We have here an example of a principle, also utilized elsewhere by the legislators,[73] to the effect that leniency was not justified where the offender's conduct had resulted in actual harm that could not be undone.

The benefit of confession was available not only to a person who had confessed an offense that he had himself committed but also to one on whose behalf, without his knowledge, a close relative had confessed. This rule has to be understood in the context of a further Confucian-inspired complex of rules dealing with the mutual concealment of offenses by family members and the prohibition placed on the bringing of formal accusations against relatives. The early Confucians, in direct contrast to the Legalists, had argued that it was the duty of the father to conceal the crime of the son and of the son to conceal the crime of the father.[74] Remonstrances should be conducted within the family and efforts made to reform the offender, but he should not be exposed to prosecution by the authorities. This idea, extended beyond father and son to include other close relatives, was adopted by the penal law of all dynasties from at least T'ang times.[75] It was made enforceable through the introduction of a prohibition on the bringing of accusations between close relatives.

Severe punishments were to be imposed on junior relatives who brought accusations against their seniors, even where the accusations were true. The punishments in the converse case of the accusation of a junior by a senior was considerably less severe. For example, it was a capital offense for a son to bring a legal accusation against his father, but the father might accuse his son with impunity. Rebellion and related offenses, on grounds of state security, were excluded from the operation of these rules. Further, where relatives had acted toward each other in such a way as to ignore the obligations imposed by kinship, through physical assault or the appropriation of property, accusations to the court were also allowed. In cases where the accusation was not permitted, the accuser was normally punished, but the accused was treated as though he had himself confessed and might accordingly escape punishment under the ordinary rules pertaining to confession.

There is a certain difficulty in establishing the relationship between the rules prohibiting the accusation of relatives and those permitting relatives to confess on behalf of another. The person accused or on whose behalf confession had been made was uniformly treated as though he had himself confessed. But the person making the confession and the person making the accusation were treated very differently. The former committed a laudable act; the latter committed an offense that might entail heavy punishment. Yet, how was one to tell whether a relative was confessing on behalf of another or bringing an accusation against him? According to a Ch'ing legal commentary, the difference lay in the intention with which the relative had acted. When he confessed on behalf of another, he was activated by love for his relative and desired to ensure that the latter was not punished for his offense. On the other hand, where he brought an accusation, he acted out of an evil desire to see that the severity of the law was applied to his relative.[76] Although circumstances might sometimes allow the authorities to determine the sentiment upon which the relative revealing the offense had acted, as where the two were known to be enemies or to have quarreled, it cannot always have been easy to discern the relative's motive. Perhaps the assumption, in line with the Confucian conception of the family, was that the person revealing the offense was intending to confess on behalf of his relative, unless there was some clear indication to the contrary.

SEXUAL RESTRAINT

We have already touched on this topic in our discussion of the value attributed in Confucian thought to the chaste woman.[77] In this section we widen the discussion and further develop the theme of female chastity. Generally, sexual intercourse outside the relationship constituted by marriage or concubinage was legally prohibited, both the man and the woman incurring liability to punishment. Sexual intercourse between relatives, who in any case were barred from marriage, was classified as one of the ten abominations. A Ch'ing legal commentary says that such an act reduced human behavior to that of the animal, as well as introducing confusion into family relationships.[78]

Where there had been consent and no force had been used, the punishment in principle for the man and the woman was the same. T'ang law sentenced each to penal servitude for one and a half years,[79] Ming and Ch'ing law to eighty blows with the heavy stick.[80] It is interesting that in this context the later law took a more lenient attitude than the earlier. In other words, the preservation of chastity by the man and the woman in ordinary circumstances, although still important, was less valued in Ming and Ch'ing times than in T'ang. The codes of all dynasties increased the punishment of the woman by one degree should she have been married, evidencing the fact that the chastity of a wife was valued more highly than that of an unmarried woman. But the man, even if married, incurred no increase in punishment.

Conversely, where the man and woman were related, the punishments in Ming and Ch'ing law tended to be more severe than those in T'ang law. For example, in T'ang law sexual intercourse between a man and his brother's wife led to both parties being exiled to twenty-five hundred *li*,[81] whereas in Ming and Ch'ing law the punishment was increased to strangulation.[82] This suggests the intervention of Neo-Confucian thinking, which particularly emphasized the importance of maintaining the behavior appropriate to one's role in the family and not "confusing" the relationships.

Where the man had induced the woman to comply with his wishes through the use of force, she was not punished, but he was punished more severely than in the case where both parties had voluntarily consented. We may note again a difference in attitude between the T'ang and the Ming/Ch'ing law. The later law, as in a number of other instances, was particularly concerned with the use of violence in society, and it imposed especially severe punishments on those who had used force to obtain what they wanted.[83] For example, in T'ang, Ming, and Ch'ing law sexual intercourse between relatives who stood in a mourning relationship of three months or closer was punished by three years penal servitude, where both parties had consented.[84] But, if the man had used force, T'ang law imposed a punishment of exile to two thousand *li* (only an increase of one degree), whereas Ming and Ch'ing law imposed the most severe of the regular punishments, beheading. A Ch'ing commentary observes[85] that, where a man, giving rein to his lust, employs force to soil the purity and chastity of a woman, the circumstances are of the utmost gravity, thus justifying a severe punishment. Once again we appear to have a reflection of the Neo-Confucian concern with the protection of female chastity, especially in the context of family relationships.

Neo-Confucian concepts of proper sexual conduct may also have contributed to the introduction at the end of the seventeenth century of legislation penalizing certain forms of homosexual conduct.[86] The legislation was revised from time to time. The punishment eventually established for actual sexual intercourse between consenting males was one hundred blows with the heavy stick and the wearing of the cangue (a wooden collar) for one month.[87] This was a heavier punishment than that imposed for the corresponding heterosexual behavior. There is evidence from decisions of the Board of Punishments that, in a case of homosexual rape, the punishment of the rapist would be decreased if the victim were an "unchaste" person, that is, if he had previously engaged in homosexual acts.[88] Although it appears clear that Ch'ing law was concerned with the protection of male chastity, the precise reasons for the introduction of the antihomosexual legislation are difficult to determine. Other factors, such as the dislike by an absolutist government of deviant behavior or repulsion for acts deemed to be unnatural, may also have played a part.[89]

We have already said something about the exaggerated importance attached to female chastity by Neo-Confucian thought.[90] Further examples of the respect paid by the law to this value may be cited from the Ch'ing code. First, there is the complex of rules, introduced during the Ch'ing, that imposed heavy punishments on persons who provoked the suicide of a woman or even her relatives through assaults on or imputations against her chastity.[91]

Suicide on account of rape attracted particularly heavy punishment for the person responsible. Where a woman who had been raped afterwards committed suicide, or where her husband, father, mother, or any other mourning relative committed suicide on account of the rape, the rapist was to be sentenced to beheading after the assizes. The punishment was reduced to strangulation after the assizes in the case of attempted rape followed by suicide.[92] However, as we have already seen in a different context,[93] the antecedent behavior of the victim was made relevant to the punishment of the rapist. If she had been previously guilty of some sexual misconduct such as adultery, the rapist escaped death, though he was still to be enslaved. Such an apparently "unchaste" victim was still deemed to be "chaste" if she could be shown to have repented of her original misconduct.[94] We have here another example of the value attached by the law to genuine regret and reformation.

Where a woman was the object of obscene remarks, filthy abuse, or even just disrespectful and overfamiliar language, and in consequence committed suicide, the offender was to be sentenced to exile. But, where she had been the recipient of improper suggestions or behavior evidencing a wish to entice her into sexual misconduct, such as where a person had gazed lewdly into her face, with the result that she committed suicide, the offender was to be sentenced to strangulation after the assizes.[95]

The distinction between "obscene remarks" and "improper suggestions" caused the Board of Punishments some difficulty. In a case from the year 1846 T'ang quarreled with Chang and was beaten by him. Afterwards, still angry, T'ang rushed to Chang's house and yelled out abuse, saying, among other things, that he would no longer sleep with Chang's wife. Mrs. Chang overheard this remark, rushed out of the house, cursed T'ang, and then in shame and anger hanged herself. The Board treated this as a case of ordinary filthy language from an ignorant rustic that carried no real implication that Mrs. Chang had been unchaste. Accordingly, T'ang was sentenced to exile.[96]

In a case of 1852 Liu, when snubbed by Fu, retorted that Fu had no right to be angry, since he lived on what his wife received from her lovers, and he made other aspersions about Mrs. Fu's conduct (generally implying that she was a prostitute). As a result Fu became suspicious and interrogated his wife. In anger she committed suicide. The Board found again (as in the previous case) that a sentence of exile was appropriate. But the reason was different. Here a definite slur had been cast upon the wife's chastity, even though she had not been present. She had only heard of Liu's aspersions secondhand, through her husband. Therefore, Liu was sentenced to exile.[97] Should these aspersions have been made directly to her, implying a wish to have intercourse or doubts as to her chastity, and she committed suicide as a result, the punishment would have been strangulation.

The code also contains a number of procedural rules designed to protect a woman's chastity or to withdraw her legal privileges on the grounds of lack of chastity. If sentenced to the punishment of a beating that was actually to be inflicted, she might normally wear an outer garment. But, should the beating be on account of illicit sexual intercourse, she was deemed already to have forfeited her modesty, and she might wear only an undergarment.[98] Furthermore, although women could redeem punishment for most offenses, illicit sexual intercourse was excluded from the operation of this privilege.[99]

Special rules also governed the circumstances under which women might be detained in prison. Unless they had been guilty of illicit sexual intercourse or of an offense entailing capital punishment, they were not to be kept in prison pending trial. Instead, they were to be entrusted to the custody of their husband or, if they had no husband, to that of their relatives and the leading citizens of their locality.[100] The Ch'ing commentary explains this privilege on the grounds that a woman cannot be imprisoned without losing her moral reputation.[101] The implication, of course, is that where she had already lost that reputation through committing the offense of illicit sexual intercourse, she no longer needed or deserved to be exempted from imprisonment.

8 Technical Qualities

The traditional law possessed a number of technical merits, matured and refined throughout many centuries. These qualities in the main represent a prime contribution on the part of the early Legalists and the succeeding statesmen and officials who inherited their concern for effective government. These men saw the need for a clear and systematic exposition of the penal rules, for the production of a legal instrument that was readily intelligible and capable of efficient use. Arguably the T'ang code, or perhaps that of the early Ming, exhibited these attributes rather better than the later codes. The sheer size and complexity of the late Ch'ing penal code, the possibly excessive degree of regulation to which it aspired, sometimes made it difficult for officials charged with its implementation to disentangle the relevant from the irrelevant.

We discuss in this chapter the rationality of the legal process as evident particularly in the system for the investigation and trial of offenses; the drafting skills displayed by the penal codes, in particular the mathematically precise way in which distinctions of status were correlated with legal consequences, and the technique of "economy of means" by which a very large number of situations were subsumed under relatively few basic classifications or certain key technical terms used to avoid detailed repetition in the stipulation of sanctions; and the combination of the general and the specific found in the formulation of the penal rules.

RATIONALITY

The traditional Chinese legal process was characterized by a rational quality already evident at the beginning of its recorded history in the early Chou. The *K'ang kao*, to which we have already made several references, can be read as a charter of substantive and procedural justice. It postulates not only a just content in the law, that is, that the law should enunciate principles of conduct accepted within the society as being morally good, but also sets out criteria for the just application of the law. The judge (conceived here in the person of the ruler or his representative) is to apply only the law, not give vent to his own prejudices or likes and dislikes. He is to take the greatest care before sanctioning the application of the mutilating punishments. In particular, he is to take as long as is necessary to ascertain the full facts and to be certain that the truth has emerged.

These injunctions are impressive. We see that as early as 1100 B.C. the judicial process was essentially rational. It was directed to the ascertainment of the facts after a careful investigation and the application of the law, already publicly known in the form of written rules,[1] to those facts. There is no trace here of what in Western thought would be termed "irrational" modes of dispute settlement through recourse to ordeals or oracles. A similar emphasis on procedural justice is found in the *Lü hsing*, another set of injunctions on the correct way for a ruler to apply punishments, written some centuries after the *K'ang kao*.[2] This document emphasizes that in cases of doubt the mutilating punishments should not be applied. At the most a redemption fine should be levied.[3]

The injunctions found in the *K'ang kao* and the *Lü hsing* also in the main governed the conduct of legal proceedings in imperial China. The procedure was inquisitorial, the magistrate having the task of ascertaining the truth from the parties and witnesses. No legal representation was permitted. Once the truth had been ascertained, the magistrate had to identify the relevant rules of the code, apply them to the facts, and determine the correct punishment for such offenses as had been committed. As we have already seen in chapter 7, for all serious cases there was a regular procedure of review by higher authority. Should errors or discrepancies be found, the case was remitted for further investigation.

Under this procedure the magistrate was faced with two basic problems: what was he to do if the facts appeared to be in doubt, and what was he to do if the code contained no rule that was precisely relevant? We will discuss in the next chapter the technique of analogy by which the second problem was largely resolved. With respect to doubt as to the facts, the position adopted by the T'ang code was different from that of the Ming and Ch'ing codes. The T'ang code followed the principle adumbrated in the *Lü hsing*. It was provided that, where there was doubt as to the facts, the statutory punishment for the offense alleged to have been committed was not to be imposed; instead redemption by payment of copper was to be permitted.[4] The fact that this provision does not reappear in the Ming and Ch'ing codes suggests that the latter did not contemplate the possibility of situations in which the facts remained in doubt. Why this should be so, requires consideration of two further matters: the use of torture, and the need for the accused to "confess" or acknowledge that he had committed the offense of which he was accused.

In T'ang law the use of torture was strictly controlled.[5] It might be applied in the form of a limited number of beatings to elicit the facts from recalcitrant parties or witnesses, but it was not necessary to compel a confession through torture. Should the facts be clear, the court might proceed to pronounce sentence even in the absence of confession. Should the facts not be clear, a confession was necessary and might be extracted through the application of a limited amount of torture.[6] In Ming and Ch'ing law the controls placed on the use of torture were less strict, a variety of implements (such as pressing sticks or head-squeezing bands) being permissible under certain circumstances. Furthermore, not only does torture appear to have been frequently used, but its abuse also appears to have been rife. One reason for the reliance on torture in Ming and Ch'ing legal proceedings seems to have been the requirement that in all cases, irrespective of the strength of the evidence, the accused confess to the crime. Unless he confessed, the magistrate was unable to proceed to the determination of the sentence. Although wise and experienced magistrates deprecated the use of torture, there was clearly a temptation to have resort to it, in order to extract a speedy confession and allow the case to go forward.[7]

From a modern Western perspective, the use of torture in legal proceedings marks a failure in rationality. There ought to be a means of ascertaining the facts or of dealing with doubtful cases that did not rely on the infliction of pain to extract evidence or a confession. What is interesting from this perspective is that the T'ang law reveals a lesser degree of irrationality than the Ming and Ch'ing. However, we must note that despite the irrationality injected into the legal process through recourse to torture, the codes did at least seek to place limits on its use. Further, we might have to recognize a possible justification in the Chinese perception that only through a moderate infliction of pain on the recalcitrant, obstructive, collusive, or deceitful party would the authorities have a chance of ascertaining the truth.[8]

We may signal not only the rationality of the trial process, subject to the exception constituted by the use of torture, but also that of the process by which the final judgment was reached, at least in such cases as were referred to the Ch'ing Board of Punishments.[9] For each case the Board received a lengthy dossier that contained inter alia depositions of the accused and witnesses together with a statement of the provincial governor's findings and recommendations. From the available reports, albeit that they are summaries of the Board's judgments, we can appreciate the meticulous way in which the Board extracted the essential features of the dossier and determined whether the facts had been properly ascertained. Where the Board, applying considerations of common sense and ordinary reason, found that the account accepted by the provincial authorities revealed discrepancies or oddities, the case was sent back to the province for reinvestigation. The Board often went to considerable lengths to demonstrate what it found unsatisfactory in the evidence presented by the province. Where it was satisfied that the provincial authorities had uncovered the true state of affairs, it constructed a judgment that tended to adopt the following pattern: (i) citation of the articles or substatutes of the code that had been utilized by the province, (ii) a full account of the facts, (iii) a summary of the recommendations as to sentence made by the provincial authorities, (iv) a statement of those facts which the Board considered to be essential for the determination of the case, and (v) the application of the law to those facts, and the determination of the sentence, with a note of the reasons for which the Board accepted or rejected the provincial recommendation.[10]

DRAFTING SKILLS

Use of Distinctions

Throughout the codes a mathematically precise system of grading is adopted with respect to the relationship between state of affairs and legal consequences. This is particularly striking where relationships of status are involved. We cite two examples from the T'ang code, one dealing with privileges and the other with the abominations of "contumacy" and "discord."

The structure of the law relating to privilege is seen at its most developed in the T'ang code.[11] The most important privilege, that of deliberation, is accorded in the first instance to relatives of the emperor, a category defined by article 7 as follows: "Included are relatives of the emperor of the sixth degree of mourning and closer. Included also are the emperor's paternal grandmother's and his mother's relatives in the fifth degree of mourning and closer. Also included are the empress's relatives in the fourth degree of mourning and closer" (p. 84).

Several points may be made with reference to this category. The first component is constituted by the relatives of the emperor to the sixth degree of mourning. This is already an unusual extension in the class of relatives to be given a legal privilege, since normally the law recognizes only relatives within the fifth degree of mourning. The emperor himself, of course, is not mentioned because he is regarded both as the source of privilege and as being "above the law." The second component is constituted by the relatives of his most important female relatives, his paternal grandmother and his mother. But here the range is one degree less than that of his own relatives, being restricted to relatives within the fifth degree of mourning. The third component is constituted by the emperor's affinal relatives. But again the range is one degree less than those of his mother and paternal grandmother, being restricted to the empress's relatives within the fourth degree of mourning.

We may also note the grant of deliberation to those of "high position," explained as comprising "active duty officials of the third rank and above, titular officials of the second rank and above, and persons with noble titles of the first rank" (p. 86). The classes of person entitled to deliberation within this category are defined in terms of their rank: the more important the office, the greater the range of degrees included. The three classes are related in the sense that the first two are each more extensive by one degree of rank than the class immediately below.

The second most important privilege is that of petition. This is granted to "relatives of the third or closer degree of mourning of the wife of the crown prince, relatives within the second or closer degree of mourning and grandsons in the male line of those entitled to deliberation, or officials or nobles of the fifth rank or higher" (pp. 89–90). We observe, first, that the relatives of the wife of the crown prince not only receive a privilege one stage lower than that accorded to the relatives of the empress, but that the range of relatives entitled to petition is further restricted to the extent of one degree of mourning. Second, we observe that the relatives of those entitled to deliberation are themselves entitled to the next level of privilege, but only if they fall within the second degree of mourning, that is, are closer by one degree than the relatives of the wife of the crown prince. Finally, officials and nobles from the fifth to the fourth, third, or second rank (depending on whether they are active duty or titular or merely have a noble title) are given the privilege immediately under that to which their more senior colleagues are entitled.

The third privilege is the entitlement to the reduction of non-capital sentences by one degree. This is accorded to "officials of the seventh rank and above, as well as to the paternal grandparents, parents, brothers, sisters, wives, sons, and grandsons in the male line of those officials and nobles permitted petition" (p. 92). The reference to officials and nobles follows the same principle as that already indicated. The enumeration of the relatives to be entitled to reduction of punishment allows us to see the two principles adopted by the code for the construction of the clauses defining those entitled to privilege, namely: (i) certain relatives of the nobles or officials entitled to a particular privilege are to be entitled to the privilege immediately below, and (ii) the lower the primary privilege, the smaller the class of relatives so entitled. These principles are evident also in the construction of the classes entitled to the fourth privilege, that of redemption by payment of copper, namely: "officials of the ninth rank and above, and including the paternal grandparents, parents, wives, sons, or grandsons in the male line of those whose official rank permits them reduction of punishment" (p. 93).

Our second example is the definition of the abominations entitled "contumacy" and "discord." The former is defined as "to beat or plot to kill [without actually killing] one's paternal grandparents or parents; or to kill one's paternal uncles or their wives, or one's paternal aunts,[12] or one's elder brothers or sisters, or one's maternal grandparents, or one's husband, or one's husband's paternal grandparents, or his parents" (p. 66). To be noted is first the distinction between beating and plotting to kill, on the one hand, and actually killing, on the other. The former is referable only to paternal grandparents or parents, whereas the latter is referable to a small group of less important relatives. Also to be noticed is the patrilineal as well as male bias in the construction of this group. Of patrilineal relatives the text mentions brothers of the father, but includes their wives because they form part of the same household; sisters of the father, but excludes their husbands because they belong to a different agnatic group; and brothers and sisters. Of matrilineal relatives it mentions only the most important, namely, maternal grandparents. Of affinal relatives it mentions only the husband and his parents or paternal grandparents, but not the wife or her close ascendants.

Discord constitutes the eighth of the abominations, contumacy being the third. The relevant article states: "Discord means to plot to kill or also to sell relatives who are of the fifth or closer degree of mourning. This section further includes beating or accusing to the court one's husband or relatives, whether of a higher generation or of the same generation but older than oneself, of the third or closer degree of mourning, or relatives of an older generation of the fourth degree of mourning" (pp. 78–79). Contumacy had covered only the plotting to kill of paternal grandparents or parents, whereas discord covers the plotting to kill (and by implication also the killing) of all relatives within the five degrees of mourning. This includes junior as well as senior relatives, a point implicit in the conjuncture of "selling" with "plotting to kill." In respect of the less serious offenses of beating and accusing to the court, only senior relatives, including the husband, are brought within the ambit of the abomination. The fact that beating and accusing are less serious offenses than plotting to kill is reflected both in the restriction to senior relatives and the more limited range of mourning (third and fourth degrees). Furthermore, the distinction between third and fourth degree mourning relatives reflects the relative importance of seniority by age and seniority by generation. Fourth degree mourning seniors by age are excluded from the ambit of the abomination, whereas fourth degree seniors by generation are included.

Economy of Means

One conspicuous organizational quality of the code may be termed "economy of means." A relatively few central rules were deployed in such a way as to encompass a very large number of situations. Underlying this achievement was the preference of the legislators for "analogy" as the means by which to resolve a new situation, a preference which accorded generally with the respect paid by the Chinese to the practices of the past. Existing rules formed the base for the creation of new rules in the sense that the latter defined the punishment for certain conduct by reference to the former.[13] This process in turn was facilitated by the employment of certain fundamental phrases and devices, the most important of which were the technical expressions "with the same punishment," "estimate as x and sentence," and "by means of x sentence," and the resort to the device of "increasing" or "decreasing" the degree of punishment. We illustrate these points in the following sections on key expressions and use of classifications.

Key Expressions. The definition in the General Principles sections of the codes of certain key expressions not only provides a good example of the level of abstraction attained by the codes, but also constitutes an important device to facilitate the statement of the law in an economic and concise form. We cite the most useful of these terms as defined in the Ch'ing code, although all codes contained similar definitions.

One article sets out the rules governing the expressions "increase/ decrease the punishment by one or more degrees." Where "increase" is used, each degree of exile or mode of execution (strangulation and beheading) is to be taken as a single degree, but where the word "decrease" is used, each of the three kinds of exile and the two modes of death constitutes a single degree. Thus, where a sentence of strangulation is to be increased by one degree, the punishment is to be beheading, but where a sentence of beheading is to be decreased by one degree, the punishment is to be exile to three thousand *li*.[14]

Another article defines the phrase "(punish) with the same punishment" (*yu t'ung ts'ui*) as referring to the situation in which persons indirectly implicated in an offense are to receive the same punishment as those primarily guilty, with the exception that if the appropriate sentence for the latter is capital, the former are entitled to a reduction of one degree, and should be sentenced only to exile, unless they have aggravated their offense by taking a bribe to protect the main offender. However, should the phrase "the same punishment" (*t'ung ts'ui*) be employed, then in all cases exactly the same punishment, even if capital, is to be imposed.[15] The same article also contrasts the sense of the two phrases "estimate as *x* and sentence" (*chun . . . lun*) and "by means of *x* sentence" (*i . . . lun*). In the former case, the offense is deemed to be less serious than *x*, and therefore the punishment will not exceed exile. In the latter, the punishment is to be exactly the same as that prescribed for offense *x*.

These terms have an important structural role in the code. They are a form of shorthand that facilitates the interlinking and cross-referencing of rules. Through their use a range of legal consequences can be invoked without the need to list them in detail for each case to which they are to be applied. As will be seen in the next chapter, the legislators frequently have recourse to analogy. When establishing a new offense they prefer to find one already settled that can be used as a model. The punishment for the new offense can then be determined by reference to the old. However, the content of the reference, the particular degree of approximation between old and new, presents many variations. Frequently the technique of increasing or decreasing the punishment by one or more degrees is used. Other possibilities are presented by phrases such as "with the same punishment," "punish the same," "estimate as x and sentence" or "by means of x sentence." The next section will provide illustrations of the way in which these expressions are used in the classification of diverse offenses under a few basic heads.

Use of Classification. A good example of the use of classification is furnished by the law of homicide. We take our material from the T'ang code, although the same basic pattern was followed in the later codes. The task that the legislators set themselves was the reduction to manageable proportions of as many as possible of the infinitely varied circumstances under which killings occurred. They achieved this task by making a basic division between five principal categories: premeditated killing (*mou sha*), intentional killing (*ku sha*), killing in a fight (*tou sha*), killing in a game (*hsi sha*), and accidental killing (*kuo-shih sha*). Other situations were then subsumed under one of the principal heads. Further flexibility was ensured through the possibility of varying the degree of punishment. In this way due regard could be given to the gravity with which the specific situation was viewed. Unfortunately, the T'ang legislators do not make explicit the reasons for the particular classifications that they adopted. It is likely that factors such as the degree of fault or the nature of the causal relationship between act and death were given some weight.[16]

Several situations were subsumed under the head of *ku sha* (intentional killing). Article 73, after prescribing the punishments for shooting arrows or hurling missiles in the direction of the imperial palace, states that, where someone has thereby been killed, the case is to be treated as *ku sha* [lit: "by means of (i) *ku sha* sentence"]. Where intimidation has resulted in death, article 261 provides that the case is to be treated as *ku sha, tou sha* (killing in a fight), or *hsi sha* (killing in a game), depending on the precise facts. The *shu-i* commentary puts a case in which one person has deliberately terrorized another in a dangerous place, with the result that the latter dies, as by falling into water or from a precipice. This is to be treated as *ku sha*. Under article 395 cases in which doctors have deliberately mixed a medicine contrary to the original prescription, with the result that the patient dies, are to be treated as *ku sha*. According to article 423, the deliberate causing of a disturbance in the market, with the result that someone is killed, is to be treated as *ku sha*, but the punishment is to be decreased by one degree, that is, it becomes exile instead of beheading.

The same formula "by means of *x* sentence" is also used to accommodate certain situations under the head of *tou sha*, viz: pushing an object into a person's ear, nose, or other bodily opening, or removing his food or clothing, and as a result causing his death (article 261); or the accidental killing of a person during a robbery (article 289). In other cases a different formula is used. After the prohibition of a certain act, there follows the statement "if as a result (of the commission of the prohibited act) someone is killed, the punishment for *tou sha* is to be decreased by a certain number of degrees." Thus, by article 392, where someone is driving a cart or riding a horse through a town without good reason, and as a result a person is killed, the punishment is to be one degree less than that for killing in a fight. By article 424, if an official neglects to repair dikes, or repairs them at the wrong season, with the result that someone is killed, the punishment is to be three degrees less than that for killing in a fight. By article 427, where someone has been killed in a collision of boats caused by an individual's faulty navigation, the punishment is also to be three degrees less than that for killing in a fight.

A similar pattern is found with respect to accidental killing (*kuo-shih sha*). Where the owner of a vicious or rabid animal has not observed the precautions stipulated by the law, and as a result the animal kills someone, the case is to be treated as *kuo-shih sha*, the same formula being employed as in the case of killings subsumed under *ku* or *tou sha* (article 207). Equally, under the article on driving carts or riding horses through towns, should the offender be on urgent public business, if someone has been killed, the homicide is to be treated as "accidental" (article 392). A different formulation is employed in article 483, which deals with the administration of beatings by supervisory officials. Should the official in the exercise of his public duties beat and bring about the death of a person, the law of accidental killing is to be followed.

Another example may be cited from the T'ang code, this time of a central concept in terms of which a number of distinct offenses were classified. Again, we should note that a similar classification was adopted by the Ming and Ch'ing codes. The concept of *tsang* ("illicit goods") is one of the key notions used by the T'ang legislators in constructing a remarkably precise and integrated set of rules. In its broadest sense *tsang* expresses either property that the law treats as having been unlawfully acquired and with respect to which it establishes a penalty, or property that has been lost, destroyed, or damaged as a consequence of someone's unlawful act.[17]

The T'ang code explicitly distinguishes between several offenses that involve *tsang*: forcible theft, ordinary theft, acceptance of bribes by an official with or without subversion of the law, acceptance of property by supervisory officials within the area of their jurisdiction, and cases where liability is imposed on account of *tsang* not falling under one of the other heads (*tso tsang*). In each of these offenses the penalty is graded according to the amount of *tsang* involved, but the ratio between amount and penalty differs. Thus, the forcible theft of goods worth a piece of cloth one *ch'ih* in length[18] is punished by penal servitude for three years, while theft of goods worth ten *p'i* or more[19] is punished by strangulation (article 281). On the other hand, the thief who does not use force is punished by sixty blows with the heavy stick for taking goods worth a piece of cloth one *ch'ih* in length and by exile with added labor for taking goods worth fifty *p'i* or more (article 282).

There are numerous offenses in the code that determine the penalty by reference to *tsang*. Scales giving the relation between *tsang* and penalty are not set out for each individual offense. Instead the code provides that the offense is to be treated in the same way as ("by means of *x* sentence"), or as comparable to ("estimate *x* and sentence"),[20] one of the six basic *tsang* offenses. In the former case the effect is to ensure that the penalty established for the main offense is also the penalty for the offense subsumed under it. In the latter case, the penal consequences of the subsidiary are not the same as those of the principal offense. We may illustrate these propositions by reference to ordinary, nonforcible theft under which many other offenses are subsumed. These offenses may be divided into two groups: those which are to be treated in the same way as theft, and those which are to be treated as comparable to it.

In the first group we have cases that bear a fairly close resemblance to theft. Thus, persons who have made a personal profit from illegal conduct are to be treated as thieves, and the punishment is to be established according to the scale of *tsang* appropriate for ordinary theft. Examples are officials in charge of inspecting government horses who have made a personal profit from their sale (article 197), market officials who establish unfair prices in the markets and thereby personally profit (article 419), persons who make a profit by exchanging private for government property or vice versa (article 290), or those who use privately made, unfair measures for the giving out or taking in of official goods and thereby make a personal profit (article 420). Similarly, one who profits from another's labor by appropriating some material product on which the latter has expended effort (for example, mown and stored grass) is to be treated as a thief (article 291). Also to be treated in the same way are certain cases in which officials "borrow" government property, that is, the borrowing of government articles by supervisory officials where no written record has been left (article 212) and the private employment by officials of corvée labor that should be applied to government service (article 247).

If the essence of theft is taken to be appropriation of another's property without his consent, we can see why a number of offenses are classified not as theft itself but as comparable to theft. The main criterion for membership of this class is the negative one of a clear failure to satisfy the conditions for theft itself. Otherwise the offenses so classified have little in common. There are several offenses in which property is obtained by intimidation or deceit. The use of blackmail or intimidation to obtain property is treated as comparable to theft, but the penalty is to be increased by one degree (article 284). The obtaining of property by deceit or through the falsification of private or government documents is to be treated as comparable to theft, but here there is to be no increase in penalty (article 374).

Other offenses treated as comparable to theft involve merely destruction or loss of property or damage to it with no necessary element of deceit or illicit profit. Possibly the connecting factor is the fact that the owner has been deprived of property where it has been lost or destroyed, just as he has where it has been extorted or fraudulently obtained from him. Thus, the deliberate killing of official or private horses or cattle is to be treated as comparable to theft (article 203), as is the loss of property caused by flooding, where someone has deliberately broken open a dike for a reason other than the theft of water (article 445).

As a final example of "economy of means" we may cite the complex of rules found in all the codes dealing with confession, mutual concealment, and accusation.[21] These rules considered as a totality provide (i) that a person who confesses that he has committed an offense, before that offense has come to light, is to be pardoned, subject to certain exceptions, (ii) that persons who "conceal" offenses committed by their relatives or help them to escape the consequences of their illegal acts are to be exempt from punishment, and (iii) that persons who accuse their relatives of having committed offenses, whether the accusation is true or false, themselves commit an offense. The three sets of rules are found in different articles of the code, and also in different sections, confession and mutual concealment being treated in the "General Principles" and accusations in the "Specific Offenses" section. Despite this spatial separation the rules interlock in the sense that the operation of any one set cannot be fully understood without reference to the other two sets. Three core notions—confession, concealment and accusation—form the substratum of a highly complex and wide-ranging network of legal consequences.

The sets of rules can be said to interlock in the following way. Where a person entitled to conceal the offense of a relative confessed on the latter's behalf, even without his knowledge, the result in law was to be the same as though he had confessed himself. Equally, where relatives entitled to mutual concealment accused each other of offenses, each again was deemed to have "confessed" on his own account. Should a person accuse a relative of committing an offense which the latter had in fact committed, the accuser himself committed an offense, but the accused was treated as though he had himself confessed. We have already drawn attention to the possible difficulty in distinguishing between "making a confession on behalf of a relative" and "accusing a relative of having committed an offense."[22]

THE GENERAL AND THE SPECIFIC

Within the individual sections of the codes, the rules differ greatly in the generality of their formulation. This is particularly evident in the Ming and Ch'ing codes, where two varieties of rules coexist: those constituting articles (*lü*) and those constituting substatutes (*li*). The former tend to be general descriptions of an offense, identifying its main components, whereas the latter identify more complex and detailed situations which, in the opinion of the legislators, required special and separate treatment. We have already briefly commented on the distinction between the *lü* and the *li*.[23] We now merely add one further example, to reinforce the importance of the *li* in the development of the law.

An article inserted in the Ming and Ch'ing sections on "Robbery and Theft" provides that, where someone without reason entered another's house at night and was killed by the householder, there was to be no liability if the latter had just stumbled upon the intruder and acted in the panic and surprise of the moment, though a punishment was prescribed for the case where the intruder was first seized and then afterwards killed.[24] This article is followed in the Ch'ing code by an important and complex series of substatutes that define in detail the liability for killing a thief under a variety of circumstances.[25] The severity of the punishment for killing thieves was made to depend on a number of factors: whether it was the owner of the property, a neighbor, or some other person who pursued and killed the thief; whether the theft took place during the night or the day; whether it occurred on the premises (house or courtyard) or outside, and, if outside, whether the thief still had the stolen property when caught; whether the thief was pursued as soon as the theft took place or only tracked down later; whether the pursuers killed, although they could have arrested, the thief; and whether the thief made armed resistance or not.

It is the profusion of *li* that made the code of the late Ch'ing technically less admirable than the T'ang or Ming codes. The earlier codes had possessed a coherence and unity that to some extent were lost in the Ch'ing. *Li* were added to the code on an ad hoc basis, whenever the Board of Punishments or the throne deemed it necessary to introduce a new rule to cover a hitherto unforeseen situation. As a result, a magistrate, trying a criminal case, was likely to be faced with a large mass of detailed rules, possibly located in different parts of the code and not always consistent.[26]

Even the articles of the codes themselves represent highly differing levels of generality. From this point of view the treatment of theft is interesting. Toward the end of the series of articles grouped under the head "Robbery and Theft" is one which opens with the general statement that the public or secret taking (of property) constitutes theft. It then proceeds to define with reference to specific kinds of property the nature of the physical act that constitutes "taking."[27] This article in conjunction with two other general articles that prescribe respectively the punishments for the forcible and secret "taking" of another's property appear, at first sight, sufficient to deal with the whole topic of theft. Yet we find that the bulk of the section is occupied by various specific articles prescribing a fixed punishment for the theft of distinct kinds of property (for example, official documents, official seals, the keys of the city gates, military weapons, horses or cattle, and the produce of fields). To the Chinese legislator there were good reasons for singling out particular kinds of property for special regulation, but to the Western lawyer the treatment of theft presents an odd combination of the general and the particular.[28]

The rules that provide punishments for the infliction of physical injury were formulated with great attention to detail, and remind us of those found in the so-called barbarian codes of Western Europe. The punishment is determined by reference not only to the status of the victim vis-à-vis the offender, but also to the nature of the implement by which the injury was inflicted and the part of the body affected.[29] Although the list of specific, highly individuated offenses of which the article is composed could be taken from a Saxon or early Norman code,[30] we should not conclude that the Chinese technique was necessarily "primitive," reflecting an ill-developed ability to generalize or make abstractions. Rather, it seems to stem from a desire for precision and accuracy, as well as a concern that the punishment should be exactly proportional to the injury caused. Unless the code itself made clear the punishment appropriate to each injury, there was danger that magistrates throughout China would come to differing decisions, thus preventing the uniform application of the penal law throughout the empire.

The fundamental reason for the frequent resort in the codes to a highly specific description of the constituents of an offense (whether in articles or substatutes) was the legislators' desire to keep the ultimate power of punishment firmly under the control of the throne and to prevent the emperor's officials from exercising an independent discretion. An official acting as judge could only impose a punishment that had been specifically prescribed in the code for the precise combination of circumstances before him. When he was in doubt, he could only propose a solution by analogy or request guidance from the throne. This is no more than an illustration of the old Legalist adage that the ruler must keep in his own hands, and never delegate, "the twin handles of reward and punishment."[31]

9 Lawmaking and Legal Reasoning

In theory the position in regard to the making of law was clear. Lawmaking power was vested in the emperor, and he alone had the responsibility for introducing new offenses. In practice, however, emperors tended to act on advice. During the Ch'ing dynasty, for which the fullest information is available, the penal code was revised from time to time, the emperor formally initiating reconsideration and then accepting the recommendations of the expert body charged with scrutiny. Substatutes were frequently added to the code, concerned mainly with variations of existing offenses. These were normally approved by the emperor on the recommendation of the Board of Punishments.[1]

Personal intervention by the emperor appears to have been usually at the stage in which the precise punishment for serious cases was required to be finally established. The emperor was accepted as having the ultimate discretion in determining the sentence. On most occasions he simply accepted the Board's recommendation, but sometimes, especially where the offense had political implications or family relationships were involved, he might vary the recommendation. Although, again, he may have taken advice from those close to him, he was always prepared to act independently. The K'ang-hsi emperor has left a vivid record of his handling of capital cases. He was especially severe toward officials who had used their position to terrorize the people or to profit from corruption or toward those guilty of cowardice in war or of treason.[2] In other cases he exercised a fine discrimination, acting in conjunction with his Grand Secretaries. We quote from Jonathan Spence's account the K'ang-hsi emperor's own words:

For example, it was clear to me that the three cases of husbands killing wives that came up in 1699 were all quite different. The husband who hit his wife with an ax because she nagged at him for drinking, and then murdered her after another domestic quarrel—how could any extenuating circumstances be found? But Pao-erh, who killed his wife for swearing at his parents; and Meng, whose wife failed to serve him properly and used foul language so that he killed her—they could have their sentences reduced. Sometimes the crime seemed unpardonable—like Chu Shang-wen killing his cousin over a small argument—yet I had the death sentence remitted out of compassion, since the murderer was already sixty-seven years of age. At other times what looked like a lighter crime proved to be serious: thus Liu-ta had killed Ma-erh with a stone, but as the Grand Secretaries explained, the victim had been struck twelve times in all, and his brains had burst out onto the ground. Liu-ta was obviously an experienced killer and should be executed. Sudden murders without a cause could sometimes be forgiven—deaths resulting from drunken brawls, for example, or a lover killing his mistress in anger when her husband tried to dun him. Or a certain crime could be pardoned in peace time: the Board of Punishments wanted the bandit Fan Sung beheaded for stealing horses from the imperial retinue, but I changed it to exile, since the nation was at peace and horse theft was therefore not so serious as it would have been in time of war.[3]

The main problem faced by the central government in all dynasties was to retain control of the administration of justice. This entailed a scrupulously exact definition of the offenses contained in the code, so that little scope for uncertainty was left to the district, prefectural, and provincial officials charged with administering the law. Essentially the idea was that local officials should do no more than carry out the wishes of the emperor as specified in the code. This was not easy to ensure, and from time to time the central government became worried at the independence it detected in the activity of its local officials. During the Sung, for example, the emperor and the court were concerned at the extent to which local tribunals relied on compilations of previous judicial decisions as a source of precedents for particular cases. This practice was perceived by the central government both as leading to unwarranted extensions in the range of imperial rulings originally given for one specific case and as subverting the authority of the statutory rules themselves.[4]

Imperial policy at all times was directed at limiting the discretion of officials who acted as judges at the local level. They were not to "invent" rules for themselves, but apply only those which emanated from the emperor. This policy was designed both to protect the authority of the emperor as the sole source of law and to ensure uniformity in the administration of the law throughout China. When dealing with recommendations submitted from the provinces, the Ch'ing Board of Punishments constantly stressed the need for consistency in the application of the penal rules. A number of important consequences followed from the implementation of the policy.

In the first place, the legislators attempted to formulate the constituents of the offense as precisely and fully as possible, so that the officials trying the case might easily identify the relevant rules to apply to the facts before them. The desire to prescribe in advance for any eventuality that might occur probably accounts for the proliferation of substatutes during the Ch'ing and the multitude of detail found in some of them.[5] Of course, it was also recognized by the central authorities that not every contingency could be envisaged and so provided for in advance. "Gaps" in the law might appear. Should they do so, the correct procedure was for the officials discovering them to submit a memorial requesting guidance or decision.

Second, the penal codes contained articles by which the central authorities sought to maintain a strict control over local officials exercising judicial functions. We cite here the articles of the Ch'ing code, but add references to those of the earlier codes. It was provided that, whenever an official pronounced a sentence in a criminal case, he must cite the article or substatute upon which he relied; failure to do so was punished with thirty blows with the light stick.[6] However, the article continues, should the emperor have issued an edict for the decision of a particular case, this was not to be cited as analogous to a provision of the code itself. Officials who, in reliance upon such edicts, had wrongfully acquitted or condemned a person were to be liable under the article on delivering a mistaken judgment.[7] The explanatory commentary stresses that the articles and substatutes of the code constituted the invariable law to be applied in the future, whereas imperial decisions for special cases simply responded to the necessity of the moment.[8]

Furthermore, judges were held strictly liable for the correctness in law of their sentences. The underlying thought here, probably Legalist in origin, appears to have been that the law prescribed certain duties for officials acting as judges. Failure to carry out those duties properly in itself entailed liability, irrespective of whether the "mistake" had been inadvertent, negligent, or deliberate. However, as was usual in the codes, a distinction was drawn between the intentional and the unintentional giving of a wrong judgment. In Ch'ing law the deliberate conviction of an innocent person or acquittal of a guilty entailed for the offending official the same sentence, that is, the punishment he had wrongfully imposed on the innocent or omitted to impose on the guilty. Should he merely have made a mistake in sentencing, irrespective of the degree of carelessness exhibited, the punishment was to be a certain number of degrees less than that incurred for the deliberately wrong judgment.[9]

Third, care was taken to ensure that officials observed the rules through the maintenance of an elaborate system of review. Built into the traditional procedures for the administration of justice was the requirement that the decisions of officials in all criminal cases except those punishable only by a beating be forwarded for reexamination to their immediate superiors in the hierarchy. For noncapital cases the regular process of review stopped at the level of the province in which the case originated. Capital cases were all sent to the Board of Punishments, and ultimately to the throne, for review.[10] The Board frequently sent a case back to the originating province for reconsideration on the grounds that the facts had not properly been ascertained or that an incorrect rule of law had been applied. To ensure that this procedure was operating properly at local levels, censors or

other imperial emissaries from time to time conducted special in-
vestigations.[11] There is no strong reason for doubting that, despite
the problem of the inefficient or corrupt official, encountered in all
legal systems, the control exercised by the central government over
its subordinate officials was not on the whole effective.[12]

ANALOGY

Although the throne in all dynasties viewed the task of its judicial
officials as restricted to the correct application to the facts of the rules
detailed in the penal code, it recognized that situations might arise
for which no predetermined rule could be found. What was the judge
to do in such a case? The solution that the throne adopted was to
permit the judge to decide the case by reference to that provision of
the code which was most analogous to the facts before him. All the
codes contained an article empowering judges to decide cases by resort to analogy. The articles are not framed in identical terms, those
of the Ming and Ch'ing codes being conceived more broadly than that
of the T'ang. We shall consider here judicial recourse to analogy as it
operated under the Ch'ing.[13]

The Ch'ing article[14] admits that the code does not contain the solution to all the possible cases that might arise. Where no exactly appo-
site provision was to be found in it, the judge was authorized to cite
another rule under which the facts could be subsumed on the grounds
that they closely resembled (pi fu) the situation primarily contemplated by the rule. In making this comparison, the judge should determine whether the punishment prescribed by the rule should be
increased or decreased for the actual case before him. His recommendation should then be forwarded to his superiors for ratification, and
the throne should be informed. A substatute of 1733 prescribed in
more detail the procedure that was to be followed where rules were
applied by analogy.[15] All such cases should be referred to the Board of
Punishments, which was to determine the final sentence, submit a
full report to the throne, and await the imperial decision. It emerges
with particular clarity that, although inferior judges or even the Board

itself might propose the application of an existing rule to a hitherto unforseen set of facts with or without a modification in the punishment, the final decision as to the appropriateness of the proposed change was reserved for the throne.

To appreciate the use made by the Board of the power to recommend the application of rules by analogy, we will draw upon some of its decisions in matters of homicide. In 1799 the following facts were submitted from Shensi province. Liu, one of the partners in a milling business, on account of the pigs kept by his partner Teng fouling the stream running by his house, formed the intention of poisoning the animals. He placed the poison inside the mill in meal which he had ascertained was destined for the pigs, but he took no special precautions, nor did he give a warning. In fact three persons ate the poisoned meal and died. Under what provision of the code should Liu be sentenced? Three rules were cited to the Board: the substatute on vicious scoundrels repeatedly molesting or causing harm to others under which the punishment was exile to four thousand *li*,[16] the article on accidental killing under which the punishment was payment of money,[17] and the article on shooting arrows in the direction of an inhabited place under which the punishment was exile to three thousand *li*.[18]

The Board examined in turn the applicability of each of these rules. The rule on vicious scoundrels, it declared, could apply only in the case of persons who had acted perversely in their native place and without any reason had molested and harmed others. As to the rule on accidental killing, this had been applied in the past to cases in which a person had planned to poison an animal, and by mistake a person ate the poison and died. However, the Board pointed out that, when the poison had actually been placed in a spot which people obviously frequented, it was difficult to say that a death which resulted from someone taking and eating the poison fell within the terms of the rubric defining "accident": what ear and eye or thought and care do not reach. If the poison had been placed in the pigs' own feeding trough, and someone by mistake had eaten it and died, then the situation could be accommodated within the rubric, and the death treated as accidental. The facts of the present case, accordingly, were held to fall within the purview of the rule on shooting arrows in the direction of an inhabited place, and Liu should be sentenced by analogy with this article to a beating of 100 blows with the heavy stick and exile to three thousand *li*.[19]

The Board does not explain why it selected the article on shooting arrows as the appropriate analogy. At first sight, the situation of placing poison for pigs seems very different from that of shooting arrows or throwing stones. However, it is probable that the Board saw the analogy in the fact that both the rule on arrows and the facts concerning the poison for pigs concerned the placing of a potentially harmful object (arrows or poison) in a place frequented by people. Further, both the shooting of arrows toward an inhabited place and the placing of poisoned meal in the mill could be regarded as highly careless, if not reckless, acts. It is likely that the Board evaluated the rule and the facts more from the concrete than the abstract (focusing on degree of fault) perspective.

In a Kiangsu case of 1830 a father killed his son, wrongly believing him to have condoned the adultery of his wife.[20] The problem for the courts was the liability of the wife, whose initial wrongful act had resulted in the death of her husband. The code contained no provision for the sentencing of the wife, whose adultery was deemed to have been the cause of her husband's death. Cited to the Board were two substatutes and one article, viz: (i) where a woman had engaged in illicit sexual intercourse, with the result that her father or mother had committed suicide, she was to be sentenced to immediate strangulation; if her husband committed suicide, the punishment was to be reduced to strangulation after the assizes, it being assumed that neither parent nor husband had condoned the illicit relationship;[21] (ii) where a son or grandson or their wives had engaged in illicit sexual intercourse or debauchery, with the result that someone had beaten and killed a noncondoning parent or paternal grandparent, the son (or other offender) was to be sentenced to immediate strangulation;[22] (iii) where an adulterer killed the husband, the adulterous wife, even though she had no knowledge of the circumstances, was to be sentenced to strangulation after the assizes.[23] The provincial governor, being unable to decide the case, had requested the Board's advice.

The governor had pointed out that these rules did not cover the situation in which the noncondoning husband was beaten and killed on account of his wife's adultery either by a third party or his own father. Examination of the rules showed that the suicide of a husband in consequence of his wife's adultery was treated more leniently than that of a parent in consequence of a daughter's debauchery. From this it was possible to deduce that, for a case in which a noncondoning husband had been beaten and killed on account of his wife's adultery, the punishment of immediate strangulation should not be imposed, since this was appropriate for the case in which a parent had been beaten and killed. However, the governor had also pointed out that, in the case where the adulterer had killed the husband, not only was his own life forfeit but the wife, even though ignorant of the circumstances, was to be sentenced to strangulation after the assizes. Where it was the father who had killed his own son on account of the latter's adulterous wife, the killer was not required by law to forfeit his life. How, then, could the law merely punish the wife with strangulation?

The Board argued that, since in this case it was the father who had killed the husband, it was difficult to apply by analogy (*pi chao*) a rule which dealt with the case in which the adulterer killed the husband. Clearly, the Board thought, the relationship between killer and victim was too different in these cases. Next, the Board drew attention to the parallelism between the rules on a parent being beaten and killed or committing suicide on account of a child's debauchery, the punishment for the child in both cases being immediate strangulation. This suggested that, where the husband on account of his wife's adultery had been beaten and killed by someone, the appropriate rule to apply by analogy was that prescribing a punishment of strangulation after the assizes for the wife, where the husband had committed suicide on account of his wife's adultery. Hence, the wife in the present case should be sentenced to strangulation after the assizes.

A Shensi case of 1838 illustrates a common and important example of analogical application.[24] A father-in-law, annoyed at a fault of his daughter-in-law, rose to beat her, slipped, fell, and sustained injuries from which he died. The provincial governor had proposed a sentence of immediate strangulation under the substatute on children accidentally killing a parent,[25] but the Board rejected this on the grounds that accidental killing required some direct contact between offender and victim (lit. "parent be killed by child"). Here the victim had slipped and died through his own act. It pointed out that the previous practice in cases of this kind had been to apply by analogy (*pi chao*) the substatute on parents in shame and anger committing suicide after a child had defied orders.[26] Hence, in the present case the daughter-in-law should be sentenced to strangulation after the assizes as prescribed by this substatute.

We may note a comment of the Japanese legal scholar Nakamura Shigeo that is applicable to this case. According to M. J. Meijer, Nakamura had distinguished two kinds of analogy: that in which a rule was applied to facts which resembled those covered by it, and that in which "the spirit of the law, the meaning of the provision, or the intention of the legislator is the basis of the analogy." An example of the latter type of analogy given by Nakamura was the application of the substatute on disobedient sons. This was applied to cases in which a parent's suicide had been caused by the offending behavior of a child, falling short of actual disobedience. Meijer expresses Nakamura's thought as "the meaning of the legislator was to ensure that sons would treat their parents with such reverence and care as should have precluded their unhappiness."[27] These remarks are equally applicable to cases in which a parent, annoyed with a child, slips and is mortally injured in an attempt to chastise the offending child.

Finally, we may note a Soochow case of 1833 concerned with the chasing of a thief who slipped and died.[28] The essential facts were that a person appointed to guard a family grave site noticed someone cutting down a tree by the graves. The watchman gave chase; the thief fled, but in his panic slipped, fell into a river, and drowned. The provincial governor had reasoned that the true cause of the thief's death was the pursuit by the watchman. Since the incident happened immediately after the theft was detected, the case was the same as though the offender had struck the victim with his hands. Hence, the governor recommended a sentence of penal servitude under the substatute on stealing property from the fields at night. The relevant portion of this substatute stated that, where a person at night stole objects from the market or fields which someone was watching, should the owner or his employees at the time of the theft pursue, beat, and kill the thief, the punishment for the killer was to be one hundred blows with the heavy stick and penal servitude for three years.[29]

The Board, when considering this recommendation, had cited to it the substatute upon which the governor had relied, the article which prescribed that there should be no liability where escaping convicts were killed immediately by their escorts,[30] and the article empowering the application of rules by analogy.[31] It pointed out that the substatute on pursuing and killing the thief specifically stated that the thief be "beaten and killed." Hence, it was not possible to subsume under it a case in which the thief died, not from a beating, but from falling into a river while fleeing to avoid capture. The Board drew a sharp distinction between the case of an initial fight in which one person pursued another with the intention of striking him, where the pursuit was treated as the cause of death should the victim fall into a river and die, and the case in which the owner, on seeing a theft, at that time rushed in pursuit. Should the thief in the latter situation unexpectedly slip, fall, and die, the pursuit could not in the same way be treated as the cause of death. The Board then added the reason to which it probably gave the most weight: "If in cases like this we simply apply the substatute concerning affrays and sentence the owner accordingly, and if all those who pursue thieves will be caught in the net of the law, this will result in indecision on their part; consequently, the thieves will become even more reckless and even less ashamed of themselves, which will have grave repercussions on their repression."[32]

Since the Board was reluctant to apply the substatute recommended by the governor, it turned to another possible model, that constituted by the article on the pursuit and arrest of escaping prisoners. Although it conceded that there was a difference between the case of the particular owner of stolen property seizing the thief, and that of officials and their subordinates seizing prisoners, the Board concluded that the circumstances contemplated by the article were not "too remote" from those found in the present case. Hence it applied the article by analogy (*pi chao*) and held that the watchman should be exempt from liability.

Starting with recognition of the fact that the code contained no rule precisely applicable to the circumstances before it, the Board had fundamentally to consider whether the pursuit, slipping, and drowning of the thief should be treated in the same way as the pursuit, slipping, and drowning of one of the parties in a fight. Whereas the governor had argued that these two cases should be treated alike, the Board found reasons for differentiating them. One reason was technical, based on the wording of the substatute that the governor had sought to apply; the other was derived from policy. The technical reason adverted to the fact that the words "beat and kill" used in the substatute did not apply to a case where the owner of stolen goods or his representative was chasing the thief, whereas the policy reason emphasized the need to repress theft. The first reason operated "negatively" in that it argued for the displacement of the substatute, whereas the second operated "positively" in that it argued for the application of the article providing that there was to be no liability where the escaping prisoner was pursued and killed. The second reason appears to have been the more important in its influence on the Board's attitude, and may indeed even have inspired the restrictive interpretation given by the Board to the words "beat and kill" of the substatute.

To some extent the reasoning by analogy employed by Ch'ing judicial officials will remind the Western student of the familiar process of interpretation of a statutory rule or the determination of the ambit of a rule established by precedent. The Chinese judge, like his Western counterpart, has before him a particular set of facts. Both have to decide whether those facts could readily be subsumed under a rule of the criminal code or, in the Anglo-American system, under a rule of the common law. If no such rule can be found, the accused has to be acquitted on the grounds that he has not committed an offense known to the law. However, even where the facts at first sight do not fall within the scope of a settled rule, it is open to the judge to decide by a process of interpretation that a particular rule should be applied.

It is at this point that we notice a difference between the Western and the Chinese reasoning. The Anglo-American judge has at his command a range of rules or principles of interpretation that will enable him to decide whether a particular rule covers the case before him or not. Through the interpretative process he narrows or widens the scope of the rule. Of course, the Chinese judge also operated in this way to a certain extent. Although he did not work with formalized rules of interpretation, he still had to decide whether given facts clearly fell within the scope of a particular provision of the code. On the whole, he was not prepared to go too far in extending the wording of a rule. This is because it was unnecessary for him to do so. He was empowered by the code to apply by analogy a rule that he deemed to be appropriate in the light of all the circumstances of the case. Whereas an Anglo-American judge may be prepared to construe a particular rule widely, the Chinese judge achieved the same objective by resort to analogy.

In both cases rules of the system (for the Anglo-American the principles of interpretation and for the Chinese the article and substatute on analogy) empower the judge to exercise a certain discretion. In both cases, too, the system provides a measure of control on the way judges exercise their discretion. Anglo-American law has a system of judicial review in which the decisions of lower-ranking judges may (subject to the appeal process) be scrutinized and revised by courts higher in the hierarchy and ultimately by the legislature. The traditional Chinese system not only had a more thoroughgoing system of review in which decisions by analogy were automatically referred to the highest judicial body, the Board of Punishments, but it also required the approval of the throne, in theory at least, for analogical extensions of the settled law.

Sometimes in the modern literature we find the question raised: does the power of the Chinese judge to resort to analogy infringe the principle *nulla poena sine lege,* in the sense that conduct is made criminal in a particular case, although no prior rule had so made it? In so far as the principle can be given any specific significance, the answer must be that resort to analogy does not, any more than the familiar Anglo-American process of statutory interpretation, run counter to it. All developed legal systems recognize that combinations of facts will be alleged by the officers in charge of the application of the law to constitute offenses, even though no existing rule has precisely envisaged them. The only question perhaps relevant to the *nulla poena* principle concerns the width of the discretion entrusted to judges and the way in which that discretion is controlled. One might have a system in which it was open to the judges on their own initiative to declare criminal whatever conduct they found to be offensive, even though no prior rule could be found to justify their decision. Such a possibility for the judicial invention of "new crimes" might be regarded as contrary to the *nulla poena* principle. But this was not the case in traditional China. Resort to analogy by judges was strictly confined within the framework of the existing set of codified rules, and in any event subject to the approval of the throne.[33]

With respect to analogy we may conclude that the throne and its advisers recognized the need for officials to exercise a judicial discretion, but they took care that its exercise was kept within strictly confined limits. In this way the throne made sure that it retained control of the "lawmaking" power. Furthermore, the Board of Punishments, which maintained an overview of developments in the various provinces, was able to monitor the way in which the law was being extended and do what it could to see that consistency and uniformity of decision was observed across the provinces. From time to time the Board, on the basis of a recommendation that an existing article or substatute should be applied by analogy, would recommend that the throne enact a new substatute. Interestingly, however, when asked by the throne to consider a memorial from a provincial governor or other high-ranking official recommending the introduction of a new substatute, the Board would often refuse to endorse the recommendation. It was aware of the need to limit the proliferation of detailed statutory rules, and it was opposed to the making of a legislative rule for every new situation that emerged. Most situations, it conceived, could be adequately handled through the mechanism of analogy in accordance with the procedure established by the code itself.

PRECEDENT

Precedent, understood in a broad sense, played an important part both in the maintenance and the operation of the traditional legal system. Great respect was paid to the institutions and achievements of the past, as evidenced in the transmission of the penal codes from one dynasty to the next. Furthermore, legal innovations, whether by way of general rule or particular imperial decision, tended to be justified by appeals to what had been done or decided in the past.[34] At this point we are concerned with precedent not in the broadest sense, but in a narrower signification, resembling that in which we speak of precedent in Anglo-American jurisprudence.

Some care is necessary in evaluating the resemblances between precedent in traditional Chinese and Anglo-American law. The latter system has complex rules determining which judicial decisions are binding on which courts. Traditional Chinese law did not possess such rules, the theory being that decisions of judicial officials possessed no binding force with reference to future cases. Even decisions of the emperor were confined to the particular case in respect of which they were given, unless it was clearly expressed that they were to take effect as a general rule. We have already noted the main reasons underlying this approach: the desire to keep lawmaking power firmly in the hands of the throne, and the need to ensure that throughout the various provinces decisions in penal cases were kept as uniform and consistent as possible.

Consequently, when we speak of the role of precedent in the reasoning of the Board of Punishments or inferior organs, we are not invoking the existence of rules that determine under what circumstances a court was bound, either by decisions of its own or by those of a superior tribunal. Rather, we are referring to the fact that the Board of Punishments, as well as the provincial authorities, did from time to time rely on decisions of the Board as pointers to the correct decision to be reached in a particular case. The cases reported in the nineteenth-century collections of the Board's decisions provide many examples of the Board's reliance on previous decisions of its own. We shall study some examples of its reasoning, but first we must consider the formal position on the use of judicial decisions as established by the code or imperial edicts. We shall confine ourselves here to the position that obtained in the Ch'ing dynasty.[35]

A substatute enacted in 1738 provided that, whereas it was in order for judicial officials to cite the regular articles (*lü*) and substatutes (*li*) of the code, leading cases (*ch'eng an*) might not indiscriminately be invoked, unless they had already been elevated to the standing of a substatute or at least a general circular (*t'ung hsing*). But, should the governors general or governors of provinces in dealing with a criminal matter find an old case (*an*) that closely resembled the one before them, they might cite it as a precedent (*li*).[36] The substatute distinguishes between "leading cases" and "general circulars," according the greater authority to the latter. General circulars were decisions of the Board which, with imperial approval, were to be given special effect through circulation to all the provincial authorities. It was intended that the latter thereafter rely on such decisions as establishing an authoritative rule, should similar facts come before them in the future. General circulars were often made substatutes. Leading cases, on the other hand, were individual decisions of the Board to which no special weight or authority attached.[37] Their existence might even be known only to the originating province and the Board itself. The wording of the substatute can be understood in the sense that the prohibition to cite leading cases as a basis for a recommendation in a criminal case applied only to the provincial authorities and not to the Board itself.[38]

An investigation of the decisions of the Board in the context of homicide shows that it frequently cited and relied on leading cases (*ch'eng an*), and further that the provincial authorities might put such cases to the Board in an attempt to maintain a position that the Board had initially opposed. Although the available records provide only a summary account of the way in which the Board handled such "precedents," we may still detect marked similarities with the practice of the American or British courts. Cases were relied on as authorities in the absence of a relevant statutory provision or as controlling the way in which an ambiguous article or substatute was to be understood. Sometimes apparently conflicting lines of authority were reconciled on their facts, or the Board accepted that there was a conflict and proposed a solution. We will illustrate these propositions with a number of examples.

First, we may consider one or two general statements of the Board on the role of leading cases. In an Anhui case of 1740 the Board, referring to the recently enacted substatute of 1733,[39] cited a decision of 1732 arising from facts similar to those before it. It observed that, although the earlier decision had not been made a substatute, it might still be adduced as relevant.[40]

In another Anhui case of 1822, dealing with a woman who had killed her daughter-in-law to prevent her from disclosing an adulterous relationship, the Board found that the provincial authorities had ignored the leading cases under which the offender in cases of this kind was sentenced to capital punishment to be commuted at the autumn assizes to permanent imprisonment. Accordingly, the Board corrected the provincial recommendation to comply with the precedents. At the same time it made certain important general observations. Generally, it said, the punishments in criminal cases were to be determined according to the articles and substatutes of the code. Where new articles or substatutes had been added, the last in point of time was to be followed. But where no statutory provision had yet been completed to deal with the case, the leading cases (*ch'eng an*) of recent years were to be carefully investigated and a decision made in accordance with them.[41]

By contrast, in a memorial of 1884, arising from a protracted disagreement with the province of Fengtien over the decision of a particular case,[42] the Board stated emphatically that it was necessary to decide lawsuits in accordance with the articles and substatutes of the code. Should these be set aside in favor of leading cases, not only would a decision be given that conflicted with the regular law, but there would be a danger of substituting for consistency in judicial decision the evil practice of bias and prejudice.[43] Here, right at the end of the imperial period, we find the Board giving a firm warning on the need to maintain priority of statute over judicial decision in the resolution of criminal cases.

We may now pass to some examples of the Board's actual use of previous decisions of its own as precedents. Not infrequently they were invoked to help in the determination of the correct classification of the offense. It might be doubtful whether a particular set of facts should be subsumed under the article on accidental killing or that on killing in a game, or whether they should be classified as "killing in a fight" or "intentional killing." The terms of the relevant statutory provisions did not always provide adequate criteria for the solution of such questions, and the Board tended to rely on previous decisions of its own, where any were available, that dealt with the point at issue.

A Kiangsu case of 1826[44] raised the question whether the facts before the court should be classified as falling under the head of "killing in a game (*hsi sha*)," entailing the punishment of strangulation after the assizes, or of "accidental killing (*kuo-shih sha*)," entailing as punishment merely the payment of money to the family of the victim. Ni and Liu were drinking together. When Liu lay down, Ni took hold of him in an effort to get him to resume drinking. Liu twisted away and refused to continue. Ni's legs were unsteady on account of the wine he had drunk, and Liu's movement caused him to slip. He fell across Liu's body, crushing his abdomen. As a result, Liu died. The provincial authorities recommended that Ni should be sentenced on the grounds of accidental killing, but the department of the Board that first reviewed the decision thought that the appropriate classification of the offense was provided by "killing in a game." The full Board now investigated its previous decisions and cited a Fengtien case of 1824 arising from a drunken bout indulged in by Li and Chao. When Li drew a knife to peel a melon, Chao, being drunk, stumbled and fell on the knife, thereby killing himself. In that case the Board had recorded a verdict of accidental killing, and it proposed that the same should be followed in the present case.

In its reply the department still urged that the appropriate sentence was under "killing in a game," and in its turn cited a leading case in which Yang was drinking with Wu. After the latter had gone to sleep, Yang told him to get up and continue drinking. Wu replied that if Yang could pull him upright he would continue. When Yang attempted this, he slipped and fell on top of Wu, causing his death. On these facts Yang was sentenced under the article on killing in a game.

The Board observed that this was an obvious case of death resulting from a wrestling bout, clearly distinguishable from the facts of the present case.

The Board concluded by affirming that the circumstances under which Liu had met his death resembled an "accident" rather than a "game." It cited three further precedents to support its view. In a Shensi case of 1823 Yang, when drunk, was wrestling with Chang. Yen intervened to stop them and pulled at Yang. In struggling to free himself, Yang slipped, fell, and received mortal injuries. Yen was sentenced on the grounds of accidental killing.[45] In a Manchurian case of 1825 Ch'en and a fellow clansman, while pasturing cattle together, started in pursuit of a hare and collided, the latter falling and suffering injuries from which he died. It was held that Ch'en should be sentenced on the grounds of accidental killing. Finally, in a Szechuan case of 1825 Li and Hsien were walking together along the edge of a river, Li being drunk and supported by Hsien. Li slipped and fell into the river taking with him Hsien who drowned. It was held that Li should be sentenced on the grounds of accidental killing.[46]

Sometimes determination of the boundary between accidental killing (kuo-shih sha) and killing by mistake (wu sha) caused problems. A good illustration is supplied by a Hu-kuang case of 1802.[47] Mrs. Liu, disgusted with the behavior of her son who was under arrest as a thief, sent him some poisoned cakes. He shared these with a fellow prisoner who died as a result. The provincial authorities had suggested that Mrs. Liu should be sentenced to exile to three thousand li. They had reached this conclusion by applying the article on killing by mistake (wu sha), under which the punishment would be beheading after the assizes.[48] In view of the circumstances, it was suggested that this be reduced by one degree to exile. The article on wu sha was not directly applicable to the case of Mrs. Liu, because it presupposed that the offender was not related to his intended victim. The department of the Board that initially reviewed the case agreed with this proposal. It cited, but distinguished, a case of 1837 from Kueichou in which woman P'an angrily threw a stone at her disobedient son. Another person suddenly appearing from behind a door was hit and killed. Woman P'an was sentenced on the grounds of accidental killing. For the department this case was relevant in that it supported the general proposition that a woman in Mrs. Liu's position should at least not be sentenced to give her life in requital.

The full Board rejected the provincial and departmental recommendation. It considered that the case of woman P'an provided the correct precedent and that Mrs. Liu should likewise be sentenced on the grounds of accidental killing. This disagreement prompted the case to be sent to the body of senior legal experts known as the Statutes Commission. The Commission supported the original recommendation. On the one hand, it distinguished woman P'an's case on the grounds that the facts had not disclosed a premeditated intention to kill. On the other, it cited two further precedents that supported the provincial and departmental position. In a Shensi case of 1793 Juan was beating his son, but by mistake he struck and killed a third person. He was sentenced to strangulation after the assizes by analogy with the article on fighting and killing a bystander by mistake.[49] In a Kansuh case of 1796 Wen, angry with his disobedient son, formed the intention of poisoning him, but by mistake poisoned a third person. He was sentenced to beheading after the assizes in accordance with the normal rule on intending to kill one person but by mistake killing another.

These precedents suggested that the ordinary article on *wu sha* should be applied by analogy to Mrs. Liu. If applied without modification, her sentence would have been beheading after the assizes. However, the Commission held that in view of the circumstances, in particular the fact that the intended victim was her own misbehaving son, she should not be sentenced to loss of life. The original proposal by the province that she should receive a reduction in punishment by one degree was deemed to be appropriate.[50]

Another classificatory problem concerned the delimitation between killing in a fight (*tou sha*) and intentional killing (*ku sha*). This may be illustrated by a Shansi case of 1811.[51] During a quarrel one person threw boiling water on another and caused his death. The Board observed that hitherto in dealing with homicide cases the classification of the offense as killing in a fight or intentional killing had not been determined solely by the nature or number of the wounds. What was decisive was the presence or absence of an intention to kill. In a case such as the present, although the victim had received numerous wounds on different parts of his body from the scalding water, these had been caused by one act constituted by the original throwing of the water. This was not comparable to a case in which numerous wounds had been inflicted by separate blows of a knife, where it was relevant to consider whether the ferocity of the attack sprang from an intention to kill. To support its conclusion that the present case should be treated as killing in a fight and not as intentional killing, the Board cited no less than six leading cases decided between the years 1800 and 1810, in which a sentence of strangulation after the assizes on the grounds of killing in a fight had been recommended, where one person threw boiling water over another in the course of a quarrel.[52]

Precedent might also control the interpretation of a particular article or substatute of the code. For example, the substatute that permitted a decrease in punishment where a person, wounded in a fight, died after the lapse of ten days contemplated only the case of two individuals fighting.[53] On its face it did not deal with the situation in which several persons had plotted to beat another. This point arose in a case of 1792 from Honan.[54] After noting the lacuna in the substatute, the Bound found that there were some relevant leading cases. In a Kwangtung case of 1789 in which two persons had each beaten and killed another, and one of the victims had died after ten days, the offender was allowed a decrease of punishment to exile. A like decision was given in a Honan case of 1791. The Board also cited a memorial from Kwangtung province dealing with a case of collective beating in which nine lives had been lost. Where one of the victims had died outside the period of ten days, a decrease to exile was permitted. In the case before the Board several persons had collectively beaten others, with the result that four lives had been lost. One of the assailants had wounded a person who died after the lapse of ten days. It was held to be appropriate, in the light of the precedents, that the offender be entitled to a reduction of punishment to exile under the substatute.

The interpretation of a substatute that imposed heavy punishments on those who schemed to take another's property and took life[55] also caused difficulty. In a Kwangtung case of 1809 the Board established that the substatute was to apply only where there had first been a desire to take another's property, coupled with a plot to kill that person to obtain the property. It did not apply where the initial scheme to take property had not involved an intention to kill, but afterwards, once the property had been taken, someone was killed to prevent disclosure. The Board had to consider the following facts. Hui commissioned Li to recover his ox from Liu, who had allegedly stolen it. Li in turn commissioned Liu's relative by marriage, Hsieh, to recover the ox, and gave him some money supplied by Hui. Hsieh lost the money gambling.[56] Since Li was not willing to let the matter rest, Hsieh formed the intention of killing him to prevent disclosure. The Board held that this was not a case in which there had been an initial intention to take property, followed by the killing of the owner and the removal of the property. Consequently, the substatute on scheming for property and taking life should not be followed. In support the Board cited several previous decisions: (i) a Hupeh case of 1803 in which a debtor subjected to abusive demands for repayment plotted to kill the creditor; (ii) a Szechuan case of 1806 in which a creditor helped himself to his debtor's property in lieu of repayment, and the latter at that time formed the intention of killing him; (iii) another Szechuan case of 1806 in which a debtor faced with demands for repayment fought with his creditor and at that time formed the intention of killing him; and (iv) a third Szechuan case of 1806 in which a debtor, unable to repay, plotted to kill his creditor. In all these cases the killer had been sentenced under the ordinary law of premeditated or intentional killing and not under the special substatute.

Where conflicting cases were adduced as precedents, the Board either distinguished them on their facts or, in the case of genuine conflict, resolved which position should be followed for the future. An example of the former approach is supplied by one of the decisions on the liability of a person who helped another to commit suicide. In a Szechuan case of 1816[57] a woman suffering from a painful and incurable illness had often declared that she did not wish to live, and ultimately she attempted to strangle herself. Not succeeding on her own, she implored her husband to help by pulling tight the cord around her neck. Despite his initial reluctance, in the end she forced him to comply with her wish. The provincial authorities recommended that the husband be sentenced to strangulation after the assizes as prescribed by the article on the intentional killing of a wife.[58] In effect they treated him as the principal (the author of the idea) in a plot between himself and his wife to kill her.

The issue before the Board was whether it was correct to sentence the husband as principal in a plot to kill his wife or merely as an accessory who had actively assisted. To resolve the issue, the Board conducted an extensive review of earlier cases that disclosed similar facts. It found that in some the person helping in the suicide had been treated as the principal (author of the idea) and in others as accessory. The Board reconciled these apparently conflicting authorities on the basis of the evidence available as to the circumstances of the suicide. One of the greatest difficulties in deciding cases of contributing to a suicide was the detection of fabricated evidence designed to show that the accused had merely assisted the deceased to carry out an intention formed by the latter, rather than having himself initiated the idea. Where there was reliable evidence to the effect that the deceased had really formed the intention to kill himself, or had attempted suicide on his own, and only afterwards sought help from another who had actually killed, the latter should be sentenced as an accessory contributing active assistance and not as principal. However, for this to be the position, the Board insisted that there be available evidence from persons other than the accused as to the state of mind of the deceased. In the present case the Board found that there were independent witnesses able to show that the wife had been unable to endure her sufferings and had expressed the wish to die. Hence, it was appropriate to sentence the husband as an accessory who had contributed active assistance (entailing a noncapital sentence) and not as principal.

The Board had to consider genuinely conflicting precedents in the context of a situation arising from mistaken killing (wu sha). The province of Soochow in 1824 submitted the following facts.[59] Chang and Chu Tsai-yen were quarrelling. Chu raised his hoe to strike Chang, who parried the blow with a stick. The result was that the hoe struck and wounded Chu Shu-kuo, a bystander who had sought to intervene to make peace. He later died from the wound. The issue before the Board was: who should be held liable for the death, Chang or Chu Tsai-jen? No article or substatute covered this situation, and the Board found that its earlier decisions conflicted. Two decided in 1810 and 1818 had held the person liable whose immediate act had resulted in the victim's death, but a third, decided in 1822, had held the person liable who could be identified from the beginning as having had the intention of causing harm. In the present case the provincial authorities had followed the two earlier precedents and proposed that Chang should be sentenced to loss of life in requital under the article on killing by mistake.[60] At first the Board was inclined to agree, but the case appears to have been referred to the Statutes Commission, and the matter came to be more fully discussed.

The Commission argued that, where in the course of a quarrel one party in resisting an attack by mistake killed a third person, it should be the party making the attack who was held liable for the death. It reasoned that, although neither of the participants in the fight had intended to harm the victim, the act of resisting, which was the immediate cause of death, was itself caused by the initial blow. Moreover, the person resisting only had the intention of avoiding harm to himself. Consequently, in accordance with the principle ts'ui tso so yu ("the cause is liable for the offense")[61] the aggressor should be treated as the cause of death and sentenced to forfeiture of life. To support its reliance on the latest of the three precedents, the Commission further adduced a decision of 1822 in which it was the person whose clothes rod fell and struck a horse, and not the rider of the animal, who was held liable, where the animal bolted and caused a third person's death.[62] Consequently, in the present case Chu Tsai-jen as the person who had struck the first blow should be sentenced to strangulation after the assizes under the article on mistaken killing.

We conclude our account of the Board's use of precedent with an example in which the Board adverts to the danger of an uncontrolled reliance on leading cases. This is the decision of 1884 to which we have already referred.[63] The essential facts were as follows. In Chang's absence his wife was removed by her father, Hao, and sold to another person in marriage. Hao then pocketed the marriage payment. On his return Chang demanded his wife back, quarrelled with Hao, and in the end stabbed him to death, the circumstances disclosing the presence of an intention to kill. Two distinct issues were raised: (i) in view of his conduct, was Hao still to be treated as a father-in-law, or had he so spurned the obligations of the relationship as in effect to put himself, vis-à-vis Chang, in the position of an unrelated person, and (ii) should Chang be sentenced on the grounds that he had without authority killed a person who had committed an offense, or on the grounds that he had intentionally killed? The provincial authorities held that Hao's action in selling Chang's wife to another "broke the bond" entailed by the relationship between father-in-law and son-in-law. Hence, he should be treated as though he were not related to Chang. There was no real dispute on this point.[64] They further held that Chang should be sentenced to strangulation after the assizes in accordance with the article on the unauthorized killing of an offender.[65] It was on this point that there was a protracted difference of opinion between the province and the Board.

The Board argued that Hao's "offense" in selling Chang's wife "broke the bond" of the relationship and therefore he should be treated as an unrelated person. But it pointed out that one could not at the same time use the "offense" for a second purpose and treat Hao as falling within the definition of "offender" under the article on the unauthorized killing of an offender. This article only applied to cases in which persons with a right to seize an adulterer, thief, or like offender had killed the latter instead of capturing him. Accordingly, it sent the case back to the province for reconsideration.

The province, despite the Board's objections, affirmed its previous position. It argued that, although there was no statutory provision in the code that clearly permitted a father-in-law who had wrongfully remarried his daughter to be treated as an offender, there were certain relevant leading cases (ch'eng an). It cited the following decisions in which the Board had upheld a conviction under the article on the unauthorized killing of an offender: (i) a mother-in-law who had remarried her daughter was beaten and killed by her son-in-law (1824); (ii) a mother-in-law who, with the connivance of her daughter, had remarried her in her husband's absence was subsequently beaten and killed by her son-in-law (1819); (iii) a son-in-law procured the death of his father-in-law after the latter had remarried his daughter to another person. The province further argued that the offense committed by Hao was in fact more serious than that of theft and so fully justified the classification of his act as the unauthorized killing of an offender.

In rejecting these arguments the Board affirmed the priority of the statutory law over leading cases, and emphasized that the article on the unauthorized killing of an offender could not be applied to the present facts. After a further exchange between province and Board in which the former refused to abandon its stand, the Board in its turn cited six previous decisions of its own from the years 1863–1877 in which a son-in-law who had fought with and killed a parent-in-law, after the latter had forced his wife to marry another, had been sentenced under the ordinary law of killing in a fight. The Board accepted that these decisions conflicted with those cited by the province. In the end the case was remitted for decision to a body composed of all the central legal organs, the Three Law Offices, which resolved the matter essentially in the way favored by the Board.

Generally we may say that there is a certain similarity between the Board's application of articles or substatutes by analogy and its use of leading cases. Where no provision of the code was directly in point, the Board was required to apply one that dealt with an analogous state of affairs. But should no such analogous rule be discernible, the Board might have recourse to previous decisions that dealt with like circumstances. The difference, of course, is that the Board was legally required to apply an appropriate statutory provision, its members being liable to punishment if they failed to do so. No such mandatory requirement existed in the case of possible precedents.

10 The Role and Justification of Punishment

We propose in this chapter to examine the reasons that the imperial Chinese authorities, whether the emperor himself or his officials, gave for the infliction of pain by state agencies upon an individual on the grounds of an offense, whether or not the offense had been committed by the individual punished. We will also touch on the extent to which the imposition of punishment might be excused or mitigated through the exercise of imperial clemency. Certain factors that might secure a mitigation in punishment, such as the status of being an official or the age, youth, or infirmity of the offender, have already been discussed.[1]

Today we are accustomed to discussing punishment in the light of the possible purposes that it might fulfill, namely, public safety and deterrence, retribution, or reform.[2] The courts might impose a punishment on an individual primarily because he was regarded as a danger to the public, and so should be removed from normal social life, or because the pain inflicted on him was believed to deter others from acting in a similar manner. On the other hand, the purpose of the punishment might be seen in the element of retribution. Where an individual has acted wickedly, he has deserved punishment, in the sense that he should suffer in proportion to the wickedness of his act. Finally, pain might be inflicted on an individual to make him see the error of his ways and so reform his behavior in the future. Not uncommonly all three objectives might be present in the mind of the judge when sentencing an offender, though sometimes one will be given prominence in the reasons expressed for the sentence.

For modern Anglo-American law we have to distinguish between the objectives of the criminal law itself in establishing certain punishments for certain offenses and those of the judge in sentencing a specific offender before him. The criminal law itself may be said to be concerned primarily with protecting the public from the dangerous propensities of individuals, hence its main purpose is deterrence. Yet we cannot discount retribution as an objective of the criminal law, particularly in the context of homicide where capital punishment used to be, and in some jurisdictions still is, prescribed. In the case of some offenses, too, the legislature may be most concerned with the possibility of reforming the offender and thus prescribe a course of action designed to promote rehabilitation. However, the hallmark of much modern criminal legislation is to leave a wide measure of discretion to the judge in determining the sentence for a particular offender. It is in calculating how to exercise his discretion that a judge has considerable scope for emphasizing a deterrent, retributive, or reformative approach or in combining two or more of these approaches.

Thus, we may point immediately to a contrast with the position in traditional China. Here the legislature in the person of the emperor defined the punishments for particular offenses in such a way that the officials entrusted with the task of trying offenses had very little discretion in determining the punishment for a particular offense. Consequently, when judicial officials gave reasons for the punishment to be imposed on an individual, they were either explaining legislative policy or making a recommendation for a legislative change or for an imperial ruling in a particular case.

The Chinese sources, whether philosophical or legal, do not analyze punishment in quite the same way as modern Western thinkers. We do not find treatises or expositions that systematically explore the possible functions of punishment. Nevertheless, the language used by philosophers, emperors, or officials can be interpreted in the light of the Western terminology: deterrence, retribution, or reform. We find statements that ascribe a deterrent purpose to punishment or, alternatively or additionally, seem to focus on the element of retribution. Equally, there are emphatic statements in declarations of official policy that point to the reformative purpose of punishment.[3]

Furthermore, we may detect in the Chinese attitude to punishment an element that superficially resembles, but must be distinguished from, retribution. This is the notion of requital. We understand the difference between retribution and requital in the sense that the former presupposes moral guilt as the basis for a deserved punishment, whereas the latter predicates punishment on the notion of the harm done by the perpetrator, irrespective of the moral quality of the act. Retribution focuses on the wickedness of the offender, whereas requital focuses on the harm done to the victim. Hence, the language of compensation and forfeiture, which we have identified in the decisions of the Board of Punishments in homicide cases, reflects more the notion of requital than that of retribution.

We cannot offer a survey of discussions of punishment in all the sources of the imperial or preimperial periods. Instead, we have selected certain early classic descriptions of the functions of punishment that furnished the models for later thinking. Then we turn to statements on punishment to be found in the penal codes or their commentaries, imperial edicts, or decisions of the Board of Punishments.

The earliest (pre-Confucian) sources reveal a view of punishment as primarily deterrent.[4] The ruler should employ a combination of moral guidance and law (punishment) in his governance of the people. Where possible the people should be taught proper behavior by reflection on the conduct of the ruler and his officials. But where such guidance by example fails to secure its intended effect, the ruler should employ punishments to secure conformity with the norms of right conduct. Although punishment in this concept is used to ensure public order and the safety of the state and its citizens, there is a strong implication in this approach that, where moral guidance has failed, resort to punishment is necessary to deter potential wrongdoers from giving way to their evil impulses. Sometimes we even find an explicit acknowledgment of this point of view. Thus, when the state of Cheng in 536 B.C. inscribed its penal laws on a bronze tripod, Shu-hsiang of Chin in a famous letter criticizing the codification observed that, while the ancient kings relied principally on the moral virtues to inculcate principles of good behavior in their subjects, they still found it necessary to have punishments to awe them into avoiding wickedness.[5]

However, in what is probably the oldest extant source on law and punishment, the *K'ang kao*, dating from the foundation of the Chou dynasty,[6] we already find sketched a view of punishment that goes beyond the purely deterrent. King Wu illustrates the need for care in the use of punishments by distinguishing between offenses committed through inadvertence and those committed deliberately. In the former case the offender should not be killed, even though his offense was great, but in the latter he should die, even though his offense was small.[7] Although King Wu is discussing the infliction of the death penalty, and so does not necessarily exclude noncapital punishment for inadvertent offenses, it does not seem too fanciful to detect an element of retributive thinking in his approach. The person who has committed an offense intentionally has acted more wickedly, and therefore deserves a greater punishment, than one who has erred merely through inadvertence.

The themes of deterrence and retribution recur in the treatment of punishment by the early Legalists and Confucians, though both schools accord the former by far the more prominent place. Indeed, it seems at first glance that in Legalist discussion only the deterrent function of punishment is admitted. We find in the writings of Lord Shang and Han Fei Tzu frequent invocation of the dictum that even the lightest offenses should be punished heavily to produce a situation in which punishment will become unnecessary in society. There is also repeated emphasis on the fact that punishments should be clearly defined and rigorously applied.[8] The following passage from the *Book of Lord Shang* makes very plain the importance ascribed in the writer's thought to the deterrent effect of punishment:

What I mean by the unification of punishments is that punishments should know no degree or grade, but that from ministers of state and generals down to great officers and ordinary folk, whosoever does not obey the king's commands, violates the edicts of the state, or rebels against the statutes fixed by the ruler, should be guilty of death and should not be pardoned. Merit acquired in the past should not cause a decrease in the punishment for demerit later, nor should good behavior in the past cause any derogation of the law for wrong done later. If loyal ministers and filial sons do wrong, they should be judged according to the full measure of their guilt, and if amongst the officials, who have to maintain the law and to uphold an office, there are those who do not carry out the king's law, they are guilty of death and should not be pardoned, but their punishment should be extended to their family for three generations. Colleagues who, knowing their offense, inform their superiors will themselves escape punishment. In neither high nor low offices should there be an automatic hereditary succession to the office, rank, lands, or emoluments of officials. Therefore, do I say that if there are severe penalties that extend to the whole family, people will not dare to try (how far they can go), and as they dare not try, no punishments will be necessary. The former kings, in making their interdicts, did not put to death, or cut off people's feet, or brand people's faces, because they sought to harm those people, but with the object of prohibiting wickedness and stopping crime, for there is no better means of prohibiting wickedness and stopping crime than by making punishments heavy. If punishments are heavy and rigorously applied, then people will not dare to try (how far they can go), with the result that, in the state, there will be no people punished.[9]

Not only does Lord Shang locate the rationale of draconian punishments in their efficacy in preventing people from having recourse to wrongdoing, but he appears to exclude altogether the relevance of a retributionist justification ("the former kings . . . did not put to death, or cut off people's feet, or brand people's faces, because they sought to harm those people").

Han Fei Tzu may not have taken so extreme a view of punishment as deterrence. On occasion his language suggests that punishment had a retributive function, albeit one that was less important than its deterrent. He wrote:

Moreover, heavy penalties are not for the sole purpose of punishing criminals. The law of the intelligent sovereign, in suppressing rebels, is not disciplining only those who are being suppressed, for to discipline only the suppressed is the same as to discipline dead men only; in penalizing robbers, it is not disciplining only those who are being penalized, for to discipline only the penalized is the same as to discipline convicts only. Hence the saying: "Take seriously one culprit's crime and suppress all wickedness within the boundaries." This is the way to attain order. For the heavily punished are robbers, but the terrified and trembling are good people. Therefore, why should those who want order doubt the efficacy of heavy penalties? [10]

This passage suggests that, while the prime object of punishing murderers and robbers was to ensure that people were so terrified that they would not commit murder or robbery, the actual criminals were also punished because they had acted wickedly and so deserved punishment.

Neither Lord Shang nor Han Fei Tzu appears to have accepted King Wu's dictum that intentional offenses should be punished capitally, whereas inadvertent offenses might be pardoned. Not only is the rejection of this proposition implicit in the statement that heavy punishments should be imposed for light offenses, but a graphic story told in both sources to illustrate the merits of harsh punishment reveals the irrelevance of intention. When Duke Wen of Chin had summoned an assembly of his lords for a certain time, one of his favorites arrived late. The duke had him cut in two at the waist to demonstrate the importance of obedience to the ruler's orders.[11]

Confucius and Mencius place far less stress than the Legalists on the use of punishment in government and hence say very little about it, preferring to dwell on the importance of properly moral conduct on the part of the ruler to the well-being of the state. Their few remarks on the subject of punishment seem to stem from the notion that in any society there are some persons who are so incorrigible that they are immune to teaching and moral guidance. The only way to induce such persons to observe proper behavior is through fear of punishment, even though this is a much less satisfactory social mechanism than genuine conviction of error and repentance. A well-known passage from the Analects of Confucius states: "If you govern the people by laws and keep them in order by penalties, they will avoid the penalties yet lose their sense of shame. But if you govern them by your moral excellence, and keep them in order by your dutiful conduct, they will retain their sense of shame, and also live up to this standard."[12]

Mencius writes of those who encourage their ruler to engage in wars: "In wars to gain land, the dead fill the plains; in wars to gain cities, the dead fill the cities. This is known as showing the land the way to devour human flesh. Hence those skilled in war should suffer the most severe punishments; those who secure alliances with other feudal lords come next, and then come those who open up waste lands and increase the yield of the soil."[13] Although we cannot rule out a possible interpretation that warmongers and others who harm the state are to be punished because they have shown that they are entirely indifferent to moral principles and so deserve to be punished for their wickedness, the primary thrust of Mencius's strictures is probably that the only way to deter persons from promoting wars and the like is the threat of heavy punishment.

The fullest and certainly the most interesting account of punishment in early Confucian writing is given by Hsün Tzu. He did not accept that human nature was fundamentally good, nor did he agree that a ruler could largely dispense with punishments in favor of moral guidance. In his essay entitled *On The Correction of Errors* Hsün Tzu offers what may even be termed a theory of punishment.[14] He desires to refute the misconception that the punishments applied by the ancient kings were no more than symbolic. It is essential, he observes, that a murderer should be punished with death and that a person who has assaulted another should be physically punished (by mutilation). A person who has committed a serious offense cannot be allowed to escape with the lightest kind of punishment. At this point in his argument Hsün Tzu states the purpose of punishment in the following terms: "The origin of all punishment is the restraint of violence, the hatred of evil, and the warning against its further occurrence."[15] This purpose can be realized only when the punishment matches or fits (*tang*) the crime. The word *tang* suggests that the degree of punishment must be directly proportional to the gravity of the offense.

There is no greater misfortune, Hsün Tzu declares, than the failure of punishment to match the deed that calls it forth. Where punishment fits the crime, there is good government; where it does not, there is bad.

Hsün Tzu also emphasizes the need for the punishment to match the crime. Where this is so, the people will be in awe (*wei*),[16] in the sense that they will accept the authority of the legal regime, since they recognize the justice of the punishments.[17] Bad government is found, and disorder ensues, where excessive punishments are imposed. As an example of excessive punishment Hsün Tzu cites the practice of putting the offender's whole family to death, even though they have not been involved in his offense.[18]

The doctrine that the punishment should match the crime, Hsün Tzu holds, has to be applied with caution. In the case of incorrigible evildoers or really serious offenses, an appropriate punishment should be imposed. But rulers should not be too hasty in their resort to punishments. Although Hsün Tzu accepts that rulers should kill the incorrigibly evil without trying to reform them, he argues that those who are merely perverse and lazy should be given an opportunity to reform. They should be encouraged by the prospect of reward and warned by the threat of punishment.[19] Generally, the ruler should furnish the people with instruction before proceeding to punishment. But once the people have been instructed, should they continue to commit offenses, then they must be punished. Otherwise it will not be possible to control depravity.[20]

In Hsün Tzu's account of the functions of punishment we can detect a deterrent and retributive—and possibly also a reformative— element. The frequent references to punishment as a warning, as being needed to restrain violence and evildoing, make plain its deterrent role. Embodied within this broad concept there seems to be a reformative aspect. The threat of punishment is intended to act as a deterrent, but at the same time it constitutes a powerful incentive to reform. By placing the possibility of physical punishment before the mind of a person who is harboring evil plans, the ruler hopes not only to deter him from the commission of evil but also to bring about a change in his moral perspective. Both the deterrent and the reformative aspects become more striking when a potential offender is not only aware of the fact that he may incur punishment but sees the punishment actually applied to another who has been detected in the commission of an offense.

The retributive function can be discerned from the insistence on matching the punishment to the crime. In part what Hsün Tzu wishes to emphasize by such a statement is the fact that the system of punishment operated by the ruler must as a whole be regarded by the people as credible. They must have trust in its efficacy and impartiality; otherwise, they will not be deterred from the commission of offenses. But it does not seem that this is all that is to be implied from the requirement that the punishment match the offense. It is also implicit in such an assertion that attention should be paid to the element of desert. A person who has committed an offense deserves to be punished, but only in proportion to the gravity of the offense. Hence, Hsün Tzu finds it impossible to accept that an innocent person, one who has not committed an offense, should be punished. The reason (although not explicitly articulated) is that such a person has not deserved punishment and thus its imposition would be unjust. Indeed, it is arguably the very fact of desert, the conviction in people's minds that the law punishes only those who have deserved to be punished, and then only to the extent of that desert, which helps to sustain the credibility of the system of punishment operated by the ruler and induce its acceptance by his subjects.[21]

Although Hsün Tzu's treatment of punishment did not furnish the direct model for the policies displayed in the penal codes and the decisions of the Board of Punishments, it no doubt had an important influence on the way later Confucian-educated officials understood and practiced the art of government. What we do see reflected in later penal policy is each of the principal elements discernible in Hsün Tzu's account of punishment: the deterrent, the retributive, and the reformative. Other influences cannot be discounted, including that of the principle of requital, especially in the context of homicide. The strongly deterrent approach of Legalist thought probably influenced the treatment of the most serious offenses against the state or the family. For such offenses the punishment of relatives was retained, although Hsün Tzu himself had expressly disapproved of such a policy. It is nevertheless interesting that the justifications presented during the imperial period for the punishment of relatives do not rely purely on its deterrent effect.[22] In exploring the reasons for the punishment of offenders or their relatives we will consider first the actual provisions of the penal codes together with their explanatory commentaries, and then the reasoning found in decisions of the Ch'ing Board of Punishments or imperial edicts issued in particular cases.

THE PENAL CODES

All the codes operated with the five standard punishments: beating with the light stick, beating with the heavy stick, penal servitude for periods from one to three years, life exile to distances of two thousand to three thousand *li*, and death by strangulation or beheading. Additional punishments were added to the codes from time to time: branding, the wearing of the cangue, exile to four thousand *li*, enslavement, castration, and death by slicing.[23] We will consider first the way in which the punishments were used to achieve the regeneration of the criminal. Then we will seek to determine the extent to which their function was intended by the legislators to be deterrent or retributive.

The relationship between punishment and reform of the offender can be traced in two distinct ways. On the one hand, there is the important rule, found in all the penal codes, that provides for exemption from or mitigation of punishment where the offender has truly repented, as evidenced by his voluntary confession prior to discovery of the offense.[24] On the other hand, the noncapital punishments might be imposed to induce in the offender a sense of shame and so secure for the future a change of conduct on his part. This notion is coupled with the belief that an offender might "renew himself" through community service. We find evidence that beating, branding, the cangue, penal servitude, and even exile were conceived as mechanisms for inducing in the offender a sense of shame and repentance.

The *shu-i* commentary of the T'ang code explains the purpose of inflicting a beating with the light stick (between ten and fifty blows) as follows: "If a person commits a small offense the law must discipline him. Therefore beating is used to shame him. . . . The stick is employed in teaching [persons to be moral]."[25] The explanatory commentary of the Ch'ing code states that the offender is lightly chastised to make an example and to cause shame to spring up in his breast.[26] This statement assigns a dual function to the punishment, that of securing repentance and that of acting as a deterrent to others. A similar dual function underlies the other light punishments used during the Ch'ing, branding and the wearing of the cangue. Consistent thieves were tattooed with characters indicating the nature of their offense. The intention was both to provide a public example to act as a deterrent and to humiliate thieves in order to procure their repentance. If they showed genuine repentance, as by helping the authorities catch other thieves, the tattooed characters might be removed.[27]

A common Ch'ing punishment, especially for thieves and adulterous women, was the wearing of the cangue, a large wooden collar placed around the neck, which effectively prevented the offender from feeding him or herself. To it was attached a placard stating the nature of the offense. Again, the intention was not only to provide a warning to the public not to commit a like offense but also to humiliate the offender to induce a sense of shame and repentance.[28]

Sometimes even penal servitude and certain forms of exile appear to have been regarded as reformative, the underlying idea being the power of work to regenerate the offender and allow him through public service to atone for and redeem his offense. The T'ang shu-i commentary notes that penal servitude is a kind of slavery that shames the offender, and it quotes a passage from the Rites of Chou suggesting that one of the purposes of the punishment was to teach the offender to improve his conduct.[29] Although a regenerative function may have been ascribed to the regular punishment of life exile,[30] nothing is said to this effect in the legal commentaries. However, it is clear that such a function was attributed to the special punishment of exile to Sinkiang introduced by the Ch'ing in the middle of the eighteenth century to provide a harsher punishment for serious offenders than ordinary exile (still falling short of death) and to assist in the colonization and development of the newly acquired frontier region situated between Tibet and Outer Mongolia. In a detailed study of this punishment Joanna Waley-Cohen has shown that the Ch'ing government was applying a fundamental Neo-Confucian principle to its penal policy, that is, the principle of regeneration through socially valuable work and good conduct ("self-renewal"). Those exiled to Sinkiang, whether as slaves or just as colonists, were given a chance to redeem themselves through their good behavior and so secure emancipation or permission to return to China proper. For example, we are told that in 1759 "the [Chien-lung] emperor affirmed that the purpose of sending convicts to Xinjiang [Sinkiang] was to clear the crowded heartland, to settle the new frontier, and, through punishment, to offer criminals a means of redeeming themselves."[31]

We have already noted the fact that those punishments designed to shame the offender into repentance and reform were also designed to act as deterrents. Although the function of deterrence is not as such emphasized in the penal codes or their commentaries, probably because it was deemed self-evident, the very existence of a penal code and its range of punishments was clearly inspired by the need to secure public order, to protect the public from indiscriminate violence, and to deter individuals from behavior held to be contrary to the norms of good conduct. But it is doubtful whether the sole function of either the institution of punishment as such or the prescription of specific punishments for individual offenses was conceived to be the deterrent. We will develop this point later in our discussion of the retributive function. For the moment we may illustrate it by adducing the main examples in the codes in which persons were punished on account of an offense committed by another, namely, the punishment of colleagues for errors committed by an official in the conduct of his duties,[32] and the punishment of relatives on account of rebellion and the like.[33] Prima facie the extension of punishment to persons other than the actual offender appears to be motivated purely by considerations of deterrence. We may also recall that the Legalists treated the punishment of relatives as the most effective possible deterrent.[34] Yet deterrence does not seem to have been the only purpose assigned by the legislators to the punishment imposed on the colleagues or relatives of an offender.

Under the rules on collegiate liability of officials, where a particular official committed an error, even though inadvertent, not only he but also his colleagues, that is, those who worked in the same office and were associated with him in the making of the erroneous decision, were subjected to punishment. One might explain this phenomenon on the grounds that colleagues were thereby encouraged to greater vigilance or indeed had even themselves committed a fault in failing to notice the error. From this perspective the primary function of the punishment of colleagues might be viewed as deterrent, in the sense that it was designed to deter officials generally from neglecting their duties. While some such thought may help to explain the survival of the system of collegiate liability for many centuries, it is doubtful whether it is the only rationale. The original viewpoint may simply have been that, where officials working together produced a wrong decision, they had all collectively committed a breach of duty calling for punishment. The basis for punishment, on this interpretation, was the breach of duty committed by each individual who had participated in making the decision, even though the actual error could be attributed to one of them alone.[35]

The punishment of relatives, which appears at the time of its inception in Legalist thought to have been conceived as the ultimate deterrent, is not presented along these lines in the commentaries to the penal codes. It is perfectly credible that emperors continued to regard the possibility of such punishment as a highly effective deterrent with respect to rebellion and the like. But the legal commentaries show that other factors were also invoked to explain the severity of the punishment.[36] The T'ang *shu-i* commentary says: "Plotting rebellion and great sedition are criminal to the utmost degree of censure and extinction. Such crimes defile the whole family and the eradication of evil must reach to the roots."[37] The implication is that the whole family in some way has shared in the evil of the individual who has rebelled, and so all deserve to be punished. Ch'ing commentaries, without speaking of the eradication of evil, justify the punishment of adult relatives on the grounds that they must personally have been at fault in that they would have known of the plot and yet have done nothing to prevent it or warn the authorities.[38] On the other hand, official dicta sometimes reflect the same point of view as the T'ang commentary.[39] Essentially what one has expressed in these commentaries and dicta is a retributive (and not just a deterrent) justification for the punishment of relatives.

Examination of the scheme of specific offenses and their punishments established by the codes makes it clear that the legislators were activated by considerations of retribution or requital as well as by those of deterrence or reform. We have already noted the great care taken to adjust the punishment to the gravity of the offense. This was not a crude operation. Situations that called for punishment were scrutinized in the greatest detail by those responsible for recommending laws. Meticulous comparisons were made with existing offenses to ensure that just the right quantum of punishment was prescribed for the newly created offense. We may recall the infinite gradations of punishment dictated by the precise relationship of the offender and the victim. Relevant in determining the gravity of the offense, and hence the punishment, was not only the question of seniority but also the length of the period for which the offender was required to mourn the victim.[40]

It is difficult to explain the scrupulous attention paid to achieving the exact fit between punishment and offense by recourse only to the notion of deterrence. Characteristically, a punishment imposed simply to deter may be far more severe than the nature of the offense appears to warrant. This had been the hallmark of the Legalist approach, which had insisted that even the lightest offenses should receive heavy punishment. The approach of the penal codes is quite different. Punishment is to be precisely in proportion to the gravity of the offense. Gravity was assessed by reference partly to the consequences of the deed, for example, whether a life had been lost or one of the fundamental human relationships infringed, and partly to the presence or absence in the offender of an intention to harm. In particular cases, too, account was taken of the overall wickedness of the act. All this suggests that some attention at least was paid to the need for retribution as well as to requital for harm, a notion not necessarily predicated on the moral guilt of the offender.[41]

We cite from the penal code three specific illustrations of nondeterrent thinking. The first is the conviction that a person who has caused the death of another should give his own life in requital. The underlying idea is that the loss of life by the victim requires to be compensated or balanced by the loss of the offender's life. This idea is vividly expressed in the highly popular literary genre of the ghost tale. Many of these tales are concerned with the avenging ghosts of those who have been killed. Where human justice has been unable to bring the perpetrator to book, the ghost of the deceased will take vengeance on the killer or a member of his family, or in some cases a descendant.[42] The law, as we have seen in an earlier chapter,[43] adopts a nuanced approach and does not require the offender in all cases actually to forfeit his life. Yet the basis from which it evolves the detailed rules on homicide is precisely the principle of requital through which the value of human life is itself affirmed.

The second illustration is taken from the rules developed under the Ch'ing to deal with persons who, in a fit of madness, had killed another. The main thrust of the complex legislation on insane killers was to ensure the safety of the public. Hence, in general those convicted of killing while mad were to be kept permanently confined in prison, and they were not to be released until it was absolutely certain that there was no further danger to the public. However, in certain cases of killing regarded as exceptionally grave, the killer was still to be put to death. These were cases in which either a close senior relative or two or more persons in one family had been killed. The reason for the exaction of the death penalty in such cases was not the desire to protect the public from the insane killer, but the wickedness of the actual deed. The only appropriate response was conceived to be the death of the perpetrator. This means, not that personal blame was ascribed to the killer, but that the gravity of the act in itself entailed the punishment of death by way of requital.[44]

Finally, we have the rule stated from time to time in the Ch'ing code in the context of the most atrocious offenses that, should the offender die before the sentence of the law could be implemented, his body was still to be subjected to the appropriate form of execution. For example, the article on the premeditated killing of a parent or paternal grandparent provides that, should the offender have died in prison, the punishment of death by slicing was still to be executed on his corpse.[45] The legal commentaries suggest that the reason for this rule was the sheer wickedness of the deed, which called for the infliction of the death penalty, even though the offender had died from natural causes. It is said that, although he has received the justice of heaven, the nature of his deed also calls for the full execution of human justice.[46] By contrast, the commentaries, when explaining the rule imposing exposure of the offender's head in certain very serious offenses, stress that the reason is to inspire fear and deter others from like conduct.[47]

When citing the treatment of insane killers or parricides, we have spoken of "the wickedness of the deed." This formulation leaves open the question of whether the thinking behind the penal rules was strictly retributive or focused more on the principle of requital. The former implies that the offender has been morally wicked and so deserves a punishment proportional to the evil of his thought. On the other hand, the latter looks at the consequences of the individual's act, and proportions the severity of the punishment to the amount of harm. When we speak of "the wickedness of the act" in the context of an insane killer, the very fact of insanity should preclude retribution, since the killer has not had an evil design. Hence, in this context the principle of requital must account for the severity of the punishment. By contrast, in the context of parricide "the wickedness of the act" imports a reference to the wickedness of the offender's intention, and hence the severity of the punishment rests on retribution. Although we have made this clear analytic distinction between retribution and requital, we may wonder whether the Chinese legislators themselves drew the distinction in such stark terms. They may have operated more with a loose notion of retribution in which strict retribution and requital both played an undifferentiated part.

THE BOARD AND THE THRONE

The dominant theme in the reasoning of the Board, when considering provisional recommendations for sentence, is the need for the equalizing or balancing (p'ing) of the facts (ch'ing) and the law (fa). We also find frequent references, not only by the Board but also by the throne itself, to the need for punishment to repress wickedness and debauchery, to give effect to some particular value such as chastity, to serve as a warning, to promote teaching and good morals, "to cover the guilt (pi ku)," or to be equitable and just (p'ing yüan or yün hsieh). Before evaluating what is to be learned from this language as to the approach to punishment of the throne and its officials, we will give some illustrations of the Board's reasoning taken mainly from cases decided from the middle of the eighteenth to the middle of the nineteenth century.

In a Yunnan case of 1778[48] a son had quarrelled with his mother's lover and killed him in a fight. In shame at the public disclosure of the adultery, both his father and mother committed suicide. Under the law then in force, where a son had committed a capital offense and his parents in consequence had committed suicide, the execution entailed by the original offense was to be immediate, that is, there was to be no possibility of reprieve. The Board therefore recommended in this case that the son should be sentenced to immediate strangulation. The throne, while admitting that the Board had correctly identified the law, held that the sentence in relation to the facts of the case was not equitable (yün hsieh, lit. "in agreement and harmony"). The son had some justification for killing his mother's lover. Were he to be sentenced to immediate strangulation, there would be no matching (p'ing) of the circumstances (shih) with principle or reason (li). The throne further pointed out that immediate execution was appropriate only where the son's own wrongful conduct had led to his parents' suicide. For this case the law should be strict, in order to make clear the meaning of punishment as an assistance to teaching.[49] In response to the throne's edict, the Board proposed a new substatute in order that for future cases the facts and the law should match and equity (yün hsieh) should be increasingly manifested.[50]

From Szechuan in 1779 the following case was reported.[51] Two nine-year-old boys, while pasturing sheep, fought, with the result that one fell and received injuries from which he died. Both the province and the Board had recommended that the survivor should be sentenced to strangulation after the assizes in accordance with the article on killing in a fight, but they adduced for the throne's consideration the substatute permitting leniency in the case of children aged ten or under who had killed another person. The throne went into the case in some detail. It observed first that the substatute permitting leniency referred only to the case in which the victim had been considerably older than the offender. It further pointed out that in the present case the offender had been in the wrong, since he had started the fight. Consequently, to pity him on account of his youth and without reflection reprieve him from death would not lead to the matching of the facts and law. The throne suggested that the proper course was to record a sentence of death, but at the autumn assizes commute the execution to imprisonment, and after a few years release the offender, once his violent nature had been tamed. It was necessary to strike the right balance in the use of punishments, so as to evidence the intent to tame the cruel and give warning to the wicked.[52]

In a Soochow case of 1792[53] a Buddhist pupil in righteous anger killed his master on account of the latter's adulterous relationship with his mother. The Board had proposed a sentence of strangulation after the assizes in accordance with the terms of the substatute on sons who killed their mother's lover.[54] However, the throne, in all the circumstances of the case, did not regard this proposal as equitable. There was no harmony between the facts and the law, since debauchery had not been adequately penalized and no allowance had been made for righteous anger. The Board was asked to reconsider the case. It eventually proposed a sentence of penal servitude that was approved by the throne.

In a Honan case of 1817[55] the Board considered the complex legislation under which the liability of the husband or relative who killed the adulterous wife or lover was to be determined. Punishment varied according to the time and place at which the killing occurred.[56] These detailed rules, the Board observed, were designed to achieve a balance between the repression of debauchery and respect for the value of human life. It found that the provincial authorities in a number of cases had not properly understood the thought underlying the sub-statutes, and hence had made mistakes in the matching (p'ing) of the facts (ch'ing) and the law (fa).

Cases involving women killing their daughters-in-law often caused difficulty. In 1822 the Board gave a full exposition of the principles that should govern this kind of homicide.[57] The province of Szechuan had submitted a case in which a woman had killed her daughter-in-law to prevent her disclosing an adulterous relationship that the older woman had been conducting. The Board had some difficulty in determining the appropriate sentence. First, it cited a substatute of 1771[58] providing that, where a daughter-in-law had discovered her mother-in-law in an act of adultery and the latter, after unsuccess-fully attempting to involve her daughter-in-law in the debauchery, had plotted to kill her to prevent disclosure, the relationship was to be disregarded, and the mother-in-law was to be sentenced to behead-ing after the assizes under the ordinary law on plotting to kill (mou sha). The imperial edict promulgating the substatute had noted that the punishment originally proposed for this offense, viz, the enslave-ment and deportation of the mother-in-law, was inadequate to ensure the protection of chastity and preserve good principles and morality. Punishment must be made clear in order to assist education. Hence, the ordinary law of mou sha was to be applied. In the autumn the case was to be placed in the list for actual execution in order to act as a warning to the wicked and demonstrate the power of the law.[59]

Next, the Board cited a substatute of 1783/1821[60] according to which a woman who took a dislike to her daughter-in-law because of some verbal disagreement, and in consequence plotted to kill her, was to be sent to a Manchu garrison as a slave. The imperial edict au-thorizing this substatute remarked that the punishment of ordinary exile previously applied in such cases was insufficient "to cover the guilt [pi ku]."[61]

The Board made its own comments on these substatutes. It ex-plained the severity of the punishment prescribed in the substatute of 1771 as a warning to the debauched and evil and as a consolation to those who have remained inflexible in their chastity.[62] It noted also that the present facts fell midway between the situations contemplated by the existing substatutes. Hitherto, the practice in dealing with women who had killed their daughters-in-law to prevent disclosure of adultery had been to sentence them to capital punishment with commutation in the autumn to permanent imprisonment. The provincial authorities had recommended simply that the mother-in-law should be sentenced to strangulation after the assizes. This should be corrected in line with previous decisions by the insertion of the proviso that the execution should be commuted to imprisonment. Finally, the matter was referred to the Supreme Court of Justice, which endorsed the Board's recommendation that the offender be sentenced to capital punishment with commutation to permanent imprisonment. In this way the matching of the facts and the law would be made clear.[63]

In 1824 the following facts were submitted to the Board from the province of Shensi.[64] Cheng became angry when his ten-year-old son continued to play with his eight-year-old friend Sun instead of going on an errand. He hurled his tobacco pipe at his son, who dodged. Instead, the pipe hit and killed Sun. The provincial governor had proposed a sentence of strangulation after the assizes under the article on fighting and by mistake killing a third person.[65] The Board pointed out that the article applied to the case where two unrelated persons were fighting, not to that in which a father was attempting to beat his son. Hence, it was not equitable (p'ing) to apply the article to the present facts. Hitherto, in cases where a parent had plotted to kill a son but by mistake had killed a third person, leniency was shown and a noncapital sentence imposed. Similarly, where a father in the course of beating his son by mistake killed a third person, there should be a decrease in punishment to make clear that the facts and the law were matched. Accordingly, the appropriate sentence for Cheng was exile to two thousand li.

Some of the decisions in cases involving multiple killings or liability of relatives ("joint liability") also offer instructive comments by the Board or the throne. In a Shantung case of 1815 in which a person had killed six members of one family, the provincial authorities had sentenced two accomplices only to exile, the principal offender having already been killed by relatives of the victim. The Board held that this recommendation was not equitable (p'ing yün) and was entirely inadequate to serve as a warning against wickedness and to redress wrongs. The governor was ordered to reconsider the case, and it appears that in the end at least one of the accomplices was sentenced to immediate beheading.[66]

With respect to the article on killing three or more persons in one family, the Board in a Kuangsi case of 1821[67] noted that the law deemed it to be insufficient "to cover the guilt" merely to exact the life of the killer in requital. Consequently, the punishment was to include the exile of his wife and children. It was then sufficient to repress wickedness and redress the wrong.

In a Shansi case of 1828[68] the Board reviewed the history of the legislation on "joint liability" imposed in offenses of multiple killings. An imperial edict of 1789 stated that, where three or more persons in one family had been killed, the sons of the killer, irrespective of age, were to be handed over to the Imperial Household department and castrated. In this way the evil would not be transmitted, and the punishment would be sufficient "to cover the guilt."[69] The meaning is that castration was sufficient to ensure discontinuance of the killer's family line without the necessity of putting the sons to death.

The Board also quoted a memorial of 1793 from the Imperial Household Department, which suggested that sons aged 15 or below should remain within the palace as eunuchs, whereas those aged 16 or above should be sent to a distant frontier region as slaves. The reason given was that young children could still be molded and influenced, whereas, in the case of the older sons, there was the fear that their wicked spirit or air (ch'i)[70] would make them difficult to control. The thought expressed here is that further punishment of the young sons was not necessary because they could be taught to improve, whereas improvement was deemed to be impossible in the case of the older sons, and so they should be placed in a position in which they might cause no harm in the future.

Running throughout all these decisions is the theme that the sentence imposing punishment should be equitable; the law and the facts should be matched. What exactly is to be understood by this concern? It appears to be clear that several rather different factors may be relevant to the equity of the punishment. Sometimes we find it stressed that the punishment must be sufficient to act as a warning to others and to reinforce teaching and good morals. Here we have an appeal to the deterrent function of punishment, but not deterrence in the Legalist sense of simply securing the good order of the state as determined by the ruler. This is only one aspect of the thinking of the Board and the throne. The other is the need to deter people from infringing proper conduct as prescribed by Confucian morality. The point of punishment is to make it abundantly clear to the emperor's subjects that they should all ensure that they learn and abide by the canons of properly moral behavior. It is thus not here a question of simple deterrence, but of deterrence coupled with the objective of teaching plain morality through the infliction of punishment. We may recall in this context the structure of the Sacred Edict in its expanded version. The emperor explains at great length the moral duties of his subjects, then quotes from the code the punishments to which they are exposed if they fail to accept and implement the imperial instructions.[71]

By contrast, language such as "redress the grievance" or "cover the guilt" imports a reference to retribution rather than deterrence. The context in which these expressions occur is usually one in which the wickedness of the offender's conduct is being stressed, wickedness arising from deliberate wrongdoing and not inadvertent error. Hence, we may speak of a conception of punishment in such cases as retributive in the sense that the moral guilt, the evil of the offender, deserves punishment in proportion to its extent. The extent of the evil may be measured by reference not only to the initial intention but also to the circumstances in which the deed has been accomplished, the degree of savagery displayed, and the like.

From retribution we have to distinguish the notion of requital often invoked in cases of homicide. The principle that a person who has caused the death of another should lose his own life in requital does not reflect a notion of punishment for moral guilt, since the degree of such guilt may be negligible, such as when death results from a fight or a game. The dominant notion, rather, is that the value that must necessarily attach to human life can only be upheld if the law is seen to require the loss of the killer's life in requital. A further element underlying the strength of the principle of requital appears to have been the widely held and deeply seated belief in the power of the victim's ghost to cause harm, if no adequate requital for his or her death has been made.[72]

Sometimes, too, punishment is deemed to match the offense only if proper regard has been had for some value deemed important by society. We have already in this context adverted to the value of human life itself. Another value frequently mentioned by the throne or the Board is that associated with female chastity. Where chastity has been threatened, the punishment of the offender should reflect the importance that society attaches to the preservation of a woman's virtue. A related matter to which the Board pays attention in determining punishment is the righteousness of the anger aroused by attacks on chastity. A son who becomes angry over his mother's adulterous relationship and kills her lover in a fight will not be treated as deserving the kind of punishment that would be appropriate if his anger had arisen from a different cause, such as a quarrel over money.

PUNISHMENT AND HARM

One of the factors taken into account by the Board or the throne in determining the appropriate punishment for a specific offense is the amount of harm actually done. Although this consideration is not given special prominence in the reasoning of judicial decisions or imperial edicts, often being incorporated within some such phrase as "repress wickedness and debauchery," it is given a distinctive role in certain rules established by the penal codes. We have already adduced one of these, namely, that which qualifies the exemption from punishment accorded an offender who has confessed prior to discovery. No exemption or mitigation is to be accorded in respect of offenses from which irreversible harm has flowed. Thus, in a case of theft, exemption can be given should the stolen property be returned, but in cases of death or physical injury, no exemption is possible, since the harm cannot be undone.[73] Other rules disclose a similar perspective, especially in the context of liability of officials. Where an official had made a bad decision, in principle all those associated with the decision were liable to punishment. However, should any of those involved in the decision realize the mistake and bring it to light prior to implementation, there was to be exemption from liability for all.[74] A special application of this rule governed the liability of judicial officials who gave a wrong judgment. The severity of the punishment depended on whether the judge had wrongfully convicted or acquitted a person. Yet in both cases there was to be a reduction in punishment of one degree (not complete exemption) should no harm have been done by the mistaken sentence. This refers to the fact that in a case of wrongful conviction the sentence should not actually have been carried out prior to discovery of the mistake, or in a case of wrongful acquittal the offender should not have been released or, if released, have been recaptured or, in either case, should have died from natural causes.[75]

CONCLUSION

Our analysis of punishment in traditional Chinese thinking differs from that offered by a number of Western scholars. A view deeply entrenched in Western scholarship is that the Chinese educated elite, responsible for the administration of justice, regarded punishment as a means of maintaining cosmic harmony. Offenses were regarded as upsetting the proper balance that should be observed between human behavior and natural phenomena. Failure on the part of humans to behave in the correct way upset the balance and might bring about disturbances in the course of natural phenomena, unless the imbalance was corrected through the implementation of appropriate punishment by the authorities of the state.[76]

We do not wish to deny that sometimes there is expressed an overt belief on the part of emperors and their officials that the widespread or atrocious perpetuation of injustices had led to unfavorable responses on the part of natural phenomena (for example, floods or droughts). We also accept that there may be a "core of truth" in the cosmic harmony theory of punishment in the sense that it focuses on the need for a response to an offense that can be described in terms of "requital" or "retribution." The point we wish to emphasize is that none of the recommendations of the Board of Punishments or the decisions of the throne that we have examined betray any sign that, in the day-to-day administration of the penal system, the punishment of offenses was regarded as a mechanism for the restoration of a disturbed cosmic harmony.[77]

Karl Bünger, a Western sinologist who has written a great deal about the traditional Chinese legal system, has asserted that punishment in China was not revenge, or retribution, or a means for retraining or educating the offender. Focusing on the old Legalist (and also Confucian) principle that the purpose of punishment was to end the need for punishment, he concludes that punishment was conceived in a purely rational sense as a means of deterrence or, in some cases, as necessary for the protection and safety of the public.[78] We accept that both deterrence and the safety of the public as well as that of the state were important objectives of punishment, but we cannot agree that a retributive or reformative function was altogether lacking. The evidence we have surveyed seems clearly to show that some punishments were conceived under a predominantly reformative aspect, although they might also have been regarded as deterrents, while the punishment of offenders generally possessed a nondeterrent and nonreformative character that is best described in terms of "retribution" or "requital." Nor can we be sure that a deep-seated instinct for revenge did not play a part in the formulation of the rules that prescribed the punishment for particularly grave offenses such as homicide.

Nor do we find compelling a recently propounded view according to which the penal process of traditional China was "disciplinary" rather than "adjudicative."[79] On this theory the only purpose of punishment was the disciplining of subordinates for disobedience to orders. The superior (here the emperor) might punish his inferiors as he pleased, whenever he considered that there was a need to reestablish hierarchical submission and control over the group. There was no conception of punishing the individual on the grounds of a specific offense, no adherence to the principle *nulla poena sine lege*,[80] and it made no difference whether it was the person who had been insubordinate or another member of the group who was disciplined. All that was necessary was that the group as a whole be kept in a state of due obedience.

It is true both that emperors and their officials were concerned that their subordinates obeyed orders and that traditional Chinese society was organized according to a strict hierarchy of inferiors and superiors. It is also true that the emperor retained a residual power of punishment that he might exercise either independently of the judicial authorities or in response to their recommendation.[81] Nevertheless, the reduction of the penal system in traditional China to the disciplining of subordinates who have failed to obey orders can only be described as a gross distortion. The very essence of the penal codes was to define the conditions under which specific offenses were committed by individuals and to prescribe the punishment appropriate to the offense. The task of the judicial authorities was to conduct a scrupulous investigation of the facts and the law to determine whether those conditions had been met and, if so, whether the correct sentence had been imposed. The emperor might vary the sentence proposed by the Board, but, except perhaps in certain political cases that directly threatened the stability of the regime, he did so in accordance with well-established principles by which the gravity of the offense and the appropriate punishment were to be determined.

NOTES

Preface

1   Richter, *Political Theory of Montesquieu*, 279.
2   See Stephens, *Order and Discipline in China*, and Vandermeersch, "An Enquiry into the Chinese Conception of the Law."
3   See, for example, Bünger, "Concluding Remarks," 313ff.
4   Cf. the perceptive observations of Ladany, *Law and Legality in China*, 33.
5   This was already noted by the sixteenth-century Jesuit Matteo Ricci. See Gernet, "Introduction," xxi.

Chapter 1: Historical Overview of the Traditional Chinese Legal System

1   Hucker, "Confucianism and the Chinese Censorial System," 185.
2   Cf. the remarks of Bünger, "Entstehung und Wandel des Rechts in China," 455, expressing reservation as to the use of the term "Confucianization of law." There is also an illuminating account of this question in Liu, "Origin and Early Development of Chinese Law and the Penal System."
3   See Creel, *Origins of Statecraft in China*, 1:450f.
4   Par. 16 in Karlgren, *Book of Documents*, 42.
5   See Creel, "Legal Institutions and Procedures during the Chou Dynasty," 35, 37 for a translation and discussion of the relevant passages.
6   A century after Lord Shang (on whom see note 9 below), the Ch'in laws of the third century B.C. show that aristocrats were punished less severely than commoners. See the observations of Hulsewé, *Remnants of Ch'in Law*, 7f.
7   Ch'ü, *Law and Society in Traditional China*, 267ff.
8   No earlier codes have survived, except in fragments.
9   Lord Shang was chief minister of the state of Ch'in in the latter part of the fourth century B.C. and a founder of the Legalist school. For an account of his life and a translation of the writings ascribed to him see Duyvendak, *Book of Lord Shang*. Han Fei Tzu was a member of the ruling house of the state of Han who died in 233 B.C. without having held important political office. His extensive writings have been translated by W. K. Liao.

10 Duyvendak, *Lord Shang*, 197, 199.

11 Cf. Ibid., 16, 19f.

12 See further chap. 6 (officials) and chap. 7 (age, youth and infirmity).

13 See the remarks of Meijer on the complexity of the Ch'ing legislation on homicide arising from adultery, *Murder and Adultery in Late Imperial China*, x, 47, 49, 123; and cf. also McKnight, *Law and Order in Sung China*, 268–69.

14 See more on moral puritanism in chap. 4 (Neo-Confucianism) and in chap. 5 (family relationships).

15 It is expressed in *San Tzu Ching* (Three Character Classic), the main primer since Sung times for young children. See Phen's edition and translation at p. 31. On this book and other manuals used for the education of children see Rawski, "Economic and Social Foundations of Late Imperial Culture," 29ff., and Wu, "Education of Children in the Sung," 322f.

16 See more on the adoption of a male heir in chap. 3 at n. 34 and in chap. 5 at nn. 42f.

17 Cf. Legge, *Chinese Classics*, 2:132; Lau, *Mencius*, 52.

18 See the terms of the valedictory edict of the Ch'ing emperor K'ang-hsi, quoted in chap. 2 at n. 16.

19 See more on the ruler's benevolence in chap. 7.

20 See more on confession by relatives in chap. 7.

21 For the Ch'ing code see Philastre 1:321; Boulais, 272; Staunton, 64; Jones, 89. The same article provides that any ordinary person who is able to explain the laws is to receive a pardon for any first offense, if inadvertently committed. This shows that the government encouraged knowledge of the provisions of the penal code on the part of the population at large. The article is taken from the Ming code (*MLCCFL*, 469), but does not appear in the T'ang.

22 Cf. generally MacCormack, "Assistance in Conflict Resolution: Imperial China."

23 For more on rules that were seldom enforced, see chap. 3.

24 This is particularly evident in the writings of the Ch'ing legal scholar Hsüeh Yun-sheng. On the general point cf. the remarks of McKnight, *Law and Order*, 34.

25 On the basis of limited space we have had to omit from our discussion one important central issue, namely, criteria of liability (causation and fault). For more detail on the topics sketched in this chapter, see *TCPL*, chaps. 1 and 2.

Chapter 2: Varieties of Law

1 Metzger, *Internal Organization of Ch'ing Bureaucracy*, 207ff. proposes a third basic category, that of the law on administrative punishments.

2 Three important case collections from the Ch'ing period are the *P'o-an hsin-pien* (A New Collection of Revised Cases), the *Hsing-an hui-lan* (Conspectus of Penal Cases), and the *Hsing-an hui-lan hsü-pien* (an extensive supplement to the Conspectus). For details on these and other collections see Chen, "Influence of Shen Chih-ch'i's *Chi-chu* Commentary upon Ch'ing Judicial Decisions," 210 n. 11, 211 n. 12. Two general Western works on the traditional law based on the *Hsing-an hui-lan* are Alabaster, *Notes and Commentaries on Chinese Criminal Law*, and Bodde and Morris, *Law in Imperial China* (which translates a selection of the cases). Both draw selectively upon the collection, without offering a systematic analysis of all the decided cases on a particular topic.

3 A conspicuous example is Marinus Meijer, a lawyer, whose writings on the law of homicide are cited in this book.

4 Those best known are precisely those that appear in the penal codes themselves.

5 See, for example, Sweeten, "Women and Law in Rural China"; Ocko, "Hierarchy and Harmony: Family Conflict as Seen in Ch'ing Legal Cases"; Lee, "Homicide et peine capitale en Chine à la fin de l'empire"; Paderni, "Le rachat de l'honneur perdu."

6 Kroker, "Rechtsgewöhnheiten in der Provinz Shantung nach *Ming shang shih hsi kuan tiao ch'a pao kao lü*."

7 For general surveys of government and administration in China throughout all dynasties see Ch'ien Mu, *Traditional Government in Imperial China*, and Hucker, *A Dictionary of Official Titles in Imperial China*, "Introduction." For more specialized studies, restricted to specific dynasties, see Bielenstein, *Bureaucracy of Han Times*; Twitchett, *Financial Administration under the T'ang Dynasty*; Kracke, *Civil Service in Early Sung China 960–1067*; Lo, *Introduction to the Civil Service of Sung China*; Hucker (ed.), *Chinese Government in Ming Times*; Hucker, *Censorial System of Ming China*; Hsieh, *Government of China (1644–1911)*; Metzger, *Internal Organization*; Liu, *Ch'ing Institutions and Society 1644–1795*; Torbert, *Ch'ing Imperial Household Department*; Ocko, *Bureaucratic Reform in Provincial China*; Wu, *Communication and Imperial Control in China*; Ch'ü, *Local Government in China under the*

Ch'ing; Chu and Saywell, *Career Patterns in the Ch'ing Dynasty*; Bart-lett, *Monarchs and Ministers*. This is not an exhaustive list.

8 They have been translated by Hulsewé, *Remnants of Ch'in Law*.

9 For a good summary of the diverse functions of a district magistrate see Yang, "Some Characteristics of Chinese Bureaucratic Behavior," 139f. Generally on the district magistrate of Ch'ing times see Watt, *District Magistrate in Late Imperial China*.

10 The clan and the village were important in all dynasties, the guild espe-cially during the Ch'ing.

11 See Wu, *Communication and Imperial Control in China*, chap. 4; Metz-ger, *Internal Organization*, 177ff.

12 The sheer complexity of the administrative rules has been said to be their greatest defect. Cf. the remarks of Ch'ien Mu, *Traditional Government*, 108f.

13 This is a point undervalued by Stephens, *Order and Discipline*; he ar-gues that traditional China had a "disciplinary" but not a "legal" system. Generally see Metzger, *Escape from Predicament*, 186f.

14 For some examples see chap. 9.

15 Metzger, *Internal Organization*, 158f.; *Escape from Predicament*, 183.

16 Spence, *Emperor of China*, 169. Cf. also the valedictory edict of the Ch'ien-lung emperor, Staunton, 477f. The phrase "Heaven's laws" refers inter alia to the fundamental social relationships enshrined in the Three Bonds, regarded as given in nature and so endorsed by Heaven. On the Mandate of Heaven in early Chinese thought see Gaurier, "Respons-abilité politique, responsabilité morale en Chine ancienne."

17 For much of the material in this section see further MacCormack, "As-sistance in Conflict Resolution: Imperial China."

18 Generally see Jamieson, *Chinese Family and Commercial Law*; Jing, "Legislation Related to the Civil Economy in the Qing Dynasty."

19 For a summary of the law on these matters see *TCPL*, chap. 10.

20 Staunton, 335–36; Jones, 294–95. Cf. also Boulais, 1380; Philastre, 2:301; and for the corresponding Ming article, *MLCCFL*, 1580.

21 Details are set out in Ming Tai-tsu's Placard of People's Instructions. See Chang, "Village Elder System of the Early Ming Dynasty," 56.

22 We leave aside here the role of the family (clan) or guild, as well as that of the local gentry.

23 See the remarks of the seventeenth-century magistrate Huang Liu-hung, *Complete Book concerning Happiness and Benevolence*, 251ff.

24 See Bodde and Morris, *Law in Imperial China*, 413ff.; Macauley, "Civil and Uncivil Disputes in Southeast Coastal China, 1723–1820."

25 See Kroker, "Rechtsgewöhnheiten," which contains a translation of the section on Shantung province.

26 Oyamatsu, *Laws and Customs in the Island of Formosa*.

27 Ibid., 16.

28 Ibid., 18.

29 On the T'ang code see Johnson, *T'ang Code*, which translates the whole of the "General Principles" section. The Sung penal code (*Sung hsing-t'ung*, on which see McKnight, *Law and Order*, 334f.) essentially reproduced the T'ang code with some added material. Although the Yüan dynasty produced no penal code as such, collections of legal materials were issued. One of these has been translated into French by Ratchnevsky, *Un code des Yüan*. The Ming code has not as yet been translated into a Western language, but it was adopted and amplified by the Ch'ing code of which there are four translations into a Western language, those of Jones, Staunton, Philastre, and Boulais. The translation into French by Philastre is the most complete.

30 Meijer, *Murder*, 1f.

31 For more detail on early terminology see MacCormack, "Law and Punishment in the Earliest Chinese Thought."

32 The old mutilating punishments in use under the Chou dynasty are listed in a pre-Han text, the *Lü Hsing*, on which see chap. 8 at n. 2. For the Han debates on the abolition of such punishments see Hulsewé, *Remnants of Han Law* 1:124ff., 334ff.

33 For example, the Ming founder, Ming Tai-tsu, devised unusual punishments for officials guilty of corruption. See Dardess, *Confucianism and Autocracy*, 244f. Under the Ch'ing castration was reintroduced as a punishment for the sons of those guilty of rebellion.

34 For more detail on the General Principles and the Specific Offenses, see chap. 3 (organization of codes).

35 For revision of the Ch'ing code see Metzger, *Internal Organization*, 84ff., 423ff.

36 On substatutes see Bodde and Morris, *Law in Imperial China*, 43f.; Metzger, *Internal Organization*, 197ff.

37 Philastre, 2:209f.; Boulais, 1268; Staunton, 311; Jones, 276. For the procedure implied by the phrase "after the assizes" see chap. 7 at n. 37.

38 Hsüeh 290.19; a translation can be found in Meijer, "Concept of *Ku-sha*,"

112f. Of the two standard death penalties, beheading was more serious than strangulation because it sent the offender into the afterlife with an incomplete body.

39 See for example Boulais 1271, 1272.

40 See Bodde and Morris, *Law in Imperial China*, 67; Metzger, *Internal Organization*, 86. The relationship between *lü* and *li* is considered further in chap. 8 at n. 23.

41 The *shu-i* is an explanatory commentary that followed each article of the code; the article itself might also contain an interlinear commentary. Both were equally authoritative.

42 Generally, see Chen, "Influence of Shen Chih-ch'i's *Chi-chu* Commentary." The most convenient Western source for the study of these commentaries is Philastre.

43 Philastre, 1:276; Staunton, 43; Jones, 74.

44 For examples see chap. 9. Even where individual decisions had been ratified by the emperor, the imperial approval was restricted to the specific case for which the decision was given.

Chapter 3: The Conservative and Symbolic Spirit of the Law

1 Ching-I Tu, "Conservatism in a Constructive Form," 188. The words quoted in the passage are from Kirk, *Conservative Mind*.

2 The miscellaneous section contains far fewer offenses than its T'ang counterpart.

3 Cf. Philastre, 2:8; Boulais, 1024; Staunton, 269–70; Jones, 237.

4 The article is the same in the Ming code (*MLCCFL*, 1306).

5 The strengthening of the central Confucian virtue of loyalty to the ruler may owe something to Neo-Confucian influence. See further in chap. 6 at nn. 2f., nn. 24f.

6 Philastre, 2:154f.; Staunton, 300f.; Jones, 265f. See also Jones, "Theft in the Qing Code," 513.

7 One interesting omission is the sentence in the *shu-i* commentary that states: "It is difficult to provide for all possible cases, and therefore the judge is to look at the particular circumstances at the relevant time and decide [whether there has been theft]." Possibly the Ming and Ch'ing legislators thought that this conferred too explicit a discretion on the judge.

8 *Chun* is a technical expression defined in a table at the beginning of the

code as expressing the fact that there is a difference between the two states of affairs being compared (here accidental killing and killing in a fight), what is common being only the punishment, here strangulation after the assizes. See also chap. 8 at n. 15.

9 Philastre, 2:222f.; Staunton, 314; Jones, 278. The portion in brackets is the "official" or "interlinear" commentary.

10 Parallels between the T'ang and later codes are often cited in the course of this book.

11 For more detail see *TCPL*, 72ff.

12 In T'ang times the highest judicial body was called the Court of Review.

13 Cf. also the remarks of Ch'ien Mu, *Traditional Government*, 44, on the influence throughout the period from the T'ang to the Ch'ing of a T'ang work on administrative law, the *T'ang hui-tien*.

14 Cf. Analect 7.1.

15 Metzger, *Internal Organization*, 84.

16 See Ch'en, *Chinese Legal Tradition under the Mongols*, xivf.

17 Cf. Philastre, 1:275. This is from the general explanatory commentary attributed to Shen Chih-ch'i.

18 A vivid and detailed account of death and funeral rites as practiced in upper-class households at the end of the Ch'ing can be found in Lowe, *Adventures of Wu*, 2:55ff.

19 These are the *Li chi* (translated by Legge) and the *I li* (translated by Steele).

20 See Ebrey, *Chu Hsi's Family Rituals*, from which the following information is drawn. For the impact of the Family Rituals in Yüan, Ming, and Ch'ing law see Ebrey, *Confucianism and Family Rituals in Imperial China*, 150f. On the use of ritual in Ch'ing times see Smith, "Ritual in Ch'ing Culture."

21 Ebrey, *Chu Hsi's Family Rituals*, xiii.

22 Ibid., 3.

23 The relationship between filial piety and loyalty to the emperor was often stressed in official writings. Cf. in particular Baller, *Sacred Edict of K'ang-hsi*, 6, 87. On the Sacred Edict see also chap. 10 at n. 71.

24 For more on the ten abominations, see chap. 4 at nn. 13f.

25 See Twitchett, *Financial Administration*, 9f.

26 For details see McKnight, *Law and Order*, 334ff.

27 Details in Bodde and Morris, *Law in Imperial China*, 77, 80f.

28 Details in *TCPL*, 278ff.

29 See Ch'ü, *Law and Society*, 91ff.

30 Oyamatsu, *Laws and Customs in the Island of Formosa*, App. VI.

31 *Li* is the Confucian term often translated as "rites" or "propriety."

32 Ch'ü, *Law and Society*, 93.

33 *TCPL*, 260ff.

34 See Wolf and Huang, *Marriage and Adoption in China, 1845–1945*, chap. 15; Waltner, *Getting an Heir*, 71ff.

35 *TCPL*, 245ff.

36 See MacCormack, "Assistance in Conflict Resolution: Imperial China." But see also the criticism of this conception of the magistrate's role in Huang, "Codified Law and Magisterial Adjudication in the Qing."

37 A notable advocate of this view was Jean Escarra, who wrote in the 1930s an influential book on Chinese law entitled *Le droit chinois* (cf. *TCPL*, 295).

38 See Johnson, *T'ang Code*, 39–40.

39 Chu Hsi, for example, quotes in the Family Rituals a source stating that broken engagements were a frequent cause of litigation (Ebrey, *Chu Hsi's Family Rituals*, 50).

40 For marriage cf. MacCormack, "Ethical Principles and the Traditional Chinese Law of Marriage," and especially Wong, *Confucian Ideal and Reality*.

41 Already in the eighteenth century Western observers had commented on the duplicate sets of weights and measures in common use to facilitate deception in commercial transactions (so the report of Montesquieu, in Richter, *Political Theory of Montesquieu*, 280–81).

42 On this work see Rickett, *Guanzi*, introduction.

43 Quoted in Fung Yu-lan, *History of Chinese Philosophy*, 1:321. For a similar view expressed by a leading Sung Neo-Confucian (Ch'eng Hao) see Chan, *Reflections on Things at Hand*, 212.

44 Cf. Metzger, *Internal Organization*, 427.

45 Cf. the example given in Sweeten, "Women and Law in Rural China," 60f., where the wife and her lover, while being taken to court, so taunted the husband and his relatives that the latter buried them alive.

Chapter 4: The Ethical Foundations of the Penal Law

1 A *li* is approximately one-third of a mile.
2 Lau, *Mencius*, 49.
3 Duyvendak, *Lord Shang*, 201–2.
4 Here "virtue" means "obedience to the law."
5 Quoted from Fung Yu-lan, *History of Chinese Philosophy*, 1:326. Cf. also Liao, *Complete Works of Han Fei Tzu*, 1:46.
6 Hsün Tzu was also the teacher of the Legalists Han Fei Tzu and Li Ssu (chief minister of the Chin empire).
7 Knoblock, *Xunzi*, 2:94–96.
8 Dardess, *Confucianism and Autocracy*, 224.
9 This is highly reminiscent of the views of Hsün Tzu. Cf. MacCormack, "Hsün Tzu on Law and Society," 77f.
10 See Dardess, *Confucianism and Autocracy*, 196ff.
11 Ibid., 223.
12 We may compare the story told in the *Lü Hsing* (on which see chap. 8 at n. 2) of the origin of punishments in the practices of the barbaric Miao people (Karlgren, *Book of Documents*, 74 par. 3).
13 Hsüeh, 4 (ii); Philastre, 1:130; Jones, 38.
14 On amnesties see chap. 7 at nn. 45f.
15 For the T'ang version see Johnson, *T'ang Code*, 62f., and for the Ch'ing equivalents Philastre, 1:122; Boulais, 45; Staunton, 3; Jones, 34.
16 Philastre, 1:122.
17 For the T'ang abomination of "great irreverence" see Johnson, *T'ang Code*, 69f., and for the Ch'ing see Philastre, 1:123; Boulais, p. 29; Staunton, 4; Jones, 35.
18 For the T'ang see Johnson, *T'ang Code*, 65f. (At 66 the phrase "or father's sisters" needs to be inserted into the translation of the commentary after the phrase "or to kill one's paternal uncles or their wives.") For the Ch'ing see Philastre, 1:122; Boulais, p. 29; Staunton, 3; Jones, 35.
19 For the T'ang see Johnson, *T'ang Code*, 78f., and for the Ch'ing see Philastre, 1:123; Boulais, p. 30; Staunton, 4; Jones, 36.
20 For the T'ang see Johnson, *T'ang Code*, 68f., and for the Ch'ing see Philastre, 1:122; Boulais, p. 29; Staunton, 3; Jones, 35.
21 For the T'ang see Johnson, *T'ang Code*, 74f., and for the Ch'ing see Philastre, 1:123; Boulais, pp. 29–30; Staunton, 4; Jones, 35.
22 For the T'ang see Johnson, *T'ang Code*, 82f., and for the Ch'ing see Philastre, 1:124; Boulais, p. 30; Staunton, 4; Jones, 36.

23 For the T'ang see Johnson, *T'ang Code*, 80f., and for the Ch'ing see Philastre, 1:123–24; Boulais, p. 30; Staunton, 4; Jones, 36. Under "unrighteousness" is also subsumed the failure by a wife to observe the mourning regulations in respect of her husband's death.

24 Johnson, *T'ang Code*, 62. The phrase translated as "morality" (*ming chiao*) is explained by Balazs, *Traité juridique du "Souei-chou,"* 127 n. 134, as expressing the obligations flowing from reputation or social position, derived from a code of honor.

25 For details see *TCPL*, chap. 11.

26 Generally see three studies by Meijer: "Price of a *P'ai-lou*," "Homosexual Offences in Ch'ing Law," and *Murder*; also Ng, "Ideology and Sexuality: Rape Laws in Qing China."

27 For details see *TCPL*, chaps. 8 and 9.

28 Philastre, 2:551. For the views of Sung officials on the dangers of gambling see McKnight, *Law and Order*, 104.

29 The details on the opium legislation are from Spence, "Opium Smoking in Ch'ing China," 154ff.

30 Philastre, 1:665.

31 Johnson, *T'ang Code*, 77 n. 165, 81 n. 188.

32 See Ebrey, *Chu Hsi's Family Rituals*, chap. 4, and cf. above chap. 3 at n. 18.

33 See Liu, *Traditional Chinese Clan Rules*, 51, 53.

34 See, for example, Escarra, *Le droit chinois*, 70; Wu, "Chinese Legal and Political Philosophy," 220; Kroker, *Die Strafe im chinesischen Recht*, 44; Weggel, *Chinesische Rechtsgeschichte*, 142, 228f.

35 For comment on the article see Bodde and Morris, *Law in Imperial China*, 159 n. 31.

36 Kroker, *Strafe*, 45, referring to the T'ang article.

37 Bodde and Morris, *Law in Imperial China*, 214f.

38 Ibid., 240.

39 Ibid., 264f.

40 Ibid., 277.

41 Ibid., 379f.

42 This has also been based on a reading of many homicide cases.

43 Specifically on the Neo-Confucian interpretation of the Three Bonds see Hsü Dau-lin, "The Myth of the 'Five Human Relations' of Confucius," 34f. Cf. also Liu, "Socioethics as Orthodoxy," 64ff.; Weggel, *Chinesische Rechtsgeschichte*, 94ff.; Li, "Ch'ing Cosmology and Popular Precepts,"

118ff. Further literature on the effect of Neo-Confucianism on the Ming and Ch'ing law is cited in chap. 5.

44 The revision was accomplished through the insertion of a commentary into the text of the relevant article (Philastre, 2:524). For details see Ng, "Ideology and Sexuality."

45 See Meijer, "Price of a P'ai-lou," 289.

46 Ng, "Ideology and Sexuality," 60. See also Paderni, "Le rachat de l'honneur perdu," 146.

47 Philastre 2:524.

48 For the original substatute on gang rape see Philastre, 2:527, DII, and for the post-1814 position see Hsüeh, 366.2, 366.12. The summary in Ng, "Ideology and Sexuality," 66 is slightly misleading. Similar considerations with respect to the value of male chastity may have been relevant to the introduction under the Ch'ing of legislation punishing homosexual acts. The prior sexual history of the victim was also a factor to be taken into account in the determination of the offender's punishment (on which Meijer, "Homosexual Offences," 114f., 127; Ng, "Ideology and Sexuality," 69). See further chap. 7 at nn. 91f. for the case in which the woman raped or a relative committed suicide. The proviso there noted as to a repentant woman being deemed "chaste" also applied to the present case.

49 Meijer, "Price of a P'ai-lou," 301ff.; "Criminal Responsibility for the Suicide of Parents in Ch'ing Law," 133f.

50 MLCCFL, 1533. The same rule applied in the case of a wife or concubine vis-à-vis her husband's parents or paternal grandparents.

51 For translations of the substatute in its final form (Hsüeh, 299.9) see Philastre, 2:255, DIX; Boulais, 1329; Meijer, "Criminal Responsibility," 110. Where the unfilial conduct amounted to stubborn insubordination, the punishment was to be immediate beheading, where there was only a simple case of disobedience to instructions, the punishment was to be strangulation after the assizes. The same was to apply in respect of wives or concubines who brought about the suicide of their husband's parents or paternal grandparents.

52 This is a reference to the population at large.

53 HAHL, 2194; Meijer, "Criminal Responsibility," 120, 132 (from which the quotation in the text has been taken).

54 T'ang article 329; Ming, MLCCFL, 1615–16.

55 Philastre, 2:351; Boulais, 1419; Staunton, 346; Jones, 304.

56 See in particular Hsüeh, 292.11, and his commentary (cf. also 319.12, 314.12, and their respective commentaries). The summary of the development given by Meijer, "Criminal Responsibility," 122 n. 50 is not entirely accurate.

57 For the values of filial piety and chastity see also the next chapter.

Chapter 5: The Fundamental Family Roles

1 For more detail and references see MacCormack, "Natural Law and Cosmic Harmony in Traditional Chinese Legal Thought."

2 Analects 12.11.

3 Only in the relationship between friends was there a principle of equality, and even here the relationship could readily be changed into one modeled on that between elder and younger brother.

4 It is interesting that one of the theses of Jonathan Ocko in his essay on "Hierarchy and Harmony" at 218, 228–29 is that maintenance of the hierarchical distinctions, in fact, conflicted with the preservation of harmony within the family.

5 Quoted according to the summary in Dardess, *Confucianism and Autocracy*, 197.

6 Ibid., 200–201, 223.

7 See chap. 4 at n. 43.

8 Lau, *Mencius*, 102 (3A.4). A slightly different version is given by Hsu Dau-lin, "The Myth of the 'Five Human Relations' of Confucius," 28.

9 The term "Three Bonds" appears first to have been used by the Han Confucian Tung Chung-shu. See Lin, "The Relationship between Ruler and Minister in the Theory of 'Three Mainstays,'" 439. Cf. also Hsu, "Myth," 30.

10 Karlgren, *Book of Documents*, 42. King Wen, the founder of the Chou dynasty, was King Wu's father.

11 For full details on the mourning regulations see the tables at the beginning of the Ch'ing penal code: Philastre, 1:71ff.; Boulais, pp. 17f.

12 See chap. 8 at nn. 11.

13 Yen Chih-t'ui, *Family Instructions for the Yen Clan*, 18.

14 See chap. 4 at n. 43; also Gulik, *Sexual Life in Ancient China*, 223, 264; Ropp, *Dissent in Early Modern China*, 39, 124f.

15 For example, Chu Hsi emphasized "parental kindness" as well as "filial piety" and "fraternal respect" as the essential requirements for the man-

agement of the family and the state (Gardner, *Chu Hsi and the Ta-hsüeh*, 110). See also Chu, "Chu Hsi and Public Instruction," 262f., 272. The most instructive source for Neo-Confucian ethical thinking, as approved by Chu Hsi, is his Elementary Learning (*Hsiao-hsüeh*), on which see Kelleher, "Back to Basics." This work has been translated into French by Charles de Harlez.

16 In some pre-T'ang laws the punishment for filicide was more severe. See Ch'ü, *Law and Society*, 41 (Northern Wei).

17 Ming, *MLCCFL*, 1616; Ch'ing, Philastre, 2:351; Boulais, 1420; Staunton, 347 (not accurate); Jones, 304.

18 Ming, *MLCCFL*, 1616; Ch'ing, Philastre, 2:351; Boulais, 1420; Staunton, 347; Jones, 304.

19 See chap. 4 at n. 54f.

20 See chap. 4 at n. 50.

21 See chap. 4 at n. 56.

22 For this substatute see chap. 4, n. 51.

23 *Hsü-pien*, 3184.

24 Ibid., 3194.

25 Ibid., 3196; Meijer, "Criminal Responsibility," 120. Other examples are cited by Ch'ü, *Law and Society*, 51–52; Meijer, "Criminal Responsibility," 116ff. Cf. also Ocko, "Hierarchy and Harmony," 215.

26 Philastre, 2:433, DI; Boulais, 1504; Meijer, "Criminal Responsibility," 112 (Hsüeh, 338.1).

27 *HAHL*, 3111; Meijer, "Criminal Responsibility," 131.

28 Meijer, "Criminal Responsibility," 131. See also generally Bodde and Morris, *Law in Imperial China*, 409ff.

29 *HAHL*, 2076, summarized by Chen, "Influence of Shen Chih-ch'i's *Chi-chu* Commentary," 193f.

30 *HAHL*, 4266.

31 *HAHL*, 4267. For the position in respect of mad persons see MacCormack, "Legal Treatment of Insane Persons in Late Imperial China."

32 Article 345, and cf. Meijer, "Criminal Responsibility," 111, 128.

33 Ming, *MLCCFL*, 1723; Ch'ing, Philastre, 2:443; Boulais, 1503; Staunton, 374; Jones, 324.

34 The commentary to the Ming article emphasizes that there is no liability where the parental command is improper (not *i*) or where the son lacks resources with which to support the parent (*MLCCFL*, 1723–24).

35 Boulais, 1505 (Hsüeh, 338.2).

36 Boulais, 93 (Hsüeh, 16.11). The substatute was first enacted in 1741 and revised at various time during the nineteenth century.

37 Summarized in Boulais, 1508.

38 Philastre, 2:354, DI (Hsüeh, 319.1).

39 Hsüeh, 411.37.

40 So stated in a case of 1817, *HAHL*, 3106. Cf. also the observations of Ocko, "Hierarchy and Harmony," 216.

41 Hsüeh, 319.11. Cf. Boulais, 1428.

42 Legge, *Chinese Classics*, 5:157. The phrase "their kindred" (*fei lei*) is rendered by Waltner, *Getting an Heir*, 67, as "the same category."

43 Cited according to Waltner, *Getting an Heir*, 74. Generally see Boulais, 386; McMullen, "Non-Agnatic Adoption," 137ff.; Waltner, *Getting an Heir*, chap. 2.

44 For the law see *TCPL*, 26off.

45 Generally see MacCormack, "Ethical Principles." For illuminating discussion of the role accorded women in Confucian ideology and the extent to which deviations occurred in practice see Birge, "Chu Hsi and Women's Education"; Handlin, "Lü K'un's New Audience"; and Rankin, "Emergence of Women at the End of the Ch'ing."

46 Lau, *Mencius*, 139.

47 For the law see *TCPL*, 268ff.

48 Article 175. See Wong, *Confucian Ideal and Reality*, 77f.

49 Ming, *MLCCFL*, 639f.; Ch'ing, Philastre, 1:491f.; Boulais, 539f.; Staunton, 107f.; Jones, 123f.

50 Cf. MacCormack, "Ethical Principles," 254–55.

51 Liu-hung, *A Complete Book concerning Happiness and Benevolence*, 448–49. Cf. Chu Hsi's observation on Sung practice cited in chap. 3, n. 39.

52 Meijer, *Murder*, 43 n. 14.

53 T'ang article 177 (Wong, *Confucian Ideal and Reality*, 80); Ming, *MLCCFL*, 655; Ch'ing, Philastre, 1:504; Boulais, 563; Staunton, 110f.; Jones, 125.

54 Commentary to article 177.

55 Ming, *MLCCFL*, 655; Chi'ng, Philastre, 1:504; Boulais, 562; Staunton, 110; Jones, 125.

56 T'ang article 189 (Wong, *Confucian Ideal and Reality*, 81f.); Ming, *MLCCFL*, 712; Ch'ing, Philastre, 1:536; Boulais, 634; Staunton, 120; Jones, 133. For the exceptions see MacCormack, "Ethical Principles," 265–66.

57 Some of these duties were also emphasized in the clan rules. See Liu, *Traditional Chinese Clan Rules*, 84ff.

58 For some exceptional cases in which the wife might take the initiative, at least in the later law, in procuring a divorce see Tai, "Divorce in Traditional Chinese Law," 98f.

59 T'ang article 190 (Wong, *Confucian Ideal and Reality*, 88); Ming, *MLCCFL*, 712; Ch'ing, Philastre, 1:536; Boulais, 636; Staunton, 120; Jones, 134.

60 For a full statement of the grounds see MacCormack, "Ethical Principles," 266f.

61 See further MacCormack, "Ethical Principles," 267.

62 Other examples in ibid., 261f.; Ch'ü, *Law and Society*, 104f.

63 Ming, *MLCCFL*, 1470; Ch'ing, Philastre, 2:177; Boulais, 1224; Staunton, 305; Jones, 269.

64 Ming, *MLCCFL*, 1597; Ch'ing, Philastre, 2:327; Boulais, 1401; Staunton, 342; Jones, 299.

65 Hsüeh, commentary to 315.3. Ch'ü, *Law and Society*, 107 errs in stating the sentence to be beheading; he confuses "striking a blow from which the husband dies" with "accidental killing."

66 Ming, *MLCCFL*, 1598; Ch'ing, Philastre, 2:327; Boulais, 1403; Staunton, 342; Jones, 299–300.

67 Philastre, 2:253, DX (Hsüeh, 299.10). In fact, this substatute is derived from a Ming model (*MLCCFL*, 1533 on which see Meijer, "Criminal Responsibility," 111).

68 Cf. MacCormack, "Suicide in Traditional Chinese Law," 41.

69 So provided by a substatute of 1725, Philastre, 2:233, DI (Hsüeh, 293.1).

70 Commentary to article 189.

71 Cf. the discussion in Spence, *Death of Woman Wang*, 100f.; T'ien, *Male Anxiety and Female Chastity*, 32f.

72 See also *TCPL*, 201ff.

73 Ming, *MLCCFL*, 1476; Ch'ing, Philastre, 2:184; Boulais, 1232; Staunton, 307; Jones, 271. The same immunity applied if the husband killed the lover alone.

74 Substatute of 1824, Philastre, 2:186, DI (Hsüeh, 285.1). Cf. the discussion in Meijer, *Murder*, 50.

75 Cf. the contrasting views of Meijer, *Murder*, 41f. and T'ien, "Review of M. J. Meijer, *Murder*," 345f.

76 T'ang, article 253; Ming, *MLCCFL*, 1476; Ch'ing, Philastre, 2:184; Boulais, 1233; Staunton, 307; Jones, 271.

77 *HAHL*, 1599–1601.

78 *HAHL*, 1611–12.

79 Cf. Spence, *Death of Woman Wang*, 70f.; T'ien, *Male Anxiety and Female Chastity*, 34f.

80 Ming, *MLCCFL*, 660; Ch'ing, Philastre, 1:507; Boulais, 570; Staunton, 112; Jones, 126.

81 Article 184 (Wong, *Confucian Ideal and Reality*, 91f.).

82 *MLCCFL*, 660–61.

83 Philastre, 1:507f.; Boulais, 573; Staunton, 113; Jones, 127.

84 On the remarriage of widows see Waltner, "Widows and Remarriage in Ming and Early Qing China," 136f.

85 Quoted from de Groot, *Religious System of China*, 2:751.

86 Cf. Boulais, 304ff.; Mann, *Widows in the Kinship, Class, and Community Structures of Qing Dynasty China*, 37f., 41f. There is also much useful material in Elvin, "Female Virtue and the State in China," and T'ien, *Male Anxiety and Female Chastity*, 4ff.; Tao, "Chaste Widows and Institutions to Support Them in Late-Ch'ing China."

87 Philastre, 1:509, DI; Boulais, 574 (Hsüeh, 105.1).

88 See chap. 4 at n. 46. For less extreme views, more favorable to the remarriage of widows, advocated by some Sung statesmen and philosophers see Handlin, "Lü K'un's New Audience," 14.

89 Cf. Waltner, "Widows and Remarriage," 129 n. 3; Mann, *Widows*, 37f.; Birge, "Chu Hsi and Women's Education," 338f.

Chapter 6: The Fundamental Social and Political Relationships

1 For governmental procedures at the highest level under the T'ang see Ch'ien Mu, *Traditional Government*, 37ff.

2 Already under the Sung there was a depreciation in the standing of ministers compared with their position under the T'ang. See Ch'ien Mu, *Traditional Government*, 69f.; McKnight, *Law and Order*, 59f.

3 Quoted from Dardess, *Confucianism and Autocracy*, 209. See also the edict of the Yung-cheng emperor promulgated in 1724, translated by Metzger, *Internal Organization*, 159f.

4 *Li Chi*, 1:90 (modified); cf. Creel, "Legal Institutions," 39, arguing that this was not authentic Confucian doctrine, but simply an expression of hope on the part of officials.

5 See *TCPL*, chap. 6 (with references, to which may be added McKnight,

Law and Order, 491 ff.). To be noted also is the fact that officials were not to be subjected to the use of torture in the course of their interrogation. The case was to be decided according to the evidence of witnesses: T'ang article 474 (applying to those entitled to the privileges of deliberation, petition, and reduction of punishment); Ming, *MLCCFL,* 1972; Ch'ing, Philastre, 2:656; Boulais, 1681; Staunton, 441–42; Jones, 376 (the exemption in Ming and Ch'ing law applying only to persons entitled to deliberation).

6 The way these were calculated can be instanced as an example of the precise grading according to rank adopted by the code: relatives of the emperor to the *sixth* degree of mourning, relatives of the emperor's mother and paternal grandmother to the *fifth* degree of mourning, and relatives of the empress to the *fourth* degree of mourning.

7 Quoted from Hulsewé, *Remnants of Han Law,* 1:287–88.

8 Ibid. (slightly modified).

9 See McKnight, "Song Legal Privileges."

10 Ming, *MLCCFL,* 189; Ch'ing, Philastre, 1:130; Boulais, 52; Staunton, 6; Jones, 38.

11 Ming, *MLCCFL,* 187f.; Ch'ing, Philastre, 1:127f.; Boulais, 50; Staunton, 5f.; Jones, 36f.

12 Philastre, 1:135f.; Boulais, 63f.; Staunton, 9; Jones, 40 (cf. also *MLCCFL,* 199f.). The range of relatives to whom "protection" was extended was more circumscribed than in T'ang law. For details see Philastre, 1:131f.; Boulais, 56f.; Staunton, 7f. (and cf. *MLCCFL,* 224f.).

13 Ming, *MLCCFL,* 215; Ch'ing, Philastre, 1:138f.; Boulais, 70; Staunton, 10; Jones, 40.

14 Ming. *MLCCFL,* 218; Ch'ing, Philastre, 1:139f.; Boulais, 71; Staunton, 11; Jones, 41. See generally the remarks of Metzger, *Escape from Predicament,* 170ff.

15 For the confusing history of the Ming and Ch'ing redemption law see Metzger, *Internal Organization,* 303ff., on which the above account is based.

16 Ibid., 86.

17 The wealthy, for example, could always petition for permission to redeem an offense by the payment of a large sum. Cf. *TCPL,* 107f.

18 See chap. 5 at n. 2.

19 Lau, *Mencius,* 68 (IB 8).

20 Quoted from Hsu, "Myth of the 'Five Human Relations' of Confucius,"

35. See also the passage from Ssu-ma Kuang (the Sung statesman) quoted by Yamashita, "The Development of Ideas on Sovereignty: From the Sung to the Ming," 46. Yamashita, in fact, asserts, "Chu Hsi Confucianism represented a theory of formalistic absolutization of the ruler" (60).

21 Cf. Lin, "Relationship between Ruler and Minister," 45off. (arguing that Han Confucianism was influenced by Legalist thinking in its interpretation of the relationship between ruler and subject).

22 It is fascinating to note that the ruler's acceptance of his position as dependent upon the protection of heaven is stated in documents separated in time by over twenty-five hundred years. We may compare King Wu's observations in the *K'ang kao* [Karlgren, *Book of Documents*, 39 (par. 4), 40 (pars. 5, 6, 7), 42 (pars. 16, 21)] and those of the K'ang-hsi emperor in his valedictory edict (Spence, *Emperor of China*, 169, 172).

23 This connection was also emphasized in the teaching of the Sacred Edict.

24 For these offenses see generally *TCPL*, 119f., 122f.

25 Article 248. The portion in brackets is the "official" or "interlinear" commentary.

26 Johnson, *T'ang Code*, 63.

27 This would include affinal or matrilineal relatives.

28 Ming, *MLCCFL*, 1306; Ch'ing, Philastre, 2:8; Boulais, 1024; Staunton, 269; Jones, 237. See chap. 3 at n. 3.

29 Boulais, 1025.

30 Cf. Hulsewé, *Remnants of Han Law*, 1:127.

31 Philastre, 2:9.

32 On the unfilial son see chap. 5.

33 Generally see the full treatment in Ch'ü, *Law and Society*, chaps. 3 and 4; Ch'ü, "Chinese Class Structure and Its Ideology."

34 On this see further Ch'ü, *Law and Society*, 201ff.

35 For a convenient account of Confucius's thought see Fung Yu-lan, *History of Chinese Philosophy*, 1:66ff. See also Ho, *Ladder of Success*, 17 (quoting Mencius).

36 The examination system dates from early T'ang times.

37 On the complexities of the state examinations during the Ch'ing see the highly readable account by Miyazaki, *China's Examination Hell*.

38 Dardess, *Confucianism and Autocracy*, 199–201. Generally see Clunas, "Regulation of Consumption."

39 Ming, *MLCCFL*, 969; Ch'ing, Philastre, 1:65of.; Boulais, 836f.; Staunton, 185f.; Jones, 180.

40 Philastre, 1:651.

41 For the substatutes see Philastre, 1:651ff.; Boulais, 841ff. For similar rules
in earlier dynasties see Ch'ü, *Law and Society*, 157ff. Cf. also the speech
recorded in the *Tso chuan* for the year 710 B.C., in Fung Yu-lan, *History
of Chinese Philosophy*, 1:36–37, which suggests that the basic idea of ex-
ternal trappings both manifesting status and conveying a moral message
was pre-Confucian.

42 On marriage prohibitions generally see Ch'ü, *Law and Society*, 158ff.

43 Article 191 (Wong, *Confucian Ideal and Reality*, 83).

44 Article 192 (ibid.). Generally see Johnson, *T'ang Code*, 28f.

45 Ming, *MLCCFL*, 704; Ch'ing, Philastre, 1:535; Boulais, 621; Staunton,
119; Jones, 133.

46 Philastre, 1:535.

47 Ming, *MLCCFL*, 698; Ch'ing, Boulais, 603; Staunton, 118; Jones, 132.

48 Miyazaki, *China's Examination Hell*, 36f.

49 Hsüeh, 6.2.

50 Boulais, 67.

51 Ibid., 68.

52 Ibid., 37. On graduates see also Ch'ü, *Local Government in China under
the Ch'ing*, 173f.; Ho, *Ladder of Success*, 26ff.; and for the Sung, Lee,
"Sung Schools and Education before Chu Hsi," 116f.

53 Details in Ch'ü, *Law and Society*, 129f.; Ho, *Ladder of Success*, 18f.

54 See Ch'ü, *Law and Society*, 132 n. 6; Boulais, 356, 359.

55 Philastre, 2:289.

56 Ibid., 291.

57 The above is a summary of a complex set of rules; details for the Ming in
MLCCFL, 1561ff., and for the Ch'ing, Philastre, 2:287ff.; Boulais, 1367f.;
Staunton, 330ff.; Jones, 290f.

58 Full details in Ch'ü, *Law and Society*, 186f.

59 Philastre, 2:309; Boulais, 1381; Staunton, 336; Jones, 295 (for the Ming
see *MLCCFL*, 1583, and for the T'ang article 320).

60 Philastre, 2:545; Boulais, 1628; Staunton, 409; Jones, 352 (for the Ming
see *MLCCFL*, 1854, and for the T'ang article 414).

61 Philastre, 2:545.

62 Article 320.

63 Article 321.

64 Article 322.

65 We omit consideration of the T'ang "personal retainer" who is treated in
a way similar to, but not quite the same as, the slave.

66 Ming, *MLCCFL*, 1470; Ch'ing, Philastre, 2:177–78; Boulais, 1226; Staun- •
ton, 306; Jones, 270.

67 Ming, *MLCCFL*, 1589; Ch'ing, Philastre, 2:313; Boulais, 1387f.; Staunton,
338; Jones, 297.

68 See chap. 4 at n. 56.

69 Reduced to "after the assizes" if he had killed a year-of-mourning relative
or maternal grandparent of the family head.

70 Philastre, 2:310.

71 All such persons were "public" slaves assigned to officials or soldiers and
are to be distinguished from "private" slaves. The reason that the commentaries say nothing about "private" slaves is that the Ming code had
forbidden the keeping of slaves by private persons, and the Ch'ing code
had retained this provision, though with a qualification that tended to
nullify it. See Meijer, "Slavery at the End of the Ch'ing Dynasty," 330f.

72 Philastre, 2:313.

73 Cf., for example, the discussion in Tanaka, "Popular Uprisings, Rent
Resistance, and Bondservant Rebellions in the Late Ming," 194ff.

74 On these questions see especially Meijer, "Slavery," and Ch'ü, *Law and
Society*, 189 n. 93. Cf. also an opinion of the Board of Punishments noted
by Oyama, "Large Landownership in the Jiangnan Delta Region during
the Late Ming-Early Qing Period," 155 n. 61.

Chapter 7: Moral Values and the Law

1 On the value of life in Buddhist thought see Greenblatt, "Chu-hung and
Lay Buddhism in the Late Ming," 100ff.

2 Cf. also MacCormack, "Cultural Values in Traditional Chinese Law," 7f.,
and "General Principles of Liability in the Late Ch'ing Law of Homicide," 16f. Even prisoners were regarded with compassion by the law. The
commentary to the Ch'ing article requiring prisoners lacking families or
relatives to be supplied with food, clothing, and medical attention states
that the death of a prisoner through lack of care is serious because a
human life has been lost. See also the discussion in McKnight, *Law and
Order*, 303f., 359ff. The imperial concern for conditions in jails to which
McKnight draws attention is another example of the influence of *jen* in
government (see below).

3 There is an interesting difference in the wording of the T'ang and Ming/
Ch'ing articles. The T'ang code (article 339) simply says that an acci-

dental killing, in accordance with the circumstances, is to be treated as redeemable. On the other hand, the Ming and Ch'ing articles specify that the sentence is to conform with that for killing in a fight (i.e., strangulation), but the punishment is then to be redeemable (Ming, *MLCCFL*, 1506; Ch'ing, Philastre, 2:222 (and cf. the commentary at 224); Boulais, 1285; Staunton, 314; Jones, 278.

4 One factor underlying this insistence is the belief that the ghost of the deceased was anxious for revenge. Cf. McKnight, *Law and Order*, 326.

5 See chap. 5 at nn. 16f. The same applied in the relationship of master and slave.

6 Philastre, 2:195; Boulais, 1249; Staunton, 308; Jones, 273. Cf. T'ang article 259; Ming, *MLCCFL*, 1481.

7 Hsüeh, 287.7 (finally revised in 1804).

8 Hsüeh, 290.8, unclearly translated by Philastre, 2:215, DV, and incorrectly by Boulais, 1273. Cf. the remarks of Meijer, "An Aspect of Retribution in Traditional Chinese Law," 214f.

9 Quoted in Hsüeh's commentary.

10 The same point is made by the Board in an Anhui case of 1827, *HAHL*, 1976.

11 For the Ch'ing article see Philastre, 2:210; Boulais, 1270; Staunton, 311; Jones, 276.

12 Certain other circumstances are also contemplated.

13 *TCPL*, 193 (with references).

14 *HAHL*, 1909.

15 For a detailed study of the substatute see Meijer, "Aspect of Retribution."

16 Wang was the person who had proposed the original plot to beat Hsia.

17 For the analogical application of articles and substatutes see chap. 9.

18 *HAHL*, 1931.

19 T'ang article 256; Ming, *MLCCFL*, 1461; Ch'ing, Philastre, 2:164; Boulais, 1221 (wrongly given as 1121); Staunton, 303; Jones, 268.

20 Philastre, 2:165, translating "facts and law" by "les sentiments naturels et la règle."

21 *HAHL*, 2056.

22 Philastre, 2:327; Boulais, 1403 (omitting the relevant clause); Staunton, 342; Jones, 300.

23 Philastre, 2:210; Boulais, 1269; Staunton, 311; Jones, 276.

24 *HAHL*, 2073.

25 Philastre, 1:185; Boulais, 131; Staunton, 24; Jones, 52.

26 *P'o-an*, 117. As a result of this decision a new substatute was enacted (Hsüeh, 22.7; Boulais, 134).

27 *HAHL*, 1844.

28 Hsüeh, 287.7.

29 *HAHL*, 1849.

30 *HAHL*, 1870, 1871. The substatute was later changed, and the provision on execution of the sons removed. For its final version see Hsüeh, 287.17; Boulais, 1253.

31 Hsüeh, 303.7 (substatute of 1809); Philastre, 2:278, DIV; Boulais, 1361.

32 Philastre, 2:247; Boulais, 1323; Staunton, 321; Jones, 282.

33 See generally MacCormack, "Suicide in Traditional Chinese Law." The importance attached to human life also underlies the rules under which a person is to be entitled to a reduction in punishment where he has injured, but not where he has killed, in self-defense. See *TCPL*, 196.

34 Generally see *TCPL*, 74ff.; MacCormack, "General Principles," 15f.

35 *TCPL*, 74, quoting Bünger.

36 Spence, *Emperor of China*, 29, 32.

37 See, for example, Alabaster, *Notes and Commentaries on Chinese Criminal Law*, 28f.; Bodde and Morris, *Law in Imperial China*, 140f.

38 Spence, *Emperor of China*, 32f. Sometimes, as in cases of treason or offenses thought to be damaging to the state, the emperor might be ruthless in ordering executions (29f.).

39 T'ang article 203; Ming, 1225; Ch'ing, Philastre, 1:762; Boulais, 988; Staunton, 245; Jones, 220.

40 Philastre, 1:764; Boulais, p. 450 n. 1.

41 Greenblatt, "Chu-hung and Lay Buddhism," 111f. For observations on the possible Buddhist influence on the law see Bünger, "Die Rechtsidee in der chinesischen Geschichte," 206, and "Entstehung und Wandel des Rechts in China," 465.

42 Schirokauer, "Chu Hsi as an Administrator," 218.

43 Chan, "Evolution of the Confucian Concept *Jen*," 295f.

44 Quoted from de Bary, *Neo-Confucian Orthodoxy*, 31 (and cf. also 85, 97). For a study of Fan's thought see Liu, "An Early Sung Reformer."

45 For a summary of the law on amnesties see *TCPL*, 125ff. Generally also see McKnight, *Quality of Mercy* and *Law and Order*, 485ff.

46 Quoted from McKnight, *Quality of Mercy*, 58 (also see chap. 6 of this work, especially 113, 119–20).

47 Details in *TCPL*, 110ff., and cf. MacCormack, "Cultural Values," 7f. See

also Bodde, "Age, Youth and Infirmity in the Law of Ch'ing China"; Waltner, "Moral Status of the Child in Late Imperial China," 679f. The rules exempting officials from torture also applied to persons aged over 70 or under 15 or those who were infirm. See chap. 6, n. 14.

48 On insanity in Ch'ing law see Ng, *Madness in Late Imperial China*, chaps. 4 and 5; MacCormack, "Legal Treatment of Insane Persons in Late Imperial China."

49 Legge, *Li Chi*, 1:66.

50 Johnson, *T'ang Code*, 169, 173.

51 *MLCCFL*, 289; Philastre, 1:187.

52 Philastre, 1:187.

53 *MLCCFL*, 295; Philastre, 1:192–93.

54 Johnson, *T'ang Code*, 162f.

55 Details and references in *TCPL*, 115f.

56 Quoted from Meijer, "Slavery," 348–49.

57 Philastre, 2:720; Boulais 1699; Staunton, 459; Jones, 399.

58 Philastre, 2:722.

59 Johnson, *T'ang Code*, 152ff.; Ming, *MLCCFL*, 267; Ch'ing, Philastre, 1:162; Boulais, 96; Staunton, 20; Jones, 49.

60 Philastre, 1:163.

61 *P'o-an*, 61.

62 Cf. also the same sentiment expressed in a case of 1840 (*Hsü-pien*, 3022), summarized in MacCormack, "Legal Treatment," 262–63.

63 Bodde and Morris, *Law in Imperial China*, 223–24. The case is interesting because it involved the death of a senior relative. The offender had been originally sentenced to immediate beheading, but, after an elaborate sequence of reviews, the punishment was eventually reduced to a beating of one hundred blows and the wearing of the cangue for sixty days, the throne giving permission for the offender to return home and look after his aged parents.

64 Boulais, 111.

65 Philastre, 2:10f.

66 Philastre, 1:669.

67 Philastre, 1:670.

68 Philastre, 1:764.

69 Johnson, *T'ang Code*, 201ff.; Ming, *MLCCFL*, 305; Ch'ing, Philastre, 1:205; Boulais, 115f.; Staunton, 27; Jones, 56. For general discussion of confession and repentance see *TCPL*, chap. 7.

70 15.29 (Soothill).

71 Johnson, *T'ang Code*, 201. Cf. also Philastre, 1:207.

72 Certain other offenses were also excluded from the scope of the article on confession.

73 See also chap. 10 at n. 73.

74 Analect 13.18

75 Johnson, *T'ang Code*, 246ff.; Ming, *MLCCFL*, 336; Ch'ing, Philastre, 1:247; Boulais, 173f.; Staunton, 34; Jones, 66.

76 Philastre, 2:435. For the rules on accusation of relatives see for the T'ang code articles 345, 346, and 346; for the Ming, *MLCCFL*, 1709; and for the Ch'ing, Philastre, 2:429; Boulais, 1495f.; Staunton, 371; Jones, 322.

77 See chap. 5.

78 Philastre, 1:124.

79 Article 410.

80 Ming, *MLCCFL*, 1833; Ch'ing, Philastre, 2:524; Boulais, 1581; Staunton, 404; Jones, 347.

81 Article 411.

82 Ming, *MLCCFL*, 1843; Ch'ing, Philastre, 2:534; Boulais, 1599; Staunton, 406; Jones, 349.

83 Cf., for example, the law on forcible theft (*TCPL*, 218).

84 References cited in notes 81 and 82.

85 Philastre, 2:525.

86 See generally Meijer, "Homosexual Offences."

87 Ibid., 110, for Meijer's translation of the 1852 substatute, part IV.

88 See Ng, "Ideology and Sexuality," 69 (summarizing a Shantung case of 1815).

89 For speculation on this point see Meijer, "Homosexual Offences," 129; Ng, "Ideology and Sexuality," 68f.

90 See chap. 4 at nn. 43f. and chap. 5 at nn. 14f.

91 For what follows see MacCormack, "Suicide," 43–44. See also Meijer, "Price of a *P'ai-lou*," 389ff.; Paderni, "Le rachat de l'honneur perdu." We may also compare the parallel case of the chaste widow who preferred suicide to remarriage (chap. 5 at nn. 84f.).

92 These rules can be found in Hsüeh, 299.14, a substatute derived from eighteenth-century enactments, consolidated in 1803. The punishment for rape itself was strangulation after the assizes, and for attempted rape, life exile.

93 See chap. 4 at nn. 47f.

94 The qualification as to chastity was introduced by a substatute of 1807/
   1862 (Hsüeh, 299.20).

95 These rules were contained in a group of eighteenth-century substatutes
   (Hsüeh, 299.14). See Philastre, 2:253, DXII, 255, DXVII.

96 *Hsü-pien*, 3223.

97 Ibid., 3237.

98 Ming, *MLCCFL*, 270; Ch'ing, Philastre, 1:172; Boulais, 127; Staunton,
   22; Jones, 50.

99 Philastre, 1:114, pars. VI and VIII; Boulais, 39, 40.

100 Philastre, 2:720.

101 Philastre, 2:721.

Chapter 8: Technical Qualities

1 See Creel, "Legal Institutions," 29, 36.

2 On the *Lü hsing* see Creel, *Origins of Statecraft*, 1:161, 463; MacCormack, "The *Lü Hsing:* Problems of Legal Interpretation."

3 Karlgren, *Book of Documents*, 77, par. 15ff.; cf. also McKnight, *Law and
  Order*, 482.

4 Article 502. Cf. *TCPL*, 89, and Johnson, "Concept of Doubt in T'ang
  Criminal Law."

5 See generally *TCPL*, 83ff.

6 In practice, of course, abuses in the use of torture occurred. For the Sung,
  operating with similar formal rules, see McKnight, *Law and Order*, 157f.

7 Cf. Alford, "Of Arsenic and Old Lace," 1204, 1206; Harrison, "Wrongful Treatment of Prisoners." On the requirement of "confession" see van
  der Sprenkel, *Legal Institutions in Manchu China*, 74; Connor, "Law
  of Evidence during the Ch'ing Dynasty," 190ff.; Stephens, *Order and
  Discipline*, 41.

8 Cf. the statement in a Ch'ing legal commentary that resort was had to
  torture when the offender's guilt was certain, but he deceitfully tried to
  cast the blame on someone else and refused to recognize his own liability (Philastre, 2:657). For the approach of liberal officials in the closing
  decade of the Ch'ing to the use of torture see Meijer, *Introduction of
  Modern Criminal Law in China*, 129f., 160f.

9 Also to be noted is the fact that officials acting as judges at all levels
  were required to state in their written reports the provision(s) of the
  code upon which they relied; failure to do so attracted punishment. See

chap. 9 at n. 6. For the contents of the dossier submitted to the Board see Paderni, "Le rachat de l'honneur perdu," 140.

10 This structure emerges with particular clarity from the reports of the Hsü-pien collection.

11 See chap. 6 at nn. 4f. The following information is drawn from Johnson, *T'ang Code.*

12 This phrase is omitted in Johnson's translation.

13 An example is supplied by the opium legislation discussed in Spence, "Opium Smoking in Ch'ing China," 154ff.

14 Philastre, 1:258; Staunton, 38; Jones, 68. See also chap. 7 at n. 64.

15 Philastre, 1:265; Staunton, 40; Jones, 71. See also Philastre, 1:98ff. for other definitions of certain key terms used in the code.

16 For more detailed discussion see MacCormack, "The T'ang Code," 140ff.

17 For this and what follows cf. MacCormack, "Concept of *Tsang* in the T'ang Code." See also *TCPL*, 210ff.

18 Johnson, *T'ang Code*, xiii; a *ch'ih* is slightly less than one foot.

19 Ibid.; a *p'i* is a piece of cloth 1.8 *ch'ih* by 40 *ch'ih.*

20 Article 53 of the T'ang code defines the phrases "estimate x and sentence" and "by means of x sentence," noting that in the former case the punishment is not to exceed exile to three thousand *li*. See Johnson, *T'ang Code*, 262–63.

21 See *TCPL*, chap. 7, and cf. also above in chap. 7 at n. 69.

22 See chap. 7 at n. 76.

23 See chap. 2 at nn. 34f.

24 For the Ch'ing article (reproducing the Ming) see Philastre, 2:246; Boulais, 1199; Staunton, 297; Jones, 263.

25 Hsüeh, 277.1–3; Philastre, 2:139, DII,III; Boulais, 1200–1201; Meijer, "Self-defense," 243–44.

26 The late Ch'ing legal scholar Hsüeh Yun-sheng devoted his Tu-li ts'un-i (Doubts Arising from the Substatutes) to an identification of the inconsistencies yielded by a study of the substatutes.

27 See chap. 3 at nn. 5f.

28 For details on the law of theft see *TCPL*, 212ff.

29 Generally see *TCPL*, 194ff.

30 Cf. Downer, *Leges Henrici Primi*, 293ff.

31 For further discussion of the imperial control of punishments see chap. 9.

Chapter 9: Lawmaking and Legal Reasoning

1 See Metzger's invaluable discussion of all aspects of Ch'ing lawmaking in *The Internal Organization of Ch'ing Bureaucracy*. On the factors that operated to control and limit imperial absolutism see Gernet, "Introduction," xxf.; Hulsewé, "Law as One of the Foundations of State Power in Early Imperial China," 12; Bünger, "Concluding Remarks," 316ff. See also chap. 2 at nn. 13f.

2 Spence, *Emperor of China*, 30.

3 Ibid., 33–34.

4 See Seidel, *Studien zur Rechtsgeschichte der Sung-Zeit*, 71f., 76 (these passages from the Sung Legal Treatise are discussed *TCPL*, 56f.).

5 Cf. the remarks of Meijer, "Criminal Responsibility," 113.

6 The punishment would be redeemable under the special provisions relating to officials. See chap. 6 at n. 15.

7 Philastre, 2:710; Staunton, 455; Jones, 396. For the T'ang see articles 484, 486, and the Ming, *MLCCFL*, 2086.

8 Philastre, 2:711. See also below on the use of "precedents" by the Board.

9 Details in Philastre, 2:669f.; Boulais, 1682f.; Staunton, 447f.; Jones, 381f. Cf. also *TCPL*, 91ff.

10 See chap. 3 at n. 11.

11 For details see Alford, "Of Arsenic and Old Lace," 1227ff.

12 Cf. ibid., 1242ff. Interestingly, a recent study of the handling of capital cases suggests that the provinces were not uniform in their submission of homicide cases to the Board of Punishments. A considerable amount of provincial autonomy, especially in the nineteenth century, appears to have been tolerated by the central government. See Lee, "Homicide et peine capitale en Chine à la fin de l'empire," 122f.

13 For the T'ang law see *TCPL*, 90.

14 Philastre, 1:276; Staunton, 43; Jones, 74.

15 Philastre, 1:277, DI; Bodde and Morris, *Law in Imperial China*, 176; Chen, "On Analogy in Ch'ing Law," 223 (Hsüeh, 44.1).

16 Boulais, 1169.

17 Philastre, 2:222; Boulais, 1285; Staunton, 314; Jones, 278.

18 Philastre, 2:239; Boulais, 1311; Staunton, 317; Jones, 280.

19 *HAHL*, 1895. As the result of a recommendation made by the Board in this case, the throne enacted a new substatute to deal with cases of persons eating poisoned food that had been intended for animals. See Philastre, 2:207, DII; Boulais, 1265 (Hsüeh, 289.2).

20 *HAHL*, 2161.

21 Hsüeh, 299.3 (substatute of 1765/1804); Philastre, 2:250, DII; Boulais, 1326.

22 Hsüeh, 338.3; Philastre, 2:444, DIV (earlier version); Boulais, 1506.

23 Philastre, 2:184; Boulais, 1233; Staunton, 307; Jones, 271.

24 *Hsü-pien*, 3184.

25 See chap. 4 at nn. 55f.

26 See chap. 4 at n. 51.

27 Review of Nakamura, 348.

28 *HAHL*, 1478.

29 See chap. 8 at n. 25.

30 Philastre, 2:580; Boulais, 1659; Staunton, 422; Jones, 361.

31 See above at note 14.

32 Meijer, "Self-defense," 235.

33 Generally on analogy see Bodde and Morris, *Law in Imperial China*, 31f., 175f., 517ff.; Moore, "Wider Lessons of Chinese Law," 233; Weggel, *Chinesische Rechtsgeschichte*, 94ff. (all generally arguing for a "wide" use of analogy in the traditional law); Valk, "Review of Bodde and Morris, *Law in Imperial China*," 471; Chen, "On Analogy in Ch'ing Law" (both taking a more restrictive approach). See also the remarks of Léon Vandermeersch, "Enquiry into the Chinese Conception of Law," 20, arguing, wrongly we think, that the existence of the "what ought not to be done" article (on which see chap. 4 at nn. 35f.) shows that the principle *nulla poena sine lege* did not operate in the traditional law.

34 See on this especially Metzger, *Internal Organization*, 161f., 185ff.

35 For the position in earlier dynasties see *TCPL*, 54ff.

36 The same term *li* is used in this substatute in two meanings: that of "substatute" and that of "precedent," Hsüeh, 415.3, Philastre, 2:712, DIII; Metzger, *Internal Organization*, 201 n. 43.

37 See Bodde and Morris, *Law in Imperial China*, 151 (leading cases), 152 (general circulars).

38 So understood by Metzger, *Internal Organization*.

39 See above at note 15.

40 *HAHL*, 1973; the Board's decision in this case gave rise to a new substatute.

41 *HAHL*, 1548 at 1558.

42 See further below at note 63.

43 *HAHL*, 4999 at 5002.

44 *HAHL*, 2025.

45 The difference between this case and that relied on by the department is presumably that Yen had only been intervening to stop a wrestling bout and had not been one of the actual participants.

46 For another example in which the Board cited precedents to determine whether the facts should be classified as "accidental killing" or "killing in a game" see *HAHL*, 2060 (Chihli case of 1817).

47 *HAHL*, 2074; Chen, "Influence of Shen Chih-ch'i's *Chi-chu* Commentary," 191f.

48 Philastre, 2:222; Boulais, 1283; Staunton, 313; Jones, 278.

49 See previous note.

50 This case was followed in a Kiangsi case of 1811 (*HAHL*, 2076; Chen, "Influence," 193f.).

51 *HAHL*, 1952.

52 See the observations of Meijer, "Concept of *Ku-sha*," 105.

53 Hsüeh, 303.7; Philastre, 2:278, DIV; Boulais, 1361.

54 *HAHL*, 2021.

55 Hsüeh, 282.4; Boulais, 1217; Meijer, *Murder*, 125–26.

56 Cf. chap. 4 at n. 28 on the "evils" of gambling.

57 *HAHL*, 1568.

58 Philastre, 2:327 (official commentary); Staunton, 342; Jones, 299.

59 *HAHL*, 2092.

60 See above at note 48.

61 For a study of the operation of this important causal principle see MacCormack, "*Ts'ui tso so yu*: A Principle of Causality in Traditional Chinese Jurisprudence."

62 For this case see Chen, "Influence," 182f.

63 See above at note 42.

64 See the official commentary inserted in the article on accusation between relatives, Philastre, 2:432; Jones, 324.

65 Philastre, 2:580; Boulais, 1659; Staunton, 422; Jones, 361.

Chapter 10: The Role and Justification of Punishment

1 See chaps. 6 and 7.

2 For a sophisticated treatment of the functions of punishment see Hart, *Punishment and Responsibility*. We would also like to acknowledge the help we have received from John Stannard's unpublished paper, "Punishment and Public Relations."

3 See the account given of Sung official thinking on the functions of punishment by McKnight, *Law and Order*, 321ff.

4 See MacCormack, "Law and Punishment in the Earliest Chinese Thought," 339f., 344f., 349f.

5 Legge, *Chinese Classics*, 5:609f.

6 See chap. 1 at n. 4.

7 Karlgren, *Book of Documents*, 40, par. 8.

8 See Duyvendak, *Lord Shang*, 203, 209, 258f., 287f. (and the remarks of Duyvendak, 60); Liao, *Han Fei Tzu*, 1:282, 293–95, and 2:242f.

9 Duyvendak, *Lord Shang*, 278, and cf. 179f.

10 Liao, *Han Fei Tzu*, 2:243.

11 Duyvendak, *Lord Shang*, 280; Liao, *Han Fei Tzu*, 2:114f. Admittedly, we should not infer too much from this anecdote, if it is to be located in the context of military discipline. See Petersen, "What's in a Name?" 10f.

12 Analect 2.3 (Soothill). On the passage see Ames, *Art of Rulership*, 117; Hansen, "Punishment and Dignity in China," 373f.

13 Lau, *Mencius*, 124 (IVA 14).

14 Dubs, *The Works of Hsuntze*, 193.

15 Ibid., 15.

16 Cf. also the different sense in which "awe" is used in the letter of Shu-hsiang summarized above at note 5.

17 Cf. the passages translated in Hsiao, *History of Chinese Political Thought*, 1:188 n. 96, 198.

18 Köster, *Hsün-tzu*, 317.

19 Dubs, *Hsuntze*, 121; Watson, *Hsün Tzu*, 33f.

20 Cf. the passage translated in Ames, *Art of Rulership*, 123.

21 For a discussion of Hsün Tzu's views on punishment see ibid., 123f.

22 See below at notes 36f.

23 See also chap. 2 at nn. 31f. and chap. 3 at nn. 26f.

24 For this rule and the limitations to which it was subject see chap. 7.

25 Johnson, *T'ang Code*, 55–56.

26 Philastre, 1:59.

27 So enacted by legislation of 1740. See generally Chen, "Local Control of Convicted Thieves in Eighteenth-Century China," 125f., 129f. (noting also that the repentance of first offenders was encouraged through the tattooing of the arms, where the characters would be hidden, rather than the face, as was usually the case).

28 Cf. ibid., 130f.

29 Johnson, *T'ang Code*, 58. There are no corresponding statements in the Ch'ing commentaries.

30 See, however, the Sung attitude to penal registration, a punishment that appears to have combined the characteristics of penal servitude and exile (McKnight, *Law and Order*, chap. 12).

31 Waley-Cohen, *Exile in Mid-Qing China*, 64. See also 35, 50, 77, 139, 158, 176, 181f., 189f., 192f., 213f.

32 For details see *TCPL*, 137ff.

33 For details see chap. 6 at nn. 24f.

34 See above at note 9.

35 Cf. *TCPL*, 142.

36 Cf. *TCPL*, 124f.

37 Johnson, *T'ang Code*, 183.

38 Philastre, 2:9f., and cf. also 2:202.

39 See the discussion of the cases below.

40 For examples of the Board's constant concern to adjust the punishment precisely to the facts see below.

41 The distinction between "retribution" and "requital" is not always observed in the literature. Cf. Meijer's "Aspect of Retribution in Traditional Chinese Law."

42 Cf. Cohen, *Tales of Vengeful Souls*, xf.

43 See chap. 7 under the head "The Value of Life."

44 See MacCormack, "Legal Treatment," 251, esp 264f.

45 Philastre, 2:177; Jones, 270. This provision, contained in the interlinear commentary, does not form part of the corresponding Ming article, and may be another example of the extraordinary severity with which the Ch'ing, influenced by Neo-Confucian thinking, treated breaches of filial piety (cf. chap. 5).

46 Philastre, 1:63.

47 Ibid., 1:47.

48 *HAHL*, 1763.

49 Ibid., 1764.

50 Ibid. 1765.

51 *P'o-an*, 117. See also chap. 7 at n. 26.

52 *P'o-an*, 120–21.

53 *HAHL*, 1769, on which Meijer, *Murder*, 108.

54 Hsüeh, 285.9, trans. Meijer, *Murder*, 107.

55 *HAHL*, 1705.

56 See Meijer, *Murder*, chaps. 4 and 5.

57 *HAHL*, 1548. See also chap. 9 at n. 41.

58 Hsüeh, 284.2, summarized Philastre, 2:184.

59 *HAHL*, 1549.

60 Hsüeh, 284.5; Philastre, 2:180, DII (original version).

61 *HAHL*, 1549.

62 Ibid., 1550.

63 Ibid., 1551.

64 Ibid., 2079.

65 See chap. 9 at n. 48.

66 *HAHL*, 1844. For further details on the case see chap. 7 at n. 27.

67 *HAHL*, 1869.

68 Ibid., 1870. See chap. 7 at n. 30.

69 *HAHL*, 1871.

70 On this Neo-Confucian term see McKnight, *Law and Order*, 24.

71 Cf. chap. 3, n. 23. On the Sacred Edict and its influence see Mair, "Language and Ideology in the Written Popularizations of the *Sacred Edict*."

72 See above at note 42.

73 See chap. 7 at n. 73.

74 See *TCPL*, 140.

75 Detail in *TCPL*, 91ff.

76 For discussion and references see *TCPL*, 41f.; MacCormack, "Natural Law and Cosmic Harmony in Traditional Chinese Legal Thought."

77 So also rightly Bünger, "Das chinesische Rechtssystem und das Prinzip der Rechtsstaatlichkeit," 146f.

78 Ibid., 146.

79 Stephens, *Order and Discipline*, esp 21ff.

80 For this principle see chap. 9 at n. 33.

81 Stephens cites the practice of the K'ang-hsi emperor, as described in Spence, *Emperor of China*, 29ff., on which see chap. 9 at nn. 2f.

BIBLIOGRAPHY

Abbreviations

Boulais   Boulais, Guy. *Manuel du code chinois*. 1924. Reprint. Taipei: Ch'eng Wen, 1966. References are to the numbered paragraphs of the text, unless prefixed with a *p*, in which case the reference is to the page.

HAHL   *Hsing-an hui-lan* (Conspectus of Penal Cases). 1886. Reprint. Taipei: Ch'eng Wen, 1968.

Hsüeh   Hsüeh, Yun-sheng. *Tu-li ts'un-i* (Doubts Arising from the Substatutes). 1905. Reprint. Taipei: Chinese Materials and Research Aids Center, 1970. The substatutes are cited according to the number assigned them in the upper margin of the work.

Hsü-pien   *Hsing-an hui-lan hsü-pien* (Supplement to Conspectus of Penal Cases). 1900. Reprint. Taipei: Wen Hai, 1970.

Jones   Jones, William C. *The Great Qing Code*. Oxford: Clarendon Press, 1994.

MLCCFL   *Ming lü chi chieh fu li* (Ming Code with Substatutes and Commentary). Taipei: Ch'eng Wen, n.d.

Philastre   Philastre, P. L. F. *Le code annamite*. 2d ed. 2 vols. 1909. Reprint. Taipei: Ch'eng Wen, 1967.

P'o-an   *P'o-an hsin-pien* (New Collection of Revised Cases). 1784. Reprint. Taipei: Ch'eng Wen, 1968.

Staunton   Staunton, George Thomas. *Ta Tsing Leu Lee; being the Fundamental Laws and a Selection from the Supplementary Statutes of the Penal Code of China*. 1810. Reprint. Taipei: Ch'eng Wen, 1966.

TCPL   MacCormack, Geoffrey. *Traditional Chinese Penal Law*. Edinburgh: Edinburgh University Press, 1990.

Alford, William P. "Of Arsenic and Old Lace: Looking Anew at Criminal Justice in Late Imperial China." *California Law Review* 72 (1984): 1180–1256.

Alabaster, Ernest. *Notes and Commentaries on Chinese Criminal Law.* 1899. Reprint. Taipei: Ch'eng Wen, 1968.

Ames, Roger T. *The Art of Rulership: A Study in Ancient Chinese Political Thought.* Honolulu: University of Hawaii Press, 1983.

Balazs, Etienne. *Le traité juridique du "Souei-chou."* Leiden: E. J. Brill, 1954.

Baller, F. W. *The Sacred Edict of K'ang-hsi.* 1924. Reprint. Orono: University of Maine, 1979.

Bartlett, Beatrice S. *Monarchs and Ministers: The Grand Council in Mid-Ch'ing China, 1723–1820.* Berkeley: University of California Press, 1991

Bielenstein, Hans. *The Bureaucracy of Han Times.* Cambridge: Cambridge University Press, 1980.

Birge, Bettine. "Chu Hsi and Women's Education." In *Neo-Confucian Education: The Formative Years,* edited by William Theodore de Bary and John W. Chaffee, 325–67. Berkeley and Los Angeles: University of California Press, 1989.

Bodde, Derk. "Age, Youth, and Infirmity in the Law of Ch'ing China." In *Essays on China's Legal Tradition,* edited by Jerome Alan Cohen, R. Randle Edwards, and Fu-mei Chang Chen, 137–69. Princeton: Princeton University Press, 1980.

Bodde, Derk, and Clarence Morris. *Law in Imperial China: Exemplified by 190 Ch'ing Dynasty Cases.* Philadelphia: University of Pennsylvania Press, 1973.

Bünger, Karl. "Die Rechtsidee in der chinesischen Geschichte." *Saeculum* 3 (1952): 192–217.

———. "Entstehung und Wandel des Rechts in China." In *Entstehung und Wandel rechtlicher Traditionen,* edited by Wolfgang Fikentscher, Herbert Franke, and Oskar Köhler, 439–72. Freiburg and Munchen: Karl Alber, 1980.

———. "Das chinesische Rechtssystem und das Prinzip der Rechtsstaatlichkeit." In *Max Webers Studie über Konfuzianismus und Taoismus,* edited by Wolfgang Schluchter, 134–73. Frankfurt am Main: Suhrkamp, 1983.

———. "Concluding Remarks on Two Aspects of the Chinese Unitary State as Compared with the European State System." In *Foundations and Limits of State Power in China,* edited by Stuart R. Schram, 313–23. Hong Kong: Chinese University Press, 1987.

Chan, Wing-tsit. "The Evolution of the Confucian Concept *Jen.*" *Philosophy East and West* 4 (1955): 295–319.

———. *Reflections on Things at Hand: The Neo-Confucian Anthology Compiled by Chu Hsi and Lü Tsu-ch'en.* New York: Columbia University Press, 1967.

Chang, George Jer-lang. "The Village Elder System of the Early Ming Dynasty." *Ming Studies* 7 (1978): 53–72.

Chen, Fu-mei Chang. "On Analogy in Ch'ing Law." *Harvard Journal of Asiatic Studies* 30 (1970): 212–24.

———. "Local Control of Convicted in Eighteenth-Century China." In *Conflict and Control in Late Imperial China*, edited by Frederic Wakeman Jr. and Carol Grant, 121–42. Berkeley and Los Angeles: University of California Press, 1975.

———. "The Influence of Shen Chih-ch'i's *Chi-chu* Commentary upon Ch'ing Judicial Decisions." In *Essays on China's Legal Tradition*, edited by Jerome Alan Cohen, R. Randle Edwards, and Fu-mei Chang Chen, 170–221. Princeton: Princeton University Press, 1980.

Ch'en, Paul Heng-chao. *Chinese Legal Tradition under the Mongols: The Code of 1291 as Reconstructed.* Princeton: Princeton University Press, 1979.

Ch'ien Mu. *Traditional Government in Imperial China: A Critical Analysis.* Translated by Chun-tu Hsüeh and George O. Totten. Hong Kong: Chinese University Press, 1982.

Chu, Raymond W., and William G. Saywell. *Career Patterns in the Ch'ing Dynasty: The Office of Governor-General.* Ann Arbor: University of Michigan Press, 1984.

Chu, Ron-Guey. "Chu Hsi and Public Instruction." In *Neo-Confucian Education: The Formative Stage*, edited by William Theodore de Bary and John W. Chaffee, 252–73. Berkeley and Los Angeles: University of California Press, 1989.

Ch'ü T'ung-tsu. "Chinese Class Structure and Its Ideology." In *Chinese Thought and Institutions*, edited by John K. Fairbank, 235–50. Chicago and London: University of Chicago Press, 1957.

———. *Local Government in China under the Ch'ing.* Stanford: Stanford University Press, 1969.

———. *Law and Society in Traditional China.* 1961. Reprint. Westport, Conn.: Hyperion Press, 1980.

Clunas, Craig. "Regulation of Consumption and the Institution of Correct

Morality by the Ming State." In *Norms and the State in China*, edited by Chun-Chieh Huang and Erik Zürcher. Leiden: E. J. Brill, 1993.

Cohen, Alvin P. *Tales of Vengeful Souls: A Sixth-Century Collection of Chinese Avenging Ghost Stories*. Taipei, Paris, and Hong Kong: Ricci Institute, 1982.

Connor, Alison Wayne. "The Law of Evidence during the Ch'ing Dynasty." Ph.D diss., Cornell University, 1979.

Creel, Herrlee G. *The Origins of Statecraft in China*. Vol. 1, *The Western Chou Empire*. Chicago and London: University of Chicago Press, 1970.

———. "Legal Institutions and Procedures during the Chou Dynasty." In *Essays on China's Legal Tradition*, edited by Jerome Alan Cohen, R. Randle Edwards, and Fu-mei Chang Chen, 26–55. Princeton: Princeton University Press, 1980.

Dardess, John W. *Confucianism and Autocracy: Professional Elites in the Founding of the Ming Dynasty*. Berkeley and Los Angeles: University of California Press, 1983.

de Bary, William Theodore. *Neo-Confucian Orthodoxy and the Learning of the Mind-and-Heart*. New York: Columbia University Press, 1981.

de Groot, J. J. M. *The Religious System of China*. 6 vols. 1894. Reprint. Taipei: Southern Materials Center, 1982.

Downer, L. J. *Leges Henrici Primi*. Oxford: Clarendon Press, 1972.

Dubs, Homer H. *The Works of Hsuntze*. 1928. Reprint. Taipei: Ch'eng Wen, 1973.

Duyvendak, J. J. L. *The Book of Lord Shang*. 1928. Reprint. London: Arthur Probsthain, 1963.

Ebrey, Patricia Buckley. *Chu Hsi's Family Rituals: A Twelfth-Century Manual for the Performance of Cappings, Weddings, Funerals, and Ancestral Rites*. Princeton: Princeton University Press, 1991.

———. *Confucianism and Family Rituals in Imperial China: A Social History of Writing about Rites*. Princeton: Princeton University Press, 1991.

Elvin, Mark. "Female Virtue and the State in China." *Past and Present* 104 (1984): 111–52.

Escarra, Jean. *Le droit chinois: Conception et evolution. Institutions legislatives et judicaires. Science et enseignement*. Pekin: Henri Veitch, 1936.

Fung Yu-lan, *A History of Chinese Philosophy*. Translated by D. Bodde. 2 vols. Princeton: Princeton University Press, 1952–53.

Gardner, Daniel K. *Chu Hsi and the Ta-hsüeh: Neo-Confucian Reflection on the Confucian Canon*. Cambridge: Harvard University Press, 1986.

Gaurier, Dominique. "Responsabilité politique, responsabilité morale en

Chine ancienne: Le fils du Ciel et le Mandat Celeste." *Revue interna-*
   tionale des droits de l'antiquité 39 (1992): 27–54.
Gernet, Jacques. Introduction to *Foundations and Limits of State Power in*
   China, edited by Stuart R. Schram, xv–xxvii. Hong Kong: Chinese Uni-
   versity Press, 1987.
Greenblatt, Kristin Yü. "Chu-hung and Lay Buddhism in the Late Ming." In
   The Unfolding of Neo-Confucianism, edited by William Theodore de
   Bary, 93–140. New York: Columbia University Press, 1975.
Gulik, Robert H. van. *Sexual Life in Ancient China: A Preliminary Survey of*
   Chinese Sex and Society from ca. 1500 B.C. till 1644 A.D. 1961. Reprint.
   Leiden: E. J. Brill, 1974.
Handlin, Joanna F. "Lü K'un's New Audience: The Influence of Women's Lit-
   eracy on Sixteenth-Century Thought." In *Women in Chinese Society,*
   edited by Margery Wolf and Roxane Witke, 13–38. Stanford: Stanford
   University Press, 1975.
Hansen, Chad. "Punishment and Dignity in China." In *Individualism and*
   Holism: Studies in Confucian and Taoist Values, edited by Donald
   Monro, 359–83. Ann Arbor: University of Michigan Press, 1985.
Harlez, Charles de. *La Siao Hio; ou, Morale de la Jeunesse avec le commen-*
   taire de Tchen-siuen. Paris: Ernest Leroux, 1889.
Harrison, Judy Feldman. "Wrongful Treatment of Prisoners: A Case Study of
   Ch'ing Legal Procedure." *Journal of Asian Studies* 23 (1964): 227–44.
Hart, H. L. A. *Punishment and Responsibility: Essays in the Philosophy of*
   Law. Oxford: Clarendon Press, 1968.
Ho Ping-ti. *The Ladder of Success in Imperial China: Aspects of Social*
   Mobility, 1368–1911. 1962. Reprint. New York: Columbia University
   Press, 1980.
Hsiao Kung-chuan. *A History of Chinese Political Thought.* Vol. 1, *From the*
   Beginnings to the Sixth Century A.D. Translated by F. W. Mote. Prince-
   ton: Princeton University Press, 1979.
Hsieh, Pao Chao. *The Government of China (1644–1911).* 1925. Reprint. New
   York: Octagon Books, 1966.
Hsu Dau-lin. "The Myth of the 'Five Human Relations' of Confucius." *Monu-*
   menta Serica 29 (1970–1971): 27–37.
Huang Liu-hung. *A Complete Book concerning Happiness and Benevolence:*
   A Manual for Local Magistrates in Seventeenth-Century China. Trans-
   lated and edited by Djang Chu. Tucson: University of Arizona Press,
   1984.
Huang, Philip. "Codified Law and Magisterial Adjudication in the Qing."

In *Civil Law in Qing and Republican China*, edited by Kathryn Bernhardt and Philip Huang, 142–86. Stanford, Calif.: Stanford University Press, 1994.

Hucker, Charles O. "Confucianism and the Chinese Censorial System." In *Confucianism in Action*, edited by David S. Nivison and Arthur F. Wright, 182–208. Stanford: Stanford University Press, 1959.

———. *The Censorial System of Ming China*. Stanford: Stanford University Press, 1966.

———. "Introduction: Governmental Organization Era by Era." In *A Dictionary of Official Titles in Imperial China*, 3–96. Stanford: Stanford University Press, 1985.

———, ed. *Chinese Government in Ming Times*. New York: Columbia University Press, 1969.

Hulsewé, Anthony. *Remnants of Han Law*. Vol. 1. Leiden: E. J. Brill, 1955.

———. *Remnants of Ch'in Law*. Leiden: E. J. Brill, 1985.

———. "Law as One of the Foundations of State Power in Early Imperial China." In *Foundations and Limits of State Power in China*, edited by Stuart R. Schram, 11–32. Hong Kong: Chinese University Press, 1987.

Jamieson, G. *Chinese Family and Commercial Law*. 1921. Reprint. Hong Kong: Vetch and Lee, 1970.

Jing, Junjian. "Legislation Related to the Civil Economy in the Qing Dynasty." In *Civil Law in Qing and Republican China*, edited by Kathryn Bernhardt and Philip Huang, 42–84. Stanford, Calif.: Stanford University Press, 1994.

Johnson, Wallace. *The T'ang Code*. Vol. 1, *General Principles*. Princeton: Princeton University Press, 1979.

———. "The Concept of Doubt in T'ang Criminal Law." In *Chinese Ideas about Nature and Society: Studies in Honour of Derk Bodde*, edited by Charles Le Blanc and Susan Blader. Hong Kong: Hong Kong University Press, 1987.

Jones, William C. "Theft in the Qing Code." *American Journal of Comparative Law* 22 (1974): 330–64.

Karlgren, Bernhard. *The Book of Documents*. Reprinted by the Museum of Far Eastern Antiquities, Bulletin 22. Stockholm, 1950.

Kelleher, M. Theresa. "Back to Basics: Chu Hsi's Elementary Learning (*Hsiao-hsüeh*)." In *Neo-Confucian Education: The Formative Stage*, edited by William Theodore de Bary and John W. Chaffee, 219–51. Berkeley and Los Angeles: University of California Press, 1989.

Kirk, Russell. *The Conservative Mind: From Burke to Santayana.* Chicago: Regnery, 1953.

Knoblock, John. *Xunzi: A Translation and Study of the Complete Works.* Vol 2, books 7–16. Stanford: Stanford University Press, 1990.

Köster, Hermann. *Hsün-tzu.* Kaldenkirchen: Steyler Verlag, 1967.

Kracke, E. A. Jr. *Civil Service in Early Sung China 960–1067.* Cambridge: Harvard University Press, 1953.

Kroker, Edward. "Rechtsgewöhnheiten in der Provinz Shantung nach *Ming shang shih hsi kuan tiao ch'a pao kao lu.*" *Monumenta Serica* 14 (1949–55): 215–302.

———. *Die Strafe im chinesischen Recht.* Opladen: Westdeutscher Verlag, 1970.

Ladany, Laszlo. *Law and Legality in China: The Testament of a China-Watcher.* Edited by Marie-Luise Näth. London: Hurst, 1992.

Lau, D. C. *Mencius.* Harmondsworth: Penguin Books, 1970.

Lee, James. "Homicide et peine capitale en Chine à la fin de l'empire: Analyse statistique préliminaire des données." *Études chinoises* 10 (1991): 113–34.

Lee, Thomas H. C. "Sung Schools and Education before Chu Hsi." In *Neo-Confucian Education: The Formative Stage,* edited by William Theodore de Bary and John W. Chaffee, 105–36. Berkeley and Los Angeles: University of California Press, 1989.

Legge, James. *Li Chi: Book of Rites.* 2 vols. Edited by Ch'ü Chai and Winberg Chai. 1885. Reprint. New Hyde Park, N.Y.: University Books, 1967.

———. *The Chinese Classics.* 5 vols. 1867. Taipei: Ch'eng Wen, undated reprint.

Li, San-Pao. "Ch'ing Cosmology and Popular Precepts." In *Cosmology, Ontology, and Human Efficacy: Essays in Chinese Thought,* edited by Richard J. Smith and D. W. Y. Kwok, 113–39. Honolulu: University of Hawaii Press, 1993.

Liao, W. K. *The Complete Works of Han Fei Tzu.* 2 vols. London: Arthur Probsthain, 1959 (vol. 1 first published 1939).

Lin, Li-hsüeh. "The Relationship between Ruler and Minister in the Theory of the 'Three Mainstays.'" *Journal of Chinese Philosophy* 17 (1990): 439–71.

Liu, Adam Yuen-chung. *Ch'ing Institutions and Society 1644–1795.* Centre of Asian Studies, University of Hong Kong, 1990.

Liu, Hui-chen Wang. *The Traditional Chinese Clan Rules.* Locust Valley, N.Y.: J. J. Augustin, 1959.

Liu, James C. "An Early Sung Reformer: Fan Chung-yen." In *Chinese Thought and Institutions*, edited by John K. Fairbank, 105–31. Chicago and London: University of Chicago Press, 1957.

Liu, Kwang-ching. "Socioethics as Orthodoxy: A Perspective." In *Orthodoxy in Late Imperial China*, edited by Kwang-ching Liu, 53–100. Berkeley and Los Angeles: University of California Press, 1990.

Liu, Yong-ping. "The Origin and Early Development of Chinese Law and the Penal System: Towards a Comprehensive Analysis of the Period of Creativity." Ph.D. diss., Oxford University, 1993.

Lo, Winston W. *An Introduction to the Civil Service of Sung China, with Emphasis on Its Personnel Administration.* Honolulu: University of Hawaii Press, 1987.

Lowe, H. Y. *The Adventures of Wu: The Life-Style of a Peking Man.* Vol. 2. Princeton: Princeton University Press, 1983.

Macauley, Melissa. "Civil and Uncivil Disputes in Southeast Coastal China, 1723–1820." In *Civil Law in Qing and Republican China*, edited by Kathryn Bernhardt and Philip Huang, 85–121. Stanford, Calif.: Stanford University Press, 1994.

MacCormack, Geoffrey. "The T'ang Code: Early Chinese Law." *Irish Jurist* 18 (1983): 132–50.

———. "Law and Punishment in the Earliest Chinese Thought." *Irish Jurist* 20 (1985): 334–51.

———. "The Concept of *Tsang* in the T'ang Code." *Revue internationale des droits de l'antiquité* 33 (1986): 25–44.

———. "Ethical Principles and the Traditional Chinese Law of Marriage." *Irish Jurist* 21 (1986): 247–71.

———. "The *Lü Hsing*: Problems of Legal Interpretation." *Monumenta Serica* 37 (1986–87): 35–47.

———. "Natural Law and Cosmic Harmony in Traditional Chinese Legal Thought." *Ratio Iuris* 2 (1989): 254–73.

———. "Suicide in Traditional Chinese Law." *Chinese Culture* 32, no. 2 (1991): 33–47.

———. "Cultural Values in Traditional Chinese Law." *Chinese Culture* 32, no. 4 (1991): 1–11.

———. "General Principles of Liability in the Late Ch'ing Law of Homicide." *Asia Pacific Law Review* 1 (1992): 13–31.

———. "The Legal Treatment of Insane Persons in Late Imperial China." *Journal of Legal History* 13 (1992): 251–69.

———. "Hsün Tzu on Law and Society." *Indian Socio-Legal Journal* 18 (1992): 73–84.

———. "*Ts'ui tso so yu:* A Principle of Causality in Traditional Chinese Jurisprudence." *Irish Jurist* 15–17 (1990–92): 194–211.

———. "Assistance in Conflict Resolution: Imperial China." Forthcoming in *Transactions of the Jean Bodin Society.*

McKnight, Brian E. *The Quality of Mercy: Amnesties and Traditional Chinese Justice.* Honolulu: University of Hawaii Press, 1981.

———. "Song Legal Privileges." *Journal of the American Oriental Society* 105 (1985): 95–106.

———. *Law and Order in Sung China.* Cambridge: Cambridge University Press, 1992.

McMullen, I. J. "Non-Agnatic Adoption: A Confucian Controversy in Seventeenth- and Eighteenth-Century Japan." *Harvard Journal of Asiatic Studies* 35 (1975): 130–89.

Mair, Victor H. "Language and Ideology in the Written Popularizations of the *Sacred Edict.*" In *Popular Culture in Late Imperial China,* edited by David Johnson, Andrew J. Nathan, and Evelyn S. Rawski, 325–59. Berkeley and Los Angeles: University of California Press, 1985.

Mann, Susan. "Widows in the Kinship, Class, and Community Structures of Qing Dynasty China." *Journal of Asian Studies* 46 (1987): 37–56.

Meijer, Marinus Johan. *The Introduction of Modern Criminal Law in China.* 1950. Reprint. Arlington, Va.: University Publications of America, 1976.

———. "The Concept of *Ku-sha* in the Ch'ing Code." In *Il diritto in Cina,* edited by Lionello Lanciotti. Firenze: Leo S. Olschki, 1978.

———. "An Aspect of Retribution in Traditional Chinese Law." *T'oung Pao* 66 (1980): 199–216.

———. "Slavery at the End of the Ch'ing Dynasty." In *Essays on China's Legal Tradition,* edited by Jerome Alan Cohen, R. Randle Edwards, and Fu-mei Chang Chen, 327–58. Princeton: Princeton University Press, 1980.

———. "Review of Nakamura Shigeo, *Studies in Ch'ing Law.*" *T'oung Pao* 66 (1980): 348–53.

———. "The Price of a *P'ai-lou.*" *T'oung Pao* 67 (1981): 288–304.

———. "Criminal Responsibility for the Suicide of Parents in Ch'ing Law." In *Leyden Studies in Sinology,* edited by Wilt L. Idema, 109–37. Leiden: E. J. Brill, 1981.

———. "Homosexual Offences in Ch'ing Law." *T'oung Pao* 71 (1985): 109–33.

———. "Self-defense." In *Thought and Law in Qin and Han China: Studies*

Dedicated to Anthony Hulsewé on the Occasion of his Eightieth Birthday, edited by Wilt L. Idema and E. Zürcher, 225–44. Leiden: E. J. Brill, 1990.

———. *Murder and Adultery in Late Imperial China: A Study of Law and Morality*. Leiden: E. J. Brill, 1991.

Metzger, Thomas A. *The Internal Organization of Ch'ing Bureaucracy: Legal, Normative, and Communication Aspects*. Cambridge: Harvard University Press, 1973.

———. *Escape from Predicament: Neo-Confucianism and China's Evolving Political Culture*. New York: Columbia University Press, 1977.

Miyazaki, Ichisada. *China's Examination Hell: The Civil Service Examinations of Imperial China*. Translated by Conrad Schirokauer. New York and Tokyo: Weatherhill, 1976.

Moore, Ronald. "The Wider Lessons of Chinese Law." *Philosophy East and West* 26 (1976): 229–35.

Ng, Vivien. "Ideology and Sexuality: Rape Laws in Qing China." *Journal of Asian Studies* 46 (1987): 57–70.

———. *Madness in Late Imperial China: From Illness to Deviance*. Norman and London: University of Oklahoma Press, 1980.

Ocko, Jonathan K. *Bureaucratic Reform in Provincial China: Ting Jih-ch'ang in Restoration Kiangsu, 1867–1870*. Cambridge: Harvard University Press, 1983.

———. "Hierarchy and Harmony: Family Conflict as Seen in Ch'ing Legal Cases." In *Orthodoxy in Late Imperial China*, edited by Kwang-ching Liu, 212–30. Berkeley and Los Angeles: University of California Press, 1990.

Oyama, Masaaki. "Large Landownership in the Jiangnan Delta Region during the Late Ming – Early Qing Period." In *State and Society in China: Japanese Perspectives on Ming-Qing Social and Economic History*, 101–63. Tokyo: University of Tokyo Press, 1984.

Oyamatsu, S. *Laws and Customs in the Island of Formosa*. 1902. Reprint. Taipei: Ch'eng Wen, 1971.

Paderni, Paola. "Le rachat de l'honneur perdu: Le suicide des femmes dans la Chine du xviiie siècle." *Études chinoises* 10 (1991): 135–60.

Petersen, Jens. "What's in a Name? On the Sources concerning Sun Wu." *Asia Major* 5 (1992): 1–31.

Phen, S. T. *The Three Character Classic*. Singapore: EPB, 1989.

Rankin, Mary Backus. "The Emergence of Women at the End of the Ch'ing: The Case of Ch'iu Chin." In *Women in Chinese Society*, edited by

Margery Wolf and Roxane Witke, 39–66. Stanford: Stanford University Press, 1975.

Ratchnevsky, Paul. *Un code des Yüan*. Paris: E. LeRoux, 1937–1977 (vols. 1–3); Paris, College de France, Institut des hautes études chinoises, 1985 (vol. 4).

Rawski, Evelyn S. "Economic and Social Foundations of Late Imperial Culture." In *Popular Culture in Late Imperial China*, edited by David Johnson, Andrew J. Nathan, and Evelyn S. Rawski, 3–33. Berkeley and Los Angeles: University of California Press, 1985.

Richter, Melvin. *The Political Theory of Montesquieu*. Cambridge: Cambridge University Press, 1977.

Rickett, W. Allyn. *Guanzi: Political, Economic and Philosophical Essays from Early China*. Vol. 1. Princeton: Princeton University Press, 1985.

Ropp, Paul S. *Dissent in Early Modern China: Ju-lin Wai-shih and Ch'ing Social Criticism*. Ann Arbor: University of Michigan Press, 1981.

Schirokauer, Conrad. "Chu Hsi as an Administrator." In *Sung Studies: In Memoriam Etienne Balazs*. Vol. 1.3, 207–36. Paris and The Hague: Mouton, 1976.

Seidel, Peter. *Studien zur Rechtsgeschichte der Sung-Zeit: Übersetzung und Kommentierung des ersten Strafrechtskapitals aus den Sung-Annalen*. Frankfurt/Main: Herg und Herchen, 1983.

Smith, Richard J. "Ritual in Ch'ing Culture." In *Orthodoxy in Late Imperial China*, edited by Kwang-ching Liu, 281–310. Berkeley and Los Angeles: University of California Press, 1990.

Soothill, William E. (trans.). *The Analects; or, The Conversations of Confucius with His Disciples and Certain Others*. London: Oxford University Press, 1941.

Spence, Jonathan D. *Emperor of China: Self-Portrait of K'ang-hsi*. New York: Arthur A. Knopf, 1975.

———. "Opium Smoking in Ch'ing China." In *Conflict and Control in Late Imperial China*, edited by Frederic Wakeman Jr. and Carolyn Grant, 143–73. Berkeley and Los Angeles: University of California Press, 1975.

———. *The Death of Woman Wang: Rural Life in China in the Seventeenth Century*. London: Weidenfeld and Nicolson, 1978.

Steele, John, trans. *The I Li or, Book of Etiquette and Ceremonial*. 1917. Reprint. Taipei: Ch'eng Wen, 1966.

Stephens, Thomas B. *Order and Discipline in China: The Shanghai Mixed Court 1911–27*. Seattle: University of Washington Press, 1992.

Sweeten, Alan Richard. "Women and Law in Rural China: Vignettes from

'Sectarian Cases' (*Chiao-an*) in Kiangsi, 1872, 1878." *Ch'ing-shih Wen-ti* (*Journal of the Society of Ch'ing Studies*) 3, no. 10 (1975–78): 49–68.

Tai, Yen-hui. "Divorce in Traditional Chinese Law." In *Chinese Family Law and Social Change in Historical and Comparative Perspective*, edited by David C. Buxbaum, 75–106. Seattle: University of Washington Press, 1978.

Tanaka, Masatoshi. "Popular Uprisings, Rent Resistance, and Bondservant Rebellions in the Late Ming." In *State and Society in China: Japanese Perspectives on Ming-Qing Social and Economic History*, edited by Linda Grove and Christian Daniels, 165–214. Tokyo: University of Tokyo Press, 1984.

T'ang-lü shu-i (T'ang Code with Commentary). Beijing: Chunghua, 1983

Tao, Chia-lin Pao. "Chaste Widows and the Institutions to Support Them in Late-Ch'ing China." *Asia Major* 4 (1991): 101–19.

T'ien Ju-k'ang. *Male Anxiety and Female Chastity: A Comparative Study of Chinese Ethical Values in Ming-Ch'ing Times*. Leiden: E. J. Brill, 1988.

———. "Review of M. J. Meijer, *Murder and Adultery in Late Imperial China*." *T'oung Pao* 77 (1991): 342–48.

Torbert, Preston M. *The Ch'ing Imperial Household Department: A Study of Its Organization and Principal Functions, 1662–1796*. Cambridge: Harvard University Press, 1977.

Tu, Ching-I. "Conservatism in a Constructive Form: The Case of Wang Kuo-wei (1877–1927)." *Monumenta Serica* 28 (1969): 188–214.

Twitchett, D. C. *Financial Administration under the T'ang Dynasty*. 2d ed. Cambridge: Cambridge University Press, 1970.

Valk, Marius H. van der. "Review of D. Bodde and C. Morris, *Law in Imperial China*." *Monumenta Serica* 28 (1969): 471–74.

van der Sprenkel, Sybille. *Legal Institutions in Manchu China: A Sociological Analysis*. London: Athlone Press, 1966.

Vandermeersch, Léon. "An Enquiry into the Chinese Conception of the Law." In *The Scope of State Power in China*, edited by Stuart R. Shram, 3–25. Hong Kong: Chinese University Press, 1985.

Waley-Cohen, Joanna. *Exile in Mid-Qing China: Banishment to Xinjiang 1758–1820*. New Haven: Yale University Press, 1991.

Waltner, Ann. "Widows and Remarriage in Ming and Early Qing China." *Historical Reflections* 8 (1981): 129–46.

———. "The Moral Status of the Child in Late Imperial China: Childhood in Ritual and Law." *Social Research* 54 (1986): 667–87.

————. *Getting an Heir: Adoption and the Constitution of Kinship in Late Imperial China.* Honolulu: University of Hawaii Press, 1990.

Watt, John R. *The District Magistrate in Late Imperial China.* New York: Columbia University Press, 1972.

Weggel, Oskar. *Chinesische Rechtsgeschichte.* Leiden: E. J. Brill, 1980.

Wolf, Arthur P., and Chieh-shan Huang. *Marriage and Adoption in China, 1845–1945.* Stanford: Stanford University Press, 1980.

Wong, Sun-ming. *Confucian Ideal and Reality: Transformation of the Institution of Marriage in T'ang China (A.D. 618–907).* Ann Arbor: UMI, 1993 (dissertation date: 1979).

Wu, John C. H. "Chinese Legal and Political Philosophy." In *The Chinese Mind: Essentials of Chinese Philosophy and Culture,* edited by Charles A. Moore, 213–37. 1967. Reprint. Honolulu: University of Hawaii Press, 1977.

Wu, Pei-yi. "Education of Children in the Sung." In *Neo-Confucian Education: The Formative Stage,* edited by William Theodore de Bary and John W. Chaffee, 307–24. Berkeley and Los Angeles: University of California Press, 1989.

Wu, Silas H. C. *Communication and Imperial Control in China: Evolution of the Palace Memorial System 1693–1735.* Cambridge: Harvard University Press, 1970.

Yamashita, Ryuji. "The Development of Ideas on Sovereignty: From the Sung to the Ming." *Acta Asiatica* 52 (1987): 45–64.

Yang, C. K. "Some Characteristics of Chinese Bureaucratic Behaviour." In *Confucianism in Action,* edited by David S. Nivison and Arthur F. Wright, 134–64. Stanford: Stanford University Press, 1959.

Yen Chih-t'ui. *Family Instructions for the Yen Clan: Yen-shih Chia-hsün.* Translated by Teng Ssu-Yü. Leiden: E. J. Brill, 1968.

INDEX

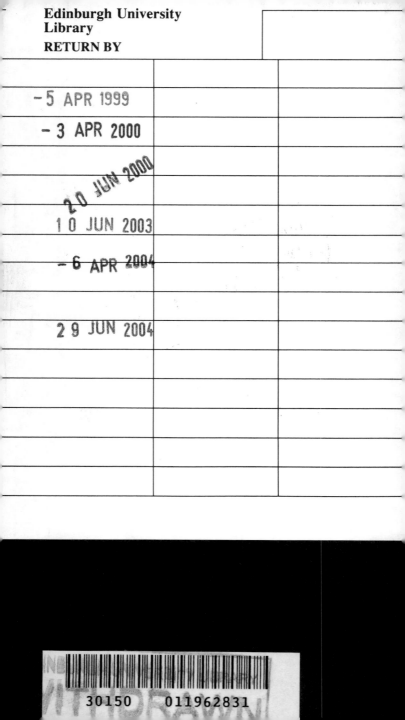